TELLING THE OLD, OLD STORY

TELLING THE OLD, OLD STORY

The Art of Narrative Preaching

David L. Larsen

CROSSWAY BOOKS • WHEATON, ILLINOIS
A DIVISION OF GOOD NEWS PUBLISHERS

Telling the Old, Old Story

Copyright © 1995 by David L. Larsen

Published by Crossway Books
    a division of Good News Publishers
    1300 Crescent Street
    Wheaton, Illinois 60187

Cover calligraphy: Timothy R. Botts

First printing, 1995

Printed in the United States of America

Library of Congress Cataloging-in-Publication Data

Larsen, David L.
    Telling the old, old story : the art of narrative preaching / David L. Larsen
        p.   cm.
    1. Preaching. 2. Storytelling—Religious aspects—Christianity.
I. Title.
BV4235.S76.L37 1995   251—dc20   94-42394
ISBN 0-89107-836-3

03	02	01	00	99	98	97	96	95
15	14	13	12	11	10	9	8	7	6	5	4	3	2	1

To our grandchildren . . .
who love to hear the story,
with the prayer they will always
love the Savior.

*"So we'll live,
And pray, and sing,
and tell old tales. . . .
As if we were God's spies. . . ."*

KING LEAR, V, III, 10-17

Table of Contents

IV. OUR SUMMONS

Introduction

Christian communicators—laypersons and clergy, teachers and preachers—are facing an increasingly complex climate and milieu for sharing the Word of God and the gospel of Jesus Christ. The widely respected historian John Lukacs, in his recent probing analysis *The End of the Twentieth Century and the End of the Modern Age*, speaks of our "state of rather catastrophic crisis" that has profoundly affected the arts, the sciences, history, and all aspects of the human journey.

This study seeks to address one significant trend in the present morass and how evangelical preaching must regard it as having both great peril and immense possibility. The upsurge of interest in narrative is widespread. My students in preaching at Trinity Evangelical Divinity School have shown great interest in dialogue on this subject, especially those in my class on narrative preaching. I owe them and my faculty colleagues an incalculable debt.

By *narrative* I am referring to one of the literary genres found in Holy Scripture. Robert Alter in his now classic work speaks of "a proper narrative event" as taking place "when the narrative tempo slows down enough for us to discriminate a particular scene."[1] Eugene Lowry helpfully shows that narrative sequence must involve a bind or some discrepancy or loss of equilibrium, an attempt at resolution, and then consequences for good or evil.[2]

In other words, a story tells about something that happened, starting with a point of tension and leading up to the satisfactory or unsatisfactory resolution of that tension. Narrative in this definition constitutes 77 percent of the Old Testament (according to Bruce Waltke), and indeed huge chunks of the New Testament are narrative according to this definition. Our task in this study is to revisit this material and its handling from the distinctive standpoint of evangelical presupposition and premise.

As always, my wife, Jean, and my family have encouraged me more than I can describe or express.

The operative and motivational plus for the preacher is aptly represented by the statue of Phillips Brooks at Trinity Church Boston, in which Brooks's left hand is on his Bible and his right hand is gesturing as he preaches. Three inches behind him is Christ, His fingers on the preacher's left shoulder. Augustus Saint-Gaudens, the sculptor, in the course of his work read a biography of Brooks and was so profoundly moved that he asked for the Gospels and was converted. So we are emboldened as messengers of the Almighty to preach Christ in the darkness of our age. The "old, old story of Jesus and His love" is surely *the greatest story ever told!*

Ad gloriam Dei.

I

OUR SOURCES

"Therefore every teacher of the law who has been instructed about the kingdom of heaven is like the owner of a house who brings out of his storeroom new treasures as well as old."

MATT. 13:52

CHAPTER ONE

Assessing the Remarkable Renaissance of Interest in Narrative

God made man because He loves stories.

ELIE WIESEL

But now bring me a minstrel. And it came to pass, when the
minstrel played, that the hand of the Lord came upon him.
And he said, Thus saith the Lord, Make this valley full of
ditches.

2 KINGS 3:15-16, KJV

You may have tangible wealth untold,
Caskets of jewels and coffers of gold.
Richer than I you could never be;
I know someone who told stories to me.

CYNTHIA PEARL MAUS

Storytelling is as old as the human family. At the beginning of
human history we find tribal storytelling. In Ur of the Sumerians
some 10,000 years ago we encounter the oral epic in full force.[1]
The ancient Minoans had their cycles of stories. Homer in Asia
Minor was one of the greatest storytellers of all times (see, for
example, *Odyssey*, VIII, 28ff.). The Hebrew people had a unique
genius for storytelling, as we shall see further.

As Ulrich Simon argues, narrative is the basis of culture,
whether we are looking at the *Gilgamesh Epic*, or Greek mythology and its Olympian heroes, or Fraser's *Golden Bough* with its
demons and gods.[2] Over fifty different kinds of bardic storytelling
have been described, featuring minstrels, skalds (among the

Norsemen), troubadours, imbongi (among the Xhosa people of South Africa), and the Wayang (a puppet show used as an ancient Javanese art form.)[3] Whatever the form (be they *Arabian Nights* or *Aesop's Fables* or tales of Robin Hood and his merry men), stories are a way in which a community and individuals in a community express who they are and what their values are.

Some go so far as to say that "knowledge is stories." Shank convincingly argues that "memory is story-based"; i.e., while not all memories are stories, understanding in a real sense "is correlating the story we are hearing with one we already know."[4] The fact that storytelling is one of the oldest arts and one of the most persistent underscores how significant and basic it is. Thus the universal appeal of story must be taken into serious consideration by every communicator. That "everybody's life is full of stories" (John Shea) establishes common ground for the thoughtful communicator. Ours is a story-shaped world, as Brian Wicker puts it. Though the point may be carried too far, Stephen Crites's early essay captured an important reality when he spoke of "The Narrative Quality of Experience."[5] So Wesley Kort can accurately speak of "the ubiquity of narrative."[6] "To be a person is to have a story," William Bausch convincingly argues.[7]

Story is a "hot medium," and the shift from orality to literacy had a serious effect on the message, as McLuhan and his disciple Postman have well shown. *The Gutenberg Galaxy* gave rise to the age of exposition, which has had an immense implication for Christian communication. The danger in a "print culture" (in which reading, essentially a rational activity, dominates) is that "oral tradition lost much of its resonance."[8] The collapse of orality was not total, of course; but many aspects of the fallout of the Enlightenment tended to "eclipse" narrative and the persons for whom narrative is an essential aspect of identity and personhood.

The instant mass communication and the "age of entertainment" of the modern era comprise but one aspect of the new age of information in which we find ourselves today. McLuhan and Powers warn of "this individualistic, decentralized, effervescent future, living at the speed of light . . . a future of generalized functional illiteracy, historical and cultural amnesia and spiritual impoverishment."[9] This is the milieu and matrix for the explosive rebirth and renewal of interest in the story, a rekindling that has reached and powerfully shaken the world of Christian communication as well.

Good storytellers are gurus in our society (persons like Garrison Keillor, Annie Dillard, Walter Wangerin, Calvin Miller, Frederick Buechner, Eugene Peterson, and many others in the Christian and non-Christian orbits). The media rhapsodize on "the storytelling renaissance," and we are told that "everyone from liberal activists to IBM is catching the tall-tale wave."[10] Indeed, there is a *Storytelling Magazine*. The older National Story League has now been augmented by the National Association for the Preservation and Perpetuation of Storytelling (NAPPS) with its annual National Storytelling Festival in Jonesborough, Tennessee. It is estimated that there are now over 300 full-time storytellers in the United States.

The reverberations in the religious world have been seismic. Of course, preachers and Christian educators have always valued and utilized the narratives of the Bible. As Leland Ryken has well said: "The Bible is God's story." Evangelicals have told the stories (and have treasured an Ethel Barrett and an Aunt Theresa), and we have used Elsie Egermeier's Bible stories for our children. Our preachers have preached narrative and have used illustrations (sometimes over-used them, as in the skyscraper sermon, one story after another); but the exegetes and homileticians of the Left have discovered story and, for reasons we shall analyze in some depth, are really going for it. We are facing here both a cultural and a theological phenomenon.

The books and treatises are pouring off the presses. Conferences are being held on "The Art of Biblical Storytelling." I read about a "Conference on Understanding, Faith and Narrative." Abingdon Press is issuing volume by volume *The Storyteller's Companion to the Bible*. Joseph Campbell's series on PBS with Bill Moyers on "myth" has given rise to a new industry. Rollo May's new book is called *The Cry for Myth*. Jamake Highwater, originator of Festival Mythos, puts it this way: "After the greed of the '80s, people in the '90s are trying to go back and reaffirm and redefine their basic beliefs, and that equals mythology."[11]

The *New Confession* of the Presbyterian Church tells us: "*Jesus Christ Stands at the Center of a Story*." It asserts: "That story is still unfolding and in faith we make it our own. It forms our memory and our hope. It tells us who we are and what we are to do. To retell it is to declare what we believe."[12]

Where are we as evangelicals in regard to all of this? What ramifications does this have for the preacher of the Word of God? What is happening and why? This volume is an effort to describe and understand the situation and to take a fresh look at the narrative genre and its value and use for us today. We must begin by seeking to trace the pathway that has led us to the present situation.

LOOKING AT THE PHENOMENON

> Let me tell the stories, and I care not who writes the textbooks. (Dr. G. Stanley Hall, pioneer adolescent psychologist)

> I will open my mouth in parables, I will utter hidden things, things from of old—what we have heard and known, what our fathers have told us. We will not hide them from their children; we will tell the next generation the praiseworthy deeds of the Lord, his power, and the wonders he has done. (Ps. 78:2-4)

The rapid rise and resurgence of interest in narrative have swept across western society. Thomas Boomershine speaks of the "Network of Biblical Storytellers" as a growing force in fostering festivals, courses, workshops, and audiocassettes for jogging.[13] As sedate and traditional a critic as Thomas Fleming in the conservative *Chronicles of Culture* warbles in an article entitled "I Love to Tell the Story": "If there were races of rational beings that think analytically and tell no stories, we and they would have nothing to say to each other."[14] We now have not only narrative preaching as a prime category, but we have narratology as a subdivision of poetics, the science of literature. We have narrative theology and narrative ethics, as well as the narrative hermeneutic and narrative spirituality. What are the factors that have shaped the current obsession with narrative?

1. *The return to narrative must be seen as part of a much larger revolution in culture and language*. After the Renaissance and the Enlightenment, human reason increasingly reigned as king. Christian thought from Tertullian and Augustine insisted that faith and revelation were keys to understanding; the latter

insisted: "Understanding is the reward of faith. Therefore seek not to understand that thou mayest believe, but believe that thou mayest understand." Anselm of Canterbury's *"credo ut intelligam"* ("I believe in order to understand") did not rule out logical demonstration (as in his ontological argument for the existence of God); but it did preserve what Gilson has called "the primacy of faith."[15] The swaggering dominance of reason rose out of the scientific Renaissance of the sixteenth century and flowered in the empiricism of David Hume and the thinking of Descartes, Spinoza, and Leibniz.

Productive as the scientific method became, rationalism was oppressive and sterile spiritually and morally. Science itself became the religion for many. Kant tried to salvage something for theology and ethics through his famous bifurcation between the noumenal and the phenomenal worlds of reality. What he did was to empty the religious creed of cognitive content, and post-Kantian, anti-intellectual agnosticism became pervasive. A Romantic revolt was inevitable as Coleridge scrounged for reality in imagination and Goethe in feeling ("Feeling is all") and Kierkegaard in an existential leap of faith. In grave danger of throwing the baby out with the bathwater, modern anti-intellectualism has revolted against reason.[16] Science has not introduced the golden age, and the mind-numbing pain and anguish of world wars and the depressions of the atomic age have created a desperate longing for feeling, affection, and love. Strangely, through this period of general reaction against the coldly and calculatingly rational, evangelical preaching, smarting from an earlier overemphasis on the emotional, has become quite rationalistic. We have been slow to pick up on what is really happening out there, and this is ominous.

2. *The recrudescence of interest in narrative follows, then, from the historical skepticism spawned by the relentless use of the critical method in biblical and theological studies.* The triumph of the evolutionary vision greatly devastated Christian supernaturalism and orthodoxy. In our century one critical school after another left little remaining in the Bible or in theology. "They have taken away my Lord and I know not where they have laid Him" became the plaintive cry of many a soul in the wake of the rationalistic riptide that roared through the religious West.

Liberalism gave itself to massive cultural accommodation.

Paul Tillich said he could not speak the creed, but he could sing it. He claimed he would consider himself a Christian even if it could be proved that Jesus never lived. Neo-orthodoxy conceded the so-called "assured results of modern criticism" but took refuge in a non-propositional, non-cognitive personal encounter.[17] The biblical theology movement of Cullmann and G. Ernest Wright placed great emphasis on the mighty acts of God and saw theology and preaching as the recital of God's acts but naively failed to see, as James Barr pointed out, that "the historical acts of God make sense only because they are set within a framework of conceptions, stories and conversations."[18] Bultmann confessed he was totally skeptical of the New Testament historical representations except that he did believe there was a Galilean Jew who was crucified outside of Jerusalem. Emil Brunner deleted the virgin birth, the empty tomb, the forty-day post-resurrection ministry, and the bodily ascension and then desperately tried (however inconsistently) to hold on to something of absolute significance in the death of Jesus on the cross.

The upshot of all of this was that for many preachers and people the cupboard was bare. There was no bread, but only a stone. Thin moralistic gruel emptied the churches. Beyond question, what we see in our time as the reassertion of story goes back to H. Richard Niebuhr's prophetic and seminal work *The Meaning of Revelation* (1941). Admittedly of "a somewhat Kantian point-of-view," Niebuhr desperately sought an escape from the dilemma of historical relativism. His famous chapter II, entitled "The Story of Our Life," argued that preaching in the early church was essentially recital. Then he developed the contrast between external history (which he had given up to the relativists) as over against internal history. His point was: revelation must be looked for in events that happen to us personally. Revelation is seen like classical drama—it makes "intelligible the course of family history." Again we are with Kierkegaard: "Truth is subjectivity." What is to keep "the story" from becoming only "my story"?

With all of our appreciation of positive increments in the present euphoric emphasis on narrative, we must recognize that some aspects of this outgrowth are plainly faddish. In taking refuge in "history-like" or purely fictional construals of narrative, devotees of "the story" need to take stock. Even advocates of the general trends acknowledge with considerable uneasiness, "Narrative interpretation offers theology a chance to duck awkward questions about the truth of the stories."[19]

3. *The renascence of interest in narrative has fostered the rise of literary criticism and aesthetic theology.* The weary preoccupation with the form of the text and the process by which the text came into being would have to eventuate into some concentration on the content of the text itself. To be distinguished from "the Bible as literature movement," this approach is yielding many rich and helpful resources to the Bible student and preacher; but the emphasis essentially takes an ahistorical or anti-historical approach to the text.[20]

An early voice in the movement was Erich Auerbach in his influential *Mimesis: The Representation of Reality in Western Literature* (1946). In his comparison of Greek classical literature with the Bible, the Bible actually comes out very well, and narrative particularly is seen as distinctive. The two-tier approach (which deals with external history on the one hand and, more importantly, with "story" on the other, with little interrelationship between them)[21] became critical for the later Karl Barth's functional idea of biblical authority, as he came to see the narrative form as the key to biblical interpretation. Indeed, new models of exegesis began to emerge out of intra-textual studies.

If Barbara Hardy is correct that "all of life is lived in narrative form," then the remarkable variety of narrative material in Scripture represents a vast repository for the Christian communicator. Down with the false sophistication that thought we could dispense with the stories of our life and destiny. Up with the real search for roots. As Robert Roth gurgles enthusiastically, "stories come alive and jump to the complexities of life . . . for stories acknowledge the place of mystery as a natural element in reality."[22]

Yet in the narrative movement as it has evolved, there is much intertwining (and at some points one must feel inter-tangling) with the New Hermeneutic and the more lately articulated New Homiletic (to be subsequently discussed), to the point that one occasionally feels hard pressed to identify just how it is that the stories of Scripture are any different from Aesop's fables. Or if the biblical accounts are "like any good novel" as some allege, and if the resurrection of Jesus Christ is really only a powerful symbol, then really how is Jesus Christ any different or any more than, say,

John LeCarre's fictional George Smiley, who is such a kind and crucial figure? The end of the neo-orthodox era came, as Ronald Thiemann and David Kelsey have attempted to show, when the idea of special revelation was swallowed up in the functional view of biblical authority derived in large part from literary or rhetorical criticism.[23] Thus appreciating something of the process by which we have come to such a full-blown and ripe experience of narrative in our time, we need to proceed to fine-line more precisely what are both the positive aspects and the perils and pitfalls in the present developments. Strengths inevitably open vulnerabilities, just as weaknesses open growth opportunities. We shall need to examine both.

IDENTIFYING THE POSITIVE FACTORS

> *Tell me a story.*
> *In this century, and moment, of mania,*
> *Tell me a story.*
> *Make it a story of great distances, and starlight.*
> *The name of the story will be Time,*
> *But you must not pronounce its name.*
> *Tell me a story of deep delight.*

ROBERT PENN WARREN

> *An old story—the glory of it is forever.*

VIRGIL

The promise of literary criticism and aesthetic theology has not been quite what an optimistic exponent predicted when he wrote about "The Coming Revolution: The New Literary Approach to New Testament Interpretation." But there have been undoubted positive increments for the Christian communicator.[24] Now, not only historical and philosophical considerations are in view, but the artistic as well, as "now the sky and the mountains and the bottom of the sea come into view."[25] As long as we are not impeded with the baggage of structuralism's jargon and working premises, we can benefit much from this research and study. We are much in debt, for instance, to Robert Alter's now classic *The Art of Biblical Narrative*, although our essential presuppositions are at variance. Acquaintance with the prophet Jeremiah's use of rhetorical devices such as inclusio, chiasm, cluster, and the finessing of argument and dialogue are immensely significant for interpretation and proclamation.[26] Our purpose in this section is to briefly survey the impressive credit side of what has been taking place in the field of narrative and story.

1. While there are radical and reprehensible practitioners in the narrative craft, and we must be discerning in our use of all sources, there is a growing number of more conservative contributors who should not be missed. Our tendency is to approach and preach every passage with the same methodology. But narrative deserves and demands unique treatment. The linear, syllogistic pattern becomes imposition on such a text rather than exposition. Although we shall want to critique their nuancing of certain issues, we must appreciate deeply Ralph Lewis's call to inductive preaching and the work of Sidney Greidanus on the various literary genres. While Paul Ricouer on the one hand sees scriptural poetic discourse as without literal truth, and Stephen Crites refuses to see the resurrection of Christ as factual, we have Gabriel Fackre writing a multi-volume narrative theology from an avowedly evangelical stance. The superlative work of Leland Ryken of Wheaton will be greatly appreciated in our treatment.

In teaching homiletics for many years I have used an essentially didactic or epistolary model for neophyte preachers. The impact of contemporary discussion has compelled me to use also a narrative model. We can do so much more with narrative and do it more intelligently and skillfully. Interestingly, Haddon Robinson in his widely used text on expository preaching does not really address the narrative genre as such. Yet in the volume of sermons more recently published and containing sermons by Robinson and some of his students, of the twelve sermons, seven are narrative (of which two are first-person sermons), and most of the sermons begin with a personal or other kind of story. We are being alerted and stimulated in the present situation to consider more efficient and effective use of our resources.

2. We are being given impetus not only to take narrative texts and stories more seriously in the interest of greater utilization of variety in our preaching, but we must see in the universal appeal of story a counteractant to our present tendency to overintellectualize Christianity. At the same time we shall vigorously argue here that any notion of jettisoning conceptual or propositional

preaching is sheer folly. What Frances Schaeffer called *Escape from Reason* will bring us into chaos and great confusion.[27] We want to maintain both propositional revelation and personal encounter. We have long sung, "Beyond the sacred page, I seek Thee, Lord." But the richness of the inspired record is more than intellectual. As Kevin Vanhoozer shares in a choice extract from the venerable Abraham Kuyper: "The rationale for the diverse literary forms in Scripture is that revelation strikes all the chords of the soul, and not just one, e.g. the rational one. This makes it clear that the historical doctrine of revelation is not the barren propositional one it is often charged with being."[28]

The Christian communicator cannot capitulate to the modern preference for images as over against ideas (this is not in reality a choice we can make, inasmuch as there cannot be images without ideas any more than you can have music without notes). Yet we would be inane were we not to take into account the need for broad appeal. If we hold to a bicameral view of the human brain, we must admit we have tended to be more left-brained in our discourse—i.e., more logical, analytic, linear, step-by-step. The challenge is to balance this with more right brain, which is imagistic, imaginative, pictorial (cf. Betty Edwards, *Drawing on the Right Side of the Brain*). Effective communication must be both, and probably we have tilted toward accumulating facts rather than sufficiently including the more spontaneously creative. The current discussion summons us to better balance, not focusing solely on the biblical words as such, but building toward what the biblical text (made up of words) teaches and says.

3. The present ferment of discussion is showing us that while we have discussed endlessly what the Bible is and how the Bible came to be, we have tended to lose what the Bible says. Widespread biblical illiteracy among laity and theologues proves this point. In his monumentally influential *The Eclipse of Biblical Narrative*, Hans Frei, the late Yale historian, documents his contention that the sense of realism in the biblical narrative was largely lost by both liberals and conservatives in the eighteenth and nineteenth centuries.[29] He convincingly shows that instead of fitting ourselves into the biblical world as represented in Scripture and feeling the excitement and force of the narrative, we have tended to neuter the text in a vain effort to fit the biblical world into our own agenda. In the process we have lost narrative real-

ism. Frei pleads for allowing the Bible to speak on its own terms. It is unified in its statement, and it is figural; i.e., like the pre-critical readers of Scripture, Frei sees Bible stories prefiguring and typifying later central biblical events. He is particularly critical of Paul Tillich and his "method of correlation" by which Tillich dips into Scripture for symbols to aid in the answers for our existentially vexed questions.

Abandon such abstraction, Frei pleads, and rather tell and retell the story! We truly owe Hans Frei a great debt of gratitude for his emphasis and clarion call, though several emphases require caution. Along with other literary scholars such as Northrop Frye and Frank Kermode (who will both be part of our subsequent discussion), Frei has a Barthian suspicion of traditional systematic theology and apologetics. None other than Meir Sternberg, the Israeli scholar, expresses concern over Frei's efforts to "neutralize" the discussions of the doctrine of inspiration and history.[30] In focusing on literary structure and truth in the narrative, Frei seems to break loose from the truth of the narrative. In a solid critique in *Christianity Today* Alister McGrath of Oxford, in light of narrative theology's virtual ignoring of the issue of truth and factuality, aptly raises the question, how can we tell the difference between fiction and history?[31]

In urging us to take the shape of the story seriously, is Frei allowing the story to be true to itself by asserting that the facticity of the narrative is unimportant? The Jewish scholar Michael Greenberg challenges Frei on this key issue: it is not irrelevant as to whether Jesus in fact did or did not exist as portrayed in the story—this is part of the very nature of the story. And as Greenberg insists, if Jesus is only a metaphor, why not someone else?[32]

Christianity, like Judaism, is a historical religion. When Paul Tillich compared the historical Jesus to a very small boy beating a very small drum after a very long parade he surrendered the faith. "History-like" is not sufficient for the biblical witness (cf. 1 John 1:1-4). Jesus as archetypal man and the examination of literary Christ-figures cannot satisfy. I take "suffered under Pontius Pilate" as historical, and I take "was crucified, dead and buried" as historical. Frei's own historical skepticism, the legacy of his modernity, makes us realize that he did not escape cultural influence any more than those in the eighteenth and nineteenth centuries who eclipsed narrative. Frei has eclipsed historicity. Brevard

Childs, whose canonical criticism shares certain salient points with Frei, his Yale colleague, nonetheless faults Frei for neglecting "chronological elements," which is of course a recognition of the criticality of temporality in real history.[33]

In his own more positive theological contribution, Frei is dubious about historical likelihood and reliability. He says: "Whether or not we know much or anything about the historical Jesus is probably a well-nigh insoluble problem."[34] Frei wants to escape "the burden of factual affirmation."[35] He essentially disparages Scripture as often naive and simple, giving its "usual pathetic, clumsy interpretation of the spoken word."[36]

Another of Frei's colleagues at Yale, George Lindbeck, leans heavily on Frei and Frei's understanding of Karl Barth. Lindbeck reflects the same reliance on historical criticism in interpreting literary texts and comes out with this conclusion in his widely read *The Nature of Doctrine*: "The Jesus of the Gospels is the Son of God, of Abraham, Isaac and Jacob, in the same strong sense that the Hamlet of Shakespeare's play is the Prince of Denmark."[37] Is that sense strong enough? Let the historical narrative stand!

WEIGHING THE PERILS OF A MINE-FIELD

Delighting and instructing at the same time. (Horace)

The Scripture stories do not, like Homer's, court our favor; they do not flatter us that they may please us and enchant us; they seek to subject us, and if we refuse to be subjected, we are rebels. (Erich Auerbach, in *Mimesis*)

Let God be true, and every man a liar. (Rom. 3:4)

The more things change, the more they stay the same. (Author unknown)

One of the striking features of the contemporary reframing of interest in narrative is the unabashed excitement many express for the text of Scripture. Erich Auerbach unequivocally celebrates the uniqueness of biblical narrative in all of literature. Meir Sternberg exults in "the Bible's rich and novel repertoire of forms." Northrop Frye shows that the Bible has exerted a great influence on the imagination of the West, even quoting William Blake's lines

"The Old and New Testaments are the Great Code of Art." Frye maintains that "the biblical images and narratives constitute the imaginative, mythological universe within which all subsequent Western literature has lived, moved and had its being."[38] Indeed, some critics and preachers who do not believe in any external or historical referent for the biblical text seem more excited and enthusiastic about the text than some of us stodgy advocates of a historical and inerrant Scripture. This is a curious and regrettable anomaly.

In the broader cultural landscape, the whole discussion of the importance of a world narrative is valuable to the Christian communicator. When Neil Postman diagnoses modern society's need for "a transcendent narrative to provide moral underpinnings," we are immeasurably heartened. Siding with Toynbee to the effect that the source of such a narrative must be religion and that "without a comprehensive religious narrative at its center a culture must decline," we can appreciate the concern for "symbol drain" in our culture and the peril of seeing "stories" lose their force.[39] Up to this juncture we are mightily impressed with how the way is being prepared for the gospel story. But is there a debit side in the movement we are describing? Might there be a sense in which general euphoria over narrative may conceal elements of the Trojan Horse? At this point I want to reference some ongoing concerns and caveats.

1. In our concern to obtain and sustain a hearing for our message, and because of the appeal and attractiveness of story, we must beware of being seduced into becoming permanent occupants of a comfort zone in our therapeutic society. Studies have demonstrated that "sermons that appeal to a variety of senses and engage the audience but that do not expound the meaning of the stories told are judged as most effective."[40] What is our motivation in preaching? Are we going to pitch it to the gallery? Are we the bearers of the message God has given, or are we stand-up comedians and entertainers? Any genre of preaching can be insipid and ineffective and meandering, but there is a special temptation in dealing with story and narrative to become frothy and lacking in substance.

Where has prophetic preaching gone in our time? This question is often asked. At what point does being "user-friendly" involve us in a tragic betrayal of the gospel? Our society is sick, and sinners languish with a disease worse than AIDS. Paul warns of a great danger: "For the time will come when men will not put up with sound doctrine. Instead, to suit their own desires, they will gather around them a great number of teachers to say what their itching ears want to hear" (2 Tim. 4:3). Jeremiah indicted the prophets and priests who "dress the wound of my people as though it were not serious. 'Peace, peace,' they say, when there is no peace" (Jer. 6:14). Many shrink back from asserting the divine demands and the divine law because this is unacceptable to unconverted people (and in today's climate is not much more acceptable to the converted). The idea of anything normative has had hard going in our post-Enlightenment time. But hasn't gospel preaching always involved an offense and a scandal? In our age of pluralism (pluralism being a synonym for our present chaotic situation) the commandments may not be popular, but isn't David Tracy's nonauthoritarian notion of authority an exercise in futility? Sidney Ahlstrom wrote of Jonathan Edwards, "He remained a kind of perpetually misunderstood stranger." Can the Christian proclaimer totally resist this role?

We shall address more extensively the present penchant to normatize the narrative genre in view of the fact that not all of the Bible is narrative. Prejudice against some genres is apparent. In his notable article "The Limits of Story," Richard Lischer argues for the place of the non-narrative in life. There are storyless places in experience. As over against those who belittle rational truth, Lischer supports Dietrich Ritschl's opposition to reducing theology to recital or story, which he sees as undermining the theological task—namely, to reflect on and clarify the tradition.[41] In this movement the Queen of the Sciences, theology, has truly become the scullery maid. The issues and questions are not quite as simple as some in the narrative movement seem to think.

2. However appealing the idea may be that we want poetry rather than prose in our age and that "the strange new world of the Bible" is inviting, there are some dangerous undercurrents in the present move to narrative. Clearly in the mode of Feuerbach who reduced all religion to imagination, the propositionalist approach of C. S. Lewis, G. K. Chesterton, and Malcolm Muggeridge is out, and "idioms for construing reality expressively not propositionally" are in. Wesley Kort is right in surmising that "lurking in the background is a doctrine of Scripture." He insists:

"Literary interests in biblical narratives require or imply a new concept of Scripture."[42] For Kort the Bible stands in a succession of texts, early and ancient. For Ellingsen contemporary experience always determines a text's meaning. For Austin Farrer revelation is not in propositions or history but in images (Tillich's *analogia imaginis*). For David Kelsey the pattern of the Bible, not the content of the Bible, is the norm. For Norman Petersen the text is more mirror than window. For Gunther Bornkamm the story of the women at the empty tomb is a legend; "But see how his story is told!"

Hans Kung basically speaks for the prevailing mood: "A story cannot be replaced by abstract ideas, neither can narrative be replaced by proclaiming and appealing, images replaced by concepts, the experience of being stirred replaced by intellectual apprehension."[43] But this denigration of ideas and logic and propositions reflecting the modern rejection of supernatural revelation leads to total subjectivity and hence chaos. It may be that in some modern art you don't need to tell a story. But any narrative representation uses ideas and propositions; and if the law of contradiction is not observed, discourse is impossible. Rationalism has failed, but rationality is of the essence, and we seek to demolish it at our own peril. Modern thinkers have attempted to unload special revelation. The decision we make as to whether the Bible is revelation will be determinative for interpretation and preaching. Thomas Torrance, vigorously parting company with Kant and Schleiermacher, argued vehemently that revelation is unique and rational and that divine revelation is absolutely prevenient.[44] So what if secularization has made Warfield's view of biblical content as authority a problem? This is the orthodox view, and it still stands.

I believe that Wingren is right in his insistence that the basic question must be, what is the essence of Christianity?[45] Luther expressed this soundly: "We continually teach that knowledge of Christ and of faith is not a human work but utterly a divine gift—this sort of doctrine which reveals the Son of God . . . is revealed by God, first by the external Word and then inwardly through the Spirit."[46] The Bultmannian view that modern man cannot understand and will not accept what the Bible says is exploded by what the Holy Spirit continues to do in our world.

I recently watched Billy Graham's preaching on television and marveled at the response of thousands to biblical proclamation. I read of Emile Cailliet's first sight of a Bible and reading it as a brilliant French scholar and coming to Christ.[47] The Bible has poetry in it, but it is more than poetry. The Bible is the powerful Word of God that transforms and changes human life.

3. A further issue must be faced. George Stroup in *The Promise of Narrative Theology* raises the question, how does narrative as such change human life? To the extent that Bultmann's idea that "the historical Jesus is irrelevant to the preaching of the kerygma" and that the Bible as the catalyst to self-understanding informs the movement, how is human experience altered by narrative? Schweitzer argued that since recital is reenactment, "to know story is to adopt a way of life consequent upon it."[48]

This is to introduce an almost gnostic idea of salvation through knowledge. Socrates believed that to know the truth is to do the truth; but this ignores the reality of human sinfulness. We need the living, historical Christ who regenerates through the Holy Spirit and who justifies through His shed blood. Information will not save—only regeneration. Hence "the events that have happened among us" (Luke 1:1, NEB) are our foundation. As Peter assures us, "We did not follow cleverly invented stories when we told you about the power and coming of our Lord Jesus Christ, but we were eyewitnesses of his majesty" (2 Peter 1:16). There are many issues and implications we have yet to explore in these and other areas of question, but we move from the datum of biblical revelation. "If Christ has not been raised, your faith is futile."

CLAIMING THE POSSIBILITIES OF THE FUTURE

We are more persuasive when we tell stories. (Roger Shank)

Tell me a story, Grandpa. (Jesse David, age 4)

The cure for boredom in the pulpit is not brilliance but reality. (P. T. Forsyth)

If anyone speaks, he should do it as one speaking the very words of God. (1 Peter 4:11a)

The deepest conviction of the Christian is that Christ was not

wrong! We have very little left in the way of live alternatives to Christ as the Ground of Trustworthiness.
(Elton Trueblood, in *A Place to Stand*)

As a preacher I am obsessed to communicate the Word of God. My concern increasingly is to say less and communicate more. What James Smart terms *The Strange Silence of the Bible in the Church* is a terrifying reality in our time—not excepting many evangelical churches that profess adherence to a high view of Scripture. We cannot rest content with mild, soporific commentaries on the biblical text.

The Bible with all of its literary genres is the Word of God and is true in all that it represents. If truth is propositional correspondence with reality, then I assert that the Bible is God's true message to lost humanity. The scissors-and-paste approach to Scripture left us with shreds. The highly subjective neo-orthodox view left us without objective criteria to determine whether the Presence we meet in dynamic encounter is God or the devil. The neo-liberal flight from historicity and supernatural revelation leaves us with Terrence Tilley's dubious rope of sand—"the lack of certainty is the good news."[49] Interestingly, a top book reviewer recently faulted man of letters Thomas Beer's "tissue of lies from beginning to end," in referring to his biography of Stephen Crane. "Beer assumed the prerogative of creative artist and invented wildly. He made up phony love affairs for Crane, forged entire letters and otherwise repeatedly broke the fact–writer's commitment to stick to the truth."[50] The same is true for Scripture and its representations of fact. Of course there is fable and parable in the Scripture that obviously make no representation as to historical fact—e.g., Nathan's story of the little sheep when confronting King David. The age of the documents does not affect this. Our premise here is unashamedly to accept the representations of Scripture as true and objective fact. The Bible is God reaching down to humankind—and what a message it is (cf. 1 Cor. 15:3-7)!

C. S. Lewis, that most extraordinarily creative person, has been indeed "a voice for old-fashioned Christian orthodoxy." As Vanhoozer shows so well, Lewis had great appreciation for both poetry and history in the Bible and held to "the actual Incarnation, Cross and Resurrection."[51] Buffeted by many diverse influences, Lewis was converted to theism in 1929; but he had serious problems with Christ and the gospel as sacrifice or propitiation. Then in 1931 he came to accept Christ and orthodox Christianity. "It really happened!" he discovered. The historical reality of Christ was pivotal for him. This reminds us of Samuel Johnson's argument against Bishop Berkeley's subjective idealism, which denied physical reality. Johnson kicked hard at a rock and exclaimed, "I refute him thus!" Thus A. N. Wilson observes of Lewis, "His full conversion released his great literary flow."[52]

The Christian communicator has the Word of Life to share—in a time when the very paradigm of communication has shifted from the Age of Exposition to the Age of Show Business, from words to images, from literary substance to ephemeral sound bites, in which "television is the command center of the new epistemology."[53] And what should our response be? Endless hand-wringings and crusades to abolish television will achieve little. Postman's solution seems to boil down to an anti-Huxleyan jeremiad.

The fact is, the Scripture has an immense trove of narrative and story, and we need to turn to it afresh and consider its optimal utilization in the communications climate of our time. We should not abandon any of the scriptural genres, and we should avoid overstatements of "the narrative structure of the faith" (Don Browning). All language is in a sense metaphorical, but the Decalogue is not exactly narrative, and neither is Romans. It is true, as Wicker says, that "We dream in narrative, daydream in narrative, remember, anticipate, hope, despair, believe, doubt, plan, revise, criticize, construct, gossip, learn, hate, and love by narrative." But this is not to say that propositions, ratiocination, conceptualization, and ideas are absent. They are essential in the process.

But Craddock goes too far when he says: "It is very important that the structure of the message be a narrative. A narrative, by its structure, provides order and meaning, and therefore I cannot stress too heavily the indispensability of narrative shape and sequence. Change the shape, for instance into a logical syllogism and . . . the function of the message as narrative is now lost. The movement from chaos to order, from origin to destiny is broken, and in its place are some ideas, well argued."[54] While not denying for a moment the power of a good story, I cannot acquiesce that only narrative structure communicates in our time. The endless blasting of discursive discourse, or the rejection of the Cartesian grid and the sermon as argument with the accompanying disparagement of reflection, are overdone.[55] To project sequences and syntagms (chain-like series) on the analogy of Russian folk-tales and classical plays (or on Zuni myths as does Levi-Strauss; cf. Galatians 1:1-10) and also impose these on Scripture is to tout the sovereignty of the reader-hearer and to bring us inevitably to the plurality of meaning and total subjective chaos.[56]

If the cohesion of narrative is the *sine qua non*, we are in a bad way. Much narrative (particularly minimalist narrative) lacks cohesion. Linear thinking may be sequential, and the syllogism or dialectic are very sequential. The notion that anyone can be totally inductive (moving from particulars to the universals) is naive; and especially for any evangelical to suppose he can obviate deductive thinking (from the universals to the particulars) is folly. The very reading of the authoritative text in the service announces the universals from which we shall advance to the particulars. Things aren't up for grabs. I shall argue in this treatment for a sound balance and blend of both inductive and deductive elements, but we must have both.

The Christian communicator must seek to utilize the powerful resources of biblical narrative as never before, and that is the subject and object of this book. As someone has well said, we should not do poorly what the Bible does so well. I shall be calling for a fresh new approach in order to maximize the pictorial and the visual elements in the biblical revelation. I am all in favor of learning from Walter Brueggemann (in his Yale Lectures entitled *Finally Comes the Poet: Daring Speech for Proclamation*)[57] and many others. We need to come alive in our preaching of scriptural narrative. We need to be concerned about more pictorial and imagistic preaching of the didactic sections of Scripture. We need to cultivate much greater skill in the use of story as illustration. Every sermon needs illustrations, but few areas are as vexed or frustrating for the preacher as "the elusive illustration" (W. E. Sangster)

What is more, James Hopewell's ideas about *Congregation: Stories and Structures* open some intriguing new doors.[58] Hopewell seeks to foster a narrative understanding of congregations, using Northrop Frye's four genres of western literature: comedy, romance, tragedy, and irony. What is our story as a community of faith? Another profitable approach is that of Peter

Morgan and his *Story Weaving*.[59] While both of these writers are mainline, the use of spinning yarns and sharing our stories (did we call them "testimonies" in the days gone by?) loom up most importantly for our common life.

In seeking revitalization and identity clarification through *Story Weaving*, Morgan demonstrates plausibly how sharing stories can enliven our common experience of prayer, worship, preaching, fellowship, witness, and service. As a story-formed community, we all need to become good storytellers. We can learn much from the new storytellers of our time, and we shall intersect with them repeatedly in the course of this volume. And in this we have ample precedent in our Jewish and Hebrew roots. The Haggadah materials are popular homilies and stories that illustrate and apply biblical teaching. We need concentration and development of similar materials in our own time and for our own areas of question and quandary.

The present hour of flux and ferment is not one in which evangelical preachers and expositors can stand pat. The homiletics of the Left are on the move. For a long time they basically used the classical approach. Now the new hermeneutic is being implemented by a new homiletic. We can obtain many insights from these happenings. Without any abandonment of historic orthodoxy we can become better communicators of the truth as it is in Jesus by tapping into biblical narrative and story with greater relish and abandon.

In all of this we need to remember that the message, the gospel, the *kerygma*, has been committed to us. But how shall we package and process it for communication? The drama critic for the *Chicago Tribune* spoke of the message of hope offered by the musical hit *Les Miserables*. He indicated, "We are desperately hungry for words of inspiration in an era where there is little shred of hope . . . [this musical] ardently and fervently conveys these sentiments . . . it is a God-send . . . [the finale] cried out hopefully . . . but would have had no impact at all if it had not been written, staged and sung with splendor." Our approach to preaching narrative is in the interest of doing so "with splendor."

CHAPTER TWO

Analyzing the Rich Treasury of Biblical Narrative

Thy Word is like a garden, Lord, with flowers bright and fair;
And every one who seeks may pluck a lovely flower there.
Thy Word is like a deep, deep mine; and jewels rich and rare
Are hidden in its mighty depths for ev'ry searcher there.

Thy Word is like a starry host: a thousand rays of light
Are seen to guide the traveler, and make his pathway bright.
Thy Word is like an armory, where soldiers may repair,
And find, for life's long battle-day, all needful weapons there.

O may I love Thy precious Word, may I explore the mine,
May I its fragrant flowers glean, may light upon me shine.
O may I find my armor there, Thy Word my trusty sword;
I'll learn to fight with ev'ry foe the battle of the Lord.

EDWIN HODDER

Since the repository of narrative wealth we turn now to assay is the Bible, it is necessary to advance our working premise as to the nature and scope of biblical authority. The influence and uniqueness of the Bible and its impact on the whole world are matters of historic record. More important for our purposes here is an understanding of why the Bible is more than inspiring literature and is in fact supernaturally inspired revelation. This perspective, as we shall seek to demonstrate, has immense implication for how we handle it and how we preach and teach it. In an age in general revolt against all authority, we shall seek to make our case for not allowing autonomous man to stand above the Bible, which is to establish human reason as a higher authority than the Scriptures, but indeed to recognize and revel in the gracious gift of divine revelation, to which we should be submissive and obedient.

We do not begin with the *a priori* that because God is perfect and wholly truthful, therefore the Scripture must be perfectly truthful. Although this argument does have an appealing appropriateness, it falls down in light of the fact that many works that have their origin in God have become flawed and besmirched through human frailty and sin (the created world and its creatures being a prime example). A better and more helpful analogy is that of the written Word and the living Word, Jesus Christ. In both, divine and human elements fuse but under such divine and providential superintendence that both the Bible and the God-Man combine genuine and authentic divine and human reality without imperfection or distortion of any kind. To be sure, for many centuries the emphasis was on the divine to the virtual denial of the human; but in modern times the pendulum has swung to the predominance of the human and the virtual exclusion or denial of the divine.

Our starting-point is really with Christ and the apostles. We begin with what may be called a primary induction. The issue is what kind of book we deal with; and, more logical and necessary than that, we begin with a consideration of what it presents itself and purports to be. Should this be dismissed as merely circular reasoning, it should be pointed out that this is a kind of circularity that is totally inescapable and normal in any inductive pursuit of truth.[1] Demonstrably Christ and the apostles viewed the Old Testament canon as an organic and authoritative whole. The cruciality of Christ's own belief in and use of the Scriptures has been well argued[2] (cf. also Matthew 5:17-18; John 5:46-47; 10:35; etc.), and in this the apostles followed, as should we (cf. 2 Tim. 3:16-17; 2 Peter 1:19-21; etc.). Very early the New Testament writings were seen to bear the same imprimatur of divine authority as did the Old Testament writings (cf. 2 Peter 3:16; etc.); and thus, with Christ and the apostles, we hold to the total trustworthiness and complete reliability of what Scripture represents, or in the plain words that become so pivotal for our approach to and utilization of the biblical materials, *the Bible can always be trusted.*

Or to put it in the language of a distinguished Old Testament scholar, Edward J. Young, "We hold to a high view of inspiration for the simple reason that the Bible teaches a high view . . . only one doctrine of inspiration is taught in the Bible, namely, that of a plenary and verbal inspiration to which the modern mind is so hostile."[3] B. B. Warfield of Princeton would urge: "The Church has always believed her Scriptures to be the Book of God, of which He was in such a sense the author that every one of its affirmations of whatever kind is to be esteemed as the utterance of God, of infallible truth and authority."[4] This view, which prevailed through the greater part of the history of the church, was an outgrowth of the Jewish understanding of the Scriptures (as seen in the Old Testament itself and reflected by the writers of the Apocrypha, Philo and Josephus) and is to be traced in the church fathers who universally affirmed the inerrancy of Scripture. We see it through the Middle Ages and in the Reformers. Although some major creeds and confessions have no article on the inspiration of Scripture (since it was no matter of controversy or debate), we hear majestic affirmation of scriptural authority in the Augsburg Confession, the Westminster Confession, and even in the Tridentine dicta.

We are here affirming our confidence in the indefectible authority of the original writings (which we possess through the science of lower or textual criticism). God employed forty different human personalities to communicate His special revelation in the library of sixty-six canonical books, which are accurate, self-consistent, non-contradictory, and in every way faithful to their intended purpose. We shall expect to find God's truth in biblical narrative as in every other genre of revealed truth. We shall marvel at the variety and diversity of style, vocabulary, and literary genius. We shall expect to find variation and divergence in the accounts (since identical descriptive language might suggest collusion, which might destroy confidence in the accounts). We shall expect to find figurative and paradoxical language, but not necessarily scientifically precise language in the description of natural phenomena.

Many difficulties and mysteries in Scripture remain (as they do in nature itself, which God has created); but one must be struck by the fact that in our modern skepticism and unbelief God has brought many faith-fortifying discoveries and archaeological finds to light that have been strengthening and corroborating for faith. Significant manuscripts of great age, the Dead Sea Scrolls, the synagogue in Capernaum, the grave of Caiaphas are but a few of those that could be cited. Faith has received great encouragement.

Hence our approach to Scripture is to be reverent, positive, and from within the commitment of faith. Ours is not a salvage operation, nor the vivisection of the Bible. Our question is not, is it true? Our question is rather, what does it mean? We gladly confess, "Your Word is truth!"

SOME NECESSARY DEFINITION

So we'll live.
    And pray, and sing, and tell old tales . . .
    As if we were God's spies . . .

        KING LEAR, V, II, 1 .10-17

CHRISTIAN IN THE HOUSE OF THE INTERPRETER:
Christian saw the picture of a very grave person hung up against the wall; and this was the fashion of it: it had eyes lifted up to heaven, the best of books was in his hand, the law of truth was upon his lips, the world was behind his back; it stood as if it pleaded with men, and a crown of gold did hang over its head. (John Bunyan)

The purpose and plea of this study is for a return to Scripture as an authoritative text possessing the most remarkable and relevant literary appeal and resources. We need to give wide berth to those theories that see Scripture as only a collection of traditions or those higher-critical views that endlessly analyze a multiplicity of authors (such as D. B. Redford, who sees in Genesis 37:18-30 a bewildering J and E alternation,[5] or Harold Bloom whose *Book of J* loses all sense of basic unity but who chirps gleefully at his discovery that J is a woman).

The bankruptcy of the legacy of higher criticism, with its inability to identify what is the Word of God in Scripture, is clear when we consider the wreckage strewn through Christendom after this demolition derby of the last several hundred years had taken place.[6] So we are told that there are no miracles or long-range prophecy in our Old Testament; that the story of Jacob's wrestling comes from a legend of a "demon" at the Jabbok ford; that Zipporah's circumcision of her son likewise comes from an old tale of a demon of the wedding night; that Elijah's pouring of the water on the altar at Carmel comes from a rain-making ceremony; that Jonah is a fable written during the exile; and that no Psalm with "any certainty" can be attributed to David.[7]

Nor can we succumb to the prevalent notion in "narrative theology" that the use of story is part of the rehabilitation of the Scripture, a way of salvaging the Bible without making the Scripture binding. We must assiduously steer clear of David Tracy's view that the Bible is but a great religious classic or James Barr's preference for a "soft idea of authority,"[8] which both become capitulations to the pluralism and relativism of our time. If Genesis 3 is only a myth, "it is impossible to affirm a doctrine of original sin."[9] Then indeed we could duck the issue of truth in our reaction against propositional truth right down the line.

Tough hurdles and many hassles are before us, and clearly even among those who profess evangelical faith in the factual representations of Scripture there are casualties and calamities. What good is a high view of Scripture if we do not read the Scripture and preach the Scripture and obey the Scripture? Christians are experiencing the same practical horizontalization as is endemic in our culture generally. A careful study of a leading evangelical publication for leaders found that in the first 434 essays of the magazine less than 1 percent referred to the Bible or Christian doctrine. A national youth leader enthralled large numbers with his daily text from the *Tales of Dracula*. We need to find the Book of the Law as they did in the days of King Josiah (cf. 2 Chron. 34–35), and then we will experience the renewal and revival we so desperately need.

As we turn to the Bible itself, we find there a number of literary genres, among which are narrative, poetry, legislation, didactic, and apocalyptic, to name but several. Our particular focus here is narrative. Leland Ryken prefers to speak of theological material, historical material, and literary material, under which he has subdivisions such as story and poetry. He sees four types of narrative or story: (1) direct narrative; (2) dramatic narrative; (3) description; and (4) commentary.[10] John Sailhamer sees the Pentateuch as a whole as narrative material, but in an earlier treatment he distinguishes four distinct literary types in the Pentateuch: narrative, poetry, law, and genealogy.[11] Meir Sternberg differentiates what he terms ideological, historiographical, and aesthetic types of biblical narrative; but in no instance does he acquiesce to an anti-didactic bias. He insists that business is never subordinate to pleasure in Scripture.[12]

In looking at narrative in Scripture as one of the chief literary genres, I would propose to speak simply of three kinds:

(1) historical narrative; (2) parabolic narrative (with no historical representation); and (3) poetic narrative, such as the Song of Miriam in Exodus 15 or the Song of Deborah in Judges 5, in which we have an historical sub-stratum with poetic and imaginative elements of language. We shall examine the rationale for this classification later as we examine with greater care specific instances. But we must first define what a narrative portion or story is.

The richness of biblical simile and metaphor and their interpretation are frequently analyzed in standard works on hermeneutics or in a volume such as G. B. Caird's *The Language and Imagery of the Bible*. The handling of literal and non-literal language is an exceedingly crucial issue, and one is reassured that Caird does not go along with Bultmann who denied that the resurrection of Christ was an event of past history but who himself insists vigorously that "the first disciples didn't believe that the resurrection is something which came to happen to them, but an event which happened to Jesus."[13]

Robert Alter in his now classic work speaks of "a proper narrative event" as taking place "when the narrative tempo slows down enough for us to discriminate a particular scene" (as over against a genealogical representation).[14] Eugene Lowry insists that narrative sequence must involve a bind or some discrepancy or the loss of equilibrium; an attempt at resolution; and then consequences for good or evil.[15] In other words, a story tells about something that happened, starting with a point of tension and finally leading up to the satisfactory or unsatisfactory resolution of that tension. Narrative in this definition constitutes 77 percent of the Old Testament (according to Bruce Waltke), and indeed even the bulk of the New Testament is narrative in this definition.

SOME PREPARATORY DIRECTION

God does not need comedians but prophets. (Author unknown)

Do your best to present yourself to God as one approved, a workman who does not need to be ashamed and who correctly handles the word of truth. (2 Tim. 2:15)

The opening of God's Word and the speaking of God's truth are awesome responsibilities and immense tasks. A submissive and humble spirit before the authority of the text is prerequisite to any real understanding of the text. The prayerful solicitation of the guidance of the Holy Spirit is essential. But further, while our focus here is the narrative genre in Scripture, we must insist that with respect to all of the genres in Scripture, the teacher or preacher must give the most thoughtful and careful attention to the characteristics of the particular genre if the passage is to be preached accurately and clearly.

The Bible is both like and unlike other books. The Bible is unlike all other books inasmuch as it is uniquely the book given to us through the supernatural processes of revelation and inspiration. In this respect it stands alone. Yet like other books it consists of words and sentences and conveys meaning in a variety of literary genres. In searching out any meaning, in the Bible or any other book, the reader is advised to inquire, what kind of literary material is this?

This is sometimes called genre criticism or genre recognition. It is imperative for the interpreter of the Psalms of the Old Testament to recognize the different kinds of parallelism employed in Hebrew poetry. Similarly, a general grasp of the characteristics of the parable genre in the Bible can save us from some very fanciful and unfortunate interpretive blunders.

The importance of genre recognition has long been accepted in literature as a whole (identifying tragedy, comedy, epic novels, and lyric verse, for instance), and a similar concern for biblical literature has existed but is now very much more being emphasized. Many students of Scripture have become the beneficiaries of the work of Professor Richard G. Moulton, long-time lecturer in this country and abroad, whose classic *The Literary Study of the Bible: An Account of the Leading Forms of Literature Represented in the Sacred Writings* is such a reverent and suggestive piece.[16] I have never been able to teach or preach the Song of Solomon the same way since I read his masterful thesis that we have in that biblical document a dramatized reminiscence in a suite of seven idyls, the personages being the King, the Bride, and her escort (the Chorus of the Daughters of Jerusalem). We cannot preach the Song of Solomon in the same way we preach the book of Romans.[17]

In our own time, writers have been relentlessly productive in giving us massive and often helpful treatments of a similar nature.

While far too concessive to modern higher-critical scholarship (and thus of limited use to the conservative expositor), the giant volume *The Literary Guide to the Bible*, edited by Robert Alter and Frank Kermode, must be seen as a point of reference in the contemporary movement.[18] In Robert Alter's wariness of "excavative scholarship" we find a congenial spirit, but nowhere in these writings do we find a recognition of anything higher than "literary force and authority." Far more satisfying is Leland Ryken's *Words of Delight: A Literary Introduction to the Bible*, to which we have already made reference.[19]

The importance of genre recognition for preaching has come through loud and clear in Walter Kaiser's *Toward an Exegetical Theology: Biblical Exegesis for Preaching and Teaching*.[20] This influential volume presses the preacher to "exegetical conscience" and shows "the special issues" raised by prophetic texts, narrative texts, and poetry. The necessity of "principalizing" the biblical narrative is forcefully made, and we shall come back to this issue again and again in the course of this study. Kaiser is brief on these issues, but most helpful.

Another landmark volume is Elizabeth Achtemeier's widely-read book *Preaching from the Old Testament*.[21] This author always calls us to greater biblicality in preaching and toward that end helpfully deals with the narrative genre, the Law (she gives a ringing indictment of the modern tendency to pass over these passages in our preaching), then the prophets, the Psalms, and the Wisdom Literature. Her unfortunate aversion to "propositional preaching" because it can become moralistic (any kind of preaching faces this danger, even narrative preaching; cf. *Aesop's Fables*) and her view that Genesis 1–11 are "symbolic in [their] entirety" leave us with keen disappointment.[22] On the other hand, her work on handling the figurative language of the Psalms is very positive.

While showing us positively how biblical writers used various rhetorical shapes to communicate their message, Thomas Long's *Preaching the Literary Forms of the Bible*[23] is undercut by his very radical notion that Scripture is interpreted in our imagination, thus losing all hermeneutical control.[24] Theologically and historically we have seen the role of imagination in relation to developing the communication of the interpreted text, not in formulating the interpretation. Long's approach is much like that of David Buttrick, who sees us preaching not from a text on a page of Scripture but from "a field of contemporary conscious-ness."[25] Interestingly Buttrick dismisses the apocalyptic genre and confesses the great difficulty his homiletic has with the Wisdom Literature and the Psalms.

A far more solid and sound work is Sidney Greidanus's *The Modern Preacher and the Biblical Text: Interpreting and Preaching Biblical Literature.* Arguing that "a genre mistake leads to faulty interpretation because the interpreter will ask the wrong questions,"[26] Greidanus treats narratives, prophetic literature, Gospels, and epistles. He has a generally high confidence in the historic reliability of Scripture. He insists that it is not enough to get the meaning of the text into the sermon, but that "We must pay attention to the total configuration of the textual form/content."[27] Unfortunately, he seems to waffle between Craddock's idea that we shouldn't need to state the application of the text or that the sermon can be with or without a theme and on the other hand the strong conviction that "A sermon ought to leave no doubt as to its specific point."[28] The bottom line in all of this is to insist that when we identify a passage as of narrative genre, we shall need to preach it as narrative and take into serious account the characteristics of biblical narrative.

SOME PRIMARY DELINEATION

> How sweet are your promises to my taste, sweeter than honey to my mouth . . . more than gold, more than pure gold. (Ps. 119:103, 127)

> . . . from infancy you have known the holy Scriptures, which are able to make you wise for salvation through faith in Christ Jesus. All Scripture is God-breathed and is useful for teaching, rebuking, correcting and training in righteousness. (2 Tim. 3:15-16)

Frequently the Old Testament has been under-utilized in the church either because of a Marcionite prejudice against it or simply from benign neglect. This is most unfortunate because after all it is Act I of the two-part drama of redemption, as John Bright termed it. Some today are even questioning the use of the expression "Old Testament" and would replace it with "Hebrew Scriptures" or "Hebrew Bible" or "First Testament." Of course, over 100 years of vicious assault on the integrity of the Old Testament hasn't helped, and the incessant emphasis on its irregularities, its exaggerations, its legendary and theological embellishments, its stories "tinted with the dye of imagination," and its alleged abundant discrepancies has left many clergy and laypeople somewhat wary.

Yet here is the Bible Jesus loved and revered and that the apostles all believed and used with power. The Old Testament is a treasure-house filled with munificent riches, not the least of which is an unequalled trove of narrative material. The succession of critical schools in this century has bequeathed us a dubious legacy overall, but literary or rhetorical criticism, if unencumbered with structuralist presuppositions, can open some fascinating doors since it has generally stood for the intentionality of the text and has argued for seeing the narratives of Scripture as carefully crafted and meaningful. I can only agree with Professor Seitz of Yale that "What is lacking in most students is a deep-seated commitment to the Old Testament in its present form. Episodes of 'Mash' or 'Cheers' are much better known."[29] There may be something a bit faddish in certain emphases in the field, but I shall endeavor to show the bottom-line gains being registered for the would-be preacher of the Old Testament text.

We find in the Old Testament narrative what is easily superior to that found in any other source. The book of Ruth is a case in point. It has been reported that Dr. Samuel Johnson, the great literary critic of two centuries ago, made a copy of Ruth and read it before a London club. "The club, thinking it was a modern composition, was loud and unanimous in its praise of the manuscript. Then Dr. Johnson informed them that it was taken from a book which they all rejected—the Bible."[30] Or we recall Charles Dickens's opinion that Jesus' story of the prodigal son is the greatest short story ever written. Or consider the fact that the book of Job continues to intrigue thoughtful people. The distinguished writer Archibald MacLeish wrote his famous play *J.B.* in 1958 based on Job, as was Robert Frost's masterful *A Masque of Reason*, written in 1945. More recently the Pulitzer prize winner William Safire has given us *The First Dissident* (which ties the book of Job to the news of today). What could better signal the relevance of the Old Testament to the issues of life in our age?

If we can steer clear of the current literary boom's dethronement of the Bible's author and His intention, as well as its concomitant insistence on the status of texts as unstable entities, and open ourselves to the stories of the Bible, we shall have found wealth untold for the aspiring communicator. We may speak of several kinds of narrative in the Old Testament.

Epical Narrative

The great epics of Homer, Virgil, Dante, and Milton have nothing on the epic-scale primal history of Genesis 1–11. This is the seed-plot of all of the Bible. The marked use of Old Testament materials by New Testament writers has its foundations right here. Apart from the historical report of the fall of our first parents in the Garden of Eden, as set forth in Genesis 3, the rest of the Bible is virtually unintelligible. Granted, the description of the creation in Genesis 1–2 (like the description of the consummation in Revelation 19–22) is so totally beyond even any analogy from our own experience that it is difficult to find language adequate to the communicative task. Yet, we must argue that the scriptural account of creation purports to do more than tell us that it was God who created all things out of nothing in the beginning; indeed, we are told aspects of *how* He did the creating (cf. Gen. 2:7).[31]

The beautiful and most striking unity of Scripture under the superintendence of its divine author can be seen in the obvious parallels between Genesis and the Gospels in the New Testament, where we have emphasis on the new genesis with the Holy Spirit bringing forth, a new Moses, a new children of Abraham, etc. The tonal themes in the Gospels move to project the divine remedy for human ruin through the Lord Jesus Christ as earlier announced (Gen. 3:15 *et al* and now at long last fulfilled); but all is predicated on a historic fall that is to be addressed in a historic redemption. Much scholarship has shown the distinctiveness and the differences of the scriptural account of the beginnings in contrast with other ancient accounts, such as the Sumerian or Egyptian. The preservation of biblical authors from contemporary error is a telling evidence for the supernatural character of this infallible book.[32] The Bible preacher can confidently share the revealed answers to the pressing questions of origins.

How enthralled I sat in Wilbur M. Smith's class as he showed how the themes of Genesis are carried through to Revelation—how the first heaven and earth are matched by a new heaven and a new earth; first rest and final rest; paradise lost and paradise regained; the tree and rivers in Eden and the tree and river in Revelation 22; husband and wife in shame and sin and then at last the Lamb and His bride. Death and curse and thorns and sorrow and the gate of the garden shut are now replaced by the curse removed through the "man of sorrows" who wore the crown of thorns; the exiles become the inheritors, and the gates of the garden city of God will never shut (Rev. 21:25). Where is there the like of the paradigmatic conflict of the first two brothers and the diverging streams of humanity climaxing in the Flood epic and in the monument to human pride and arrogance at the Tower of Babel?

The poetic seams in the creation narrative, as some have called them, do not belie historic supernaturalism or the propositional errorlessness of Scripture. The narratives are intensely theological but thoroughly historical. The Bible is a mighty and a majestic reservoir of God's revealed truth.

Historical Narrative

Standard commentaries (like that by Keil and Delitzsch) and devotional commentaries (like those by W. H. Griffith Thomas on Genesis and A. W. Pink) can give immense assistance in laying out the narrative portion and expounding it. Pink is overly addicted to typology, but interestingly enough the whole narrative movement (led by Hans Frei) is much given to "figural language" on a scale many of us thought we would never see again. The significant work of Leonard Goppelt on typology will be assessed when we come to our discussion on narrative hermeneutic.

A newer kind of resource now available with particular helpfulness in the long stretches of Old Testament narrative is seen in John Sailhamer's massive and important *The Pentateuch as Narrative*, and also in his work on the books of Chronicles.[33] Influenced by Brevard Childs and "canonical criticism" with its emphasis on the text and inter-textuality, Sailhamer clearly affirms that we are dealing with "historical narrative texts." Like Childs and this school generally, Sailhamer is leery about going beyond the text itself to the event or backgrounding of the event. This is an important caution for our approach to Scripture; but fortunately Sailhamer does not rule out relevant extrabiblical material that may be helpful in interpretation (he draws on Kitchen's insights into Egyptian sorcery, p. 253 and on the Amarna Letters as affording insights into what manna was, p. 275, etc.). This is only proper and helpful.

Strongly emphasizing literary parallelisms, wordplays, numerical symbolism, recurring themes, and chiastic coordination, Sailhamer is exceedingly helpful in helping us see the narrative shape of the documents along with narrative links. At times he seems a little strained in his parallels between the Garden of Eden and the Tabernacle in the Wilderness (p. 100). Would any of this ever really occur to the serious reader of the text apart from the ingenious suggestion of the narratologist? Do we have too much *sensus plenior* here? What does this do to the perspicacity of Scripture? The parallels between Pharaoh's recalcitrance and the Balaam cycle seem more evident to this reader, although no one was ever more helpful on the whole matter of the hardening of Pharaoh's heart than Alfred Edersheim's treatment in his *Bible History*.[34]

While similarly scoring Exodus as theological narrative, George A. F. Knight shows a sharp contrast to Sailhamer's evangelical theology as he argues that the events narrated in Exodus are not necessarily factual. That Bible book, he says, is a human composition, a saga preserving human memories containing unacceptable elements (who shall make the determination?), though in the last analysis containing nothing final.[35] Better than this to open these veins of spiritual ore is *The Daily Study Bible* (Old Testament, edited by John C. L. Gibson). This matches Professor Barclay's highly popular New Testament series and, like his, occasionally shows an anti-supernaturalistic bias. Nonetheless, there is good help here on unpackaging the narrative process. More reliable yet is the *Bible Student's Commentary* from the Netherlands. Goslinga, for instance, on Joshua, Judges, and Ruth, is forthrightly against butchering the text. He strongly emphasizes Joshua as a type of Christ and is most helpful on the vivid narrative style of Ruth.[36] This series interacts with contemporary questions in a most satisfying manner, all things taken into consideration.

Biographical Cycles

Attended by serious perils (as will be developed in the chapter devoted entirely to biblical biography), we would want nevertheless to list this incomparably rich type of narrative in our brief cataloging effort. Leland Ryken quotes Henry R. Luce, the founder of *Time* magazine, commenting on his periodical's great interest in stories about people, to this effect: *"Time* didn't start this emphasis on stories about people; the Bible did."[37] We have only to review the depth and diversity of the story cycles on Abraham, Jacob, Joseph, Moses, Samuel, the kings, Elijah, Elisha, etc. Biblical heroes or anti-heroes are unlike the personalities in Homer's writings. Bible characters tell us about God. No wonder these narratives have continued to fascinate and intrigue writers of all backgrounds. Soren Kierkegaard could not escape Abraham and Isaac in *Fear and Trembling*, and Thomas Mann, the great German writer, gave 1,000 pages to Joseph and his brothers. Whether it is the floating axhead story or the narrative biographical chapters in Daniel, Jacob Licht was absolutely correct when he insisted: "Their excellence is a matter of common experience, not of aesthetic theory."[38]

Topical Narrative

In this category I would want to highlight the mixture of biographical/historical, just as we have a mixture of narrative/instructive and narrative/legislative. Here I am thinking of the great revivals of the Old Testament—the visits of God in mighty power among His people. Or I am thinking of the more thematic Wisdom Literature, like Job on suffering, Koheleth (the Preacher, in Ecclesiastes) in his search for the *summum bonum*, or Canticles (the Song of Songs), which is really a glorious love ballad, of one passage of which (8:6-7) Professor Saintsberry of Glasgow used to say, "It is the greatest passage on the eternity of love in all of literature." He paid further tribute: "It is the absolutely perfect English prose. There is nothing to compare with it." These are the narrative riches we possess in our Bibles.

Prophetical Narrative

What an indescribably relevant and rich holding we possess in the major and minor prophets of the Old Testament. Large sections are obviously admonitory in nature, but they are in many cases intertwined and interthreaded with the story of the prophet. In some instances we have what may even seem to be bizarre acts of prophets such as Isaiah, Jeremiah, Ezekiel, and Hosea. Hosea's marriage becomes a picture of Israel's spiritual infidelity and then of the Lord's desire for spiritual restoration. Ezekiel, the mystic among the prophets, knew when the temple in Jerusalem was destroyed, because on that day the wife of his youth died. These symbolic acts become *verbum visibile*.[39]

The choice kind of resource available to us may be found often in a series like *The Communicator's Commentary*—see John Guest's helpful work on Jeremiah/Lamentations.[40] The base is good exegesis, but there is also positive help on the daring imagery and crucial application out of the forty years of Jeremiah's ministry. Here is full measure, pressed down, running over.

SOME EXTRAORDINARY DESCRIPTION

> For I resolved to know nothing while I was with you except Jesus Christ and him crucified. . . . He is before all things and in him all things hold together . . . in whom are hidden all the treasures of wisdom and knowledge. (The Apostle Paul, in 1 Corinthians 2:2; Colossians 1:17; 2:3)

> The West has lost Christ, that is why it is dying, that is the only reason. (Dostoevsky)

> I have one passion—it is He and He alone! (Zinzendorf)

When we come to the New Testament, we come to the climactic and final act in the drama of divine revelation and redemption. This is Act II in the promise/fulfillment sequence of Scripture. John Bright is surely right when he insists that "Christ is indeed to us the crown of revelation through whom the true significance of the Old Testament becomes finally apparent."[41] The interdependence of the two testaments is clearly demonstrated in the 1,378 quotations and allusions from the Old Testament in the New. Here is the conclusive and defining word from God (Heb. 1:1-3). Christ is event and word. The interrelationship of the living Word and the written Word and the preached Word is soon made clear. The christological nature of all Christian discourse is not argued here but follows from our agreement with Luther that Scripture is the garment of Christ.[42] The Bible is the cradle of Christ.

While numerous literary genres are seen in the rich variety of New Testament material, the critical mass is clearly the narratives of the four Gospels and Acts. We find sections of narrative even in the epistles, such as the autobiographical prologue in

Philippians 1:12-30, which corresponds strikingly to the *narratio* often found in Greek rhetorical works. We shall give careful attention to the narrative aspects of the apocalyptic genre in chapter 12. Recalling the words that the angel Gabriel spoke in Marc Connelly's *Green Pastures*—"Everything nailed down is coming loose!"—we can readily agree with Walter Brueggemann that our times of "the terrible ungluing" find apocalyptic most meaningful and relevant.[43]

In our assaying of the indescribably extensive wealth of the "old, old story of Jesus and His love," we stand as the beneficiaries of mountains of helpful standard commentaries, background materials, and centuries of able and effective sermonic exposition. Graham Scroggie's *A Guide to the Gospels* has helped us grasp details. J. Arthur Baird's audience criticism has assisted us in nuancing the discourses of the Lord Jesus that exist in all four Gospels in significant patterns of narrative and discourse.[44] The devastating wreckage left in the wake of redaction criticism cautions us about the importance of right presuppositions in any effort to recreate and understand the process by which the documents of the New Testament were developed. What is represented as historical happening cannot be seen as fiction with a theological purpose (on the analogy of Jewish midrashic practice).[45]

The Gospels of the New Testament have been built on the basic facts and events that are foundational to Christian faith (Luke 1:1-4). They, along with the book of Acts, are representations of events by eyewitnesses (Acts 5:32). Randel Helms's book *Gospel Fictions*, with its wholesale dismissal of the supernatural, rises out of his view that the Gospels are literature serving a theological purpose.[46] When the Gospels are approached with the poetics of the novel, we may be attempting to appeal to those who do not find the factual representations therein plausible; but we are then in grave danger of going off-track and neglecting "the scandal of historical particularity," as D. A. Carson argues so persuasively.[47] The reader-response approach sees Scripture as a mirror, whereas in fact it is more essentially a window through which we perceive divine-human realities. The impasse of this unbridled subjectivity is seen in Sampson's *Meeting Jesus*, which invites us to imagine what Jesus was like with minimal suggestions from Scripture and, having given short shrift to the resurrection, concludes with: "Is this the way it happened? We cannot know. We have suggestions. The rest is up to our imaginations. One person's imagination can be quite comfortable with what another finds unreal, unimaginable."[48] So the end product is a document with less integrity than Thucydides' *History of the Peloponnesian War* or Livy's *Annals of Rome*. Rather, let us say: "Lord, I believe. Help my unbelief."

The Gospel of Matthew

Almost all students of Matthew are familiar with Krister Stendahl's theory that this gospel is the product of the catechetical interests of "The School of St. Matthew," primarily intent on demonstrating the fulfillment of Old Testament prophecy. Whatever may be the fact of that matter, the reader of the first gospel always sits in stunned and bewildered wonder before the sheer majesty of the portrait that Matthew, the tax collector/apostle, gives us of Christ, the Messianic King. Rather than being impressed by problems and alleged conflictions, I am awed by the beauties and skills of the arrangement and by the very Jewishness of this transitional gospel, by what Merrill Tenney spoke of as *The Genius of the Gospels*. I would agree with D. E. Aune who maintained that "gospel" is a special genre, a medley of many elements which then blend into a "gospel . . . a presentation of 'the good news' of Jesus the Messiah."[49]

There is nothing here of what Brueggemann termed "Joseph Campbell's seductive, debilitating reductionism . . . of 'journey' or 'hero,'" but rather a Holy Spirit-superintended report and interpretation, of which Demarest and Lewis rightly state: "The information Jesus taught in human concepts and languages was conceptually true—consistent and factual. In humbling Himself to become a human, Jesus adapted Himself to the human level, but did not accommodate Himself to human sin or error. In prayer to the Father He exclaimed: 'I gave them the words you gave me. . . . Your word is truth' (John 17:8, 17)."[50] Students of Matthew's gracious chapters should use the best of classic and also more recent commentaries, such as those by my colleagues D. A. Carson in *The Expositor's Bible Commentary* series or Scot McKnight in *The New International Critical Commentary* series or Michael Green's fine expository study[51] and then use a superb tool like Walter Liefeld's analysis of "narrative and composition patterns" for help with structure.[52]

Sensitivity to the Jewish background can be built by reference to Rabbinic Judaism;[53] the ties to the patterns of Greek rhetoric should also be explored.[54] Recent narrative criticism has much enrichment to offer if used discerningly. The Lutheran scholar John Paul Heil has given us a most stimulating study of *The Death and Resurrection of Jesus: A Narrative-Critical reading of Matthew 26-28*. Heil traces three major sections in this portion, progressing "in a dynamically alternating sequence forming seven sets of narrative sandwiches."[55] The concern about "rhetorical effect" can be of unimaginable benefit to the expositor. The atomizing tendency in critical studies has yielded at this point to a sense of whole narrative. Such close and careful attention to patterns in the composition can open new doors and help us to get away from our homiletical lullabies in the preaching of the great sections of Scripture so central in our understanding and experience of redemption. Just as the preacher seeks to employ structure to further and forward the message, so indeed the divine and human authors of Scripture have utilized narrative structure.

The Gospel of Mark

The charm of Mark's gospel with its brisk, proactive stance has much appeal. With its conflict stories, its nineteen miracles, and its five parables, its powerful passion and resurrection narrative, this gospel is always alluring to preachers with busy, time-compacted lifestyles. Yet this treatise is more than a collection of short stories. We are often victimized by a kind of "piecemeal approach," which would almost imply a kind of random, if not haphazard, approach by the writer, as if there were no master scenario apart from a rough correspondence to the chronology of Jesus' life. Yet, years ago I remember how electrified I was to recognize how brilliantly the instances of the healing of the blind persons were placed in relationship to the spiritual myopia of the followers of our Lord. The perfection of Scripture is such that we can properly expect the skills of the artist and the jeweler in arrangement.

Differing opinions on the overall structure and purpose press us to serious evaluation. Werner Kelber, of a more skeptical bent, for example, leaves us feeling a bit leery of his sharp bifurcation between the historical and the religious. He sees much reinterpreting and even reconceptualizing of Jesus. He quite unsatisfyingly sees the Gospel of Mark as a polemic against the Jerusalem church. He sees in the boat trips within the gospel the unfolding of the logic of Gentile inclusion.[56] In the last analysis he is not optimistic, given the disciples' hardness of heart, blindness of eyes, and deafness of ears.

Much more appealing is the case of Robert Gundry in his recent commentary on Mark, which he subtitles *A Commentary on His Apology for the Cross.*[57] This is an engaging and refreshing understanding and reflects the contemporary concern to represent more than the details and fine points as so admirably done by a Vincent Taylor or an H. B. Sweet. This quest for compositional cohesion must be most carefully done, lest we impose overarching categories artificially. Yet Mark 10:45 may well be the key verse of the entire gospel. This is what may be called "narrative propane." This necessitates that preaching be more than "a mild, soporific commentary on a biblical text."

The Gospel of Luke and the Book of Acts

Foreseeably the contributions of the Gentile physician who accompanied the Apostle Paul on many of his widespread itinerations have proved to be particularly attractive to the practitioners of literary and rhetorical criticism. That narrative requires art is especially in evidence here. As Professor Scott of Northwestern University used to say: "Luke was not only a doctor and an historian but one of the world's greatest men of letters. He wrote the clearest and the best Greek written in that century."[58]

Like Kelber's treatment of Mark, its twin, O. C. Edwards, Jr.'s work on Luke is for those not technically trained. The absorbing focus is always on the story line, with a deemphasis on the historical line.[59] Storytelling helps make what may be unacceptable more palatable, as all communicators know. But can it relieve us of the need to advance logical arguments sustained by historical evidence?

In an impressive duo of volumes, Robert Tannehill gives us what he calls *The Narrative Unity of Luke-Acts: A Literary Interpretation.* I cite this work as an example out of the Niagara being published, since this gifted author argues that Luke-Acts "is the longest and most complex narrative in the New Testament. It was written by an author of literary skill and rich imagination who had a complex vision of Jesus Christ and of the mission in which he is the central figure."[60] Typically unconcerned with history, the writer nonetheless sees the unity and the theology of this two-volume work by Luke. At long last we have the gospel account out of the chop-shop.

An even more nuanced approach is David P. Moessner's intriguing study of the central part of Luke (9:51–19:44), the journey to Jerusalem. Entitling his work *Lord of the Banquet*, the author seeks to draw the parallel between Moses and Jesus, between Deuteronomy and our Lord's purpose.[61] Whether or not Moessner convinces us about the travel narrative or not, some fascinating ideas about the *gestalt* of Luke's narrative are presented. What treasures of truth we have in God's Word!

The Gospel of John

Of especially high quality is R. Alan Culpepper's fine piece, *Anatomy of the Fourth Gospel: A Study in Literary Design*.[62] This work does not supplant the old reliables or the newer and magisterial commentary by D. A. Carson.[63] Culpepper does not deny there is any history in John, but he steadfastly holds to a distinction between objective history and narrative history. He is helpful because he grapples with plot development in John. Have we not all marveled at the use of selectivity in the seven vignettes of miracle, meeting, and message in this gospel? Yet, we are totally resistant to the idea that the Gospel of John is a many-lobed novel. We must most adamantly insist that there are continents of difference between the fairy tales about Herne the Hunter as circulated in the times of Henry VIII and the actual event of the defeat of the Spanish armada in the same century.

The wells of anecdote may run dry or we may sustain incendiary rhetoric by one means or another. But without the unimpeachable reality of the historical, supernatural, living Christ we have no message and no power. Our Bibles in their entirety present us with an inexhaustible source of truth for proclamation and practice. Let us say, "I trust in your word" (Ps. 119:42b).

CHAPTER THREE

Advancing Excellence in Expounding Biblical Narrative

With preaching Christianity stands or falls.

P. T. FORSYTH

The reason for the great weight that the Reformers laid on preaching was not educational or social but theological.

T. H. L. PARKER

Praedicatio verbi dei est verbum dei (The preaching of the Word of God is the Word of God).

SECOND HELVETIC CONFESSION

God is the preacher.

MARTIN LUTHER, IN HIS TABLE TALKS

The task of the sermon is to create space for the Word of God ... preaching must be exposition of Holy Scripture.

KARL BARTH, IN HOMILETICS

Preach the Word.

2 TIM. 4:2A

The Christian Church is a textual community. Everything we are or do stands in vital relationship to the written Word of God. The preaching of the Word of God is at the very center of the worship and praise of the people of God and is absolutely crucial for their health and growth. We have surveyed something of the renewal of interest in the not unsubstantial narrative sections of Scripture, and we have sought to take stock of something of the rich inventory of narrative in the Bible. Our concern now moves to the more effective and powerful preaching of these narrative sections. With such a trove of remarkable story for preaching, we should not want, as has been said, to do poorly what the Scripture itself does so well.

The pulse of preaching tends to fluctuate in the Church. But I would want to argue that throughout church history, while preaching is by no means the only factor in the mix, where preaching has been strong, the Church has been strong; and conversely, where preaching has been weak, the Church has been weak. Many times a premature obituary has been written for preaching. Not only adversaries from without, but even some erstwhile evangelicals have maintained a steady hostility toward preaching and have seized every opportunity to denigrate it. Clyde Fant lists some magazine titles that reflect something of the typical impatience with preaching, such as "Why Sermons Make Us Go to Sleep" or "Is Preaching Obsolete?" or "The Futility of Sermons" or "A Halt to Preaching."[1] In point of fact, many sermons are dreadful or dull. Many a preacher's preaching efforts fall into a homiletical black hole or suffer a homiletical free-fall with disastrous consequences.

Two sharply contrasting traditions in preaching stand face to face in our time. There is a preaching tradition that stands essentially in the stream of the Enlightenment and is horizontal and human being-centered. The other tradition, to which we here totally subscribe, stands in the stream of the Reformation and is God-centered, with a prior and dominant vertical. Liberalism basically lost the Bible in its theology from below and with its flagrant use of destructive higher criticism. The homiletics of the Left is now desperately trying to retrieve something biblical through narratology. Book reviews, commentaries on current events, and the bully pulpit on social issues were emptying the churches. Life-situation preaching ran out of gas to the degree that it was simply another self-help technique.

Conservatives in growing churches have stressed biblical preaching; and God, as He has promised, has blessed His Word. Still, evangelical preaching has tended to be extremely hortatory and often moralistic. Expository preaching has been hard work and has often been strings of pearls—clusters of sermonettes with a lack of inner coherence and unity and frequently only vaguely relevant. We have been better with what the text meant then than with what the text means now. Our preaching has often failed to strike the "preaching arc" connecting "the two worlds" of which John Stott has so well spoken.

In well-meant but definitely misguided efforts to be relevant and popular and "with" what is happening in our therapeutic society, evangelicals are tending to horizontalize preaching by psychologizing or sociologizing the text—for example, turning the book of Nehemiah into a guide on management theory, thus losing the critical vertical dimension. One gifted young preacher turns John 11 concerning the raising of Lazarus from the dead into a homily on sympathy and support for the bereaved, totally omitting any reference to the miracle or the claim of Jesus in 11:25-26. This is imposition of the most glaring kind. Is not the author's intention to present Christ's climactic seventh and final miracle and that which precipitates the final resolve of the religious establishment to silence Jesus (John 11:53)? Happy instruction about empathizing with the sorrowing may be incidentally mentioned, but to restrict the focus to that is to miss the "gut" of this text.

Our brief here is for the expository preaching of the narrative sections of Scripture. This is not to say that other kinds of biblical preaching (topical, textual-topical, or textual) do not have their proper and appropriate place;[2] but it is to assert that allowing the text to shape the sermon has every advantage, and preaching *lectio continua* (expository series) models for a congregation how the Scripture is properly handled and hence how they may use Scripture themselves. Nothing can be better than to take a natural thought-unit, articulate its center of gravity in a clear proposition or "big idea," and then develop it through the natural order of the text, drawing both main points and subpoints from the text in its context. Let the proportion and tone of the sermon correspond to the proportion and tone of the text; in other words, don't build a temple where the text has only built a tent.

We must not allow any considerations to move us away from sound and careful exegesis of the text, whatever the genre. One modern pulpit icon purported to preach on John 21 and indicated that the sea in which the fishermen labored in such futility represents the unconscious mind and that turning the nets to the right side of the boat means the right-brained, more creative approach, which will bring us awareness of Christ. Such folly!

No better is the preacher who raised the question as to "Why Moses Struck the Rock" in Numbers and responded with the theory that Moses lost his temper because he had been deeply wounded as a baby when his mother put him out on the Nile in the ark of papyrus. Since we all have these deep wounds and are dysfunctional, we can understand the dynamics. However, this is an unconscionable twisting of Scripture. Such a flattening out of the scriptural text will bring us a "famine of hearing the words of the Lord" (Amos 8:11).

The need of this hour is to advance excellence in the expounding of Scripture, and we shall examine now the three components of expounding biblical narrative.

READING THE STORY

> Intelligent reading of Scripture is the best preaching. (Bishop Wordsworth)

> Until I come, devote yourself to the public reading of Scripture, to preaching and to teaching. (1 Tim. 4:13)

> They read from the Book of the Law of God, making it clear and giving the meaning so that the people could understand what was being read. (Neh. 8:8)

The first ingredient in advancing excellence in the handling of biblical narrative must be attention to the more effective reading of the biblical story. If we read the story well, we shall more likely tell the story well, and this will add up to preaching the story well. So much public reading of the Scripture is careless and expressionless. A preacher is reported to have observed to an actor that audiences seemed to pay more attention to the actor than to the preacher. The actor replied that actors try to present fiction as if it were actually the truth, while preachers often present the truth as if it were fiction. The place for us to begin is in what frequently seems to be a mono-mood reading of the exciting biblical narrative.

While it is certainly possible to overdo expression in the interpretive reading of Scripture, the more common problem is reading without any sense of undulation, no hills or valleys, no moments of effective intensity. Some aspire to read without interpretation, but this is not possible. Any reading of Scripture is an interpretation. As Bartow correctly observes in his thoughtful analysis of this issue, "Neutrality is also an interpretation. It is the purveying of an attitude or mood . . . there is no way just to say words or to speak ideas without suggesting how people are to hear and respond to these words and ideas."[3]

On the other hand, I have heard preachers, like the late Donald Grey Barnhouse of Philadelphia, lace his reading of the text of Scripture with running commentary and exegetical insight before the actual sermonic exposition. A case can be made for separating the reading of the Scripture from the exposition of the Scripture. Let the Word stand as it was written, and then let the human communicator lead out its meaning. For this reason I prefer that the Bible be held up in the hands of the reader so all may clearly perceive that it is the Word of God that is being read and further allowing some ongoing eye contact for greater engagement with the congregation.

We are discussing here what is called in speech and rhetoric oral interpretation. One of the foremost textbooks in this important field, written by Lee and Gura, defines interpretation as "the art of communicating to an audience a work of literary art in its intellectual, emotional and aesthetic entirety."[4] This is the text I have used for some years in training young preachers how to free up in order to flow. Inhibited and clutched, many preachers stand like a stick and speak like zombies, with little inflective variation or expression. I work with preachers to read Psalm 100 as celebrative, or Psalm 23 as more introspective and pensive, with Psalm 23:4 marking a turning point. We need to feel the discovery of the divine presence in the valley of the shadow. We need to read Psalm 22 as pathos. The chapters of Lamentations and the crucifixion narratives in the Gospels present immense opportunity for oral interpretation. How can we read about the suffering and passion of our divine Savior without reverent and solemn expression? Read Acts 27, which describes Paul's voyage, and hear the winds howl; or read the story of the flood in the days of Noah in such a way as to make the audience hear the rain pelting down upon the roof of the ark.

A trainer of preachers once observed that an important criterion of fitness for ministry was to ask the neophyte preacher to read Genesis 3. He would listen carefully to hear the reading of God's question to our fallen parent—"Adam, where are you?" Does the preacher have heart, empathy, sensitivity? Is the preacher racing through material, or is the preacher conveying something of the anguish of God? Which word should have emphasis? To give equal emphasis to all of the words flattens out the passage. Emphasis on "where" seems to imply that the omniscient God needs information. A case could be made for stress on either "are" or "you" or shades of emphasis on both. Careful study of the passage and evaluation of the meaning of the passage are essential.

Parents and grandparents reading stories to little children is great preparation for the kind of reading preachers need to do. My former colleague Thomas E. McComiskey has given us a helpful volume on *Reading Scripture in Public*, in which he has a superb chapter on "sense-structure" in the narrative material of Scripture. Even the reading of Scripture calls for the identification of the main idea of the narrative, which, as we shall discuss in our next chapter, is not always an easy exercise. Helpful exercises enhance the benefits of this fine treatment.[5]

The idea and history of play-acting make some uneasy at any suggestion of the correlation of skills. But an able actor is one who interprets and communicates the personality of another. How could we conceivably read Judah's heroic appeal on behalf of Benjamin in the Egyptian court (Gen. 44:18-34) or David's lament on hearing of the death of Absalom (2 Sam. 18:33) in a matter-of-fact manner?

Every vocal skill is called for in this task, from appropriate relaxation techniques to foster more productive diaphragmatic breathing, to the development and projection of clearer tonal quality and voice timbre. Vocal monotony is soporific. Untrained speakers are especially prone to talk too fast. Too much head-bobbing or body sway are distracting. Exercises in breath control, volume projection, and greater resonantal richness are to be found in virtually every solid book on speech. Then go for the jugular of the meaning of the passage and prepare the public reading. The first step toward maximally effective use of biblical narrative is to work on reading the story well.

TELLING THE STORY

No privilege is so great as teaching the soul of a child. (Unknown)

Impress them on your children. Talk about them when you sit at home and when you walk along the road, when you lie down and when you get up. (Deut. 6:7)

"In the future when your descendants ask their fathers, 'What do these stones mean?' tell them, 'Israel crossed the Jordan on dry ground.'" (Josh. 4:21)

The next challenge beyond the reading of the story well is the telling of the story, and nothing better focuses our task than telling the story to children. However, I have noticed that in the "children's pulpit" in the average church service it is the adults who seem to be the most avidly attentive. We are touching here also the impact of the anecdote and the sequential illustration in the sermon itself. Jesse Jackson is one contemporary political figure who never forgets the power of the anecdote. Most used by preachers have no music or cadence whatever.

Frank O'Conner has well reminded us that there are three elements in the story: (1) exposition, (2) development, and (3) drama. The aspiring storyteller would be well advised to read the fairy tales of the Grimm Brothers and Hans Christian Andersen, *Arabian Nights*, the King Arthur legends, and others. For younger children, who models effective storytelling better than Beatrix Potter? We raised our children on *My Book House*[6] edited by Olive Beaupre Miller, as well as on the Bible stories. Such gifted storytellers as Paul Gallico (*The Snow Goose*) or Nathaniel Hawthorne (*The Great Stone Face* and *Behind the Minister's Black Veil*) or Margery Williams (*The Velveteen Rabbit*) are superb models. Bruno Bettelheim's study on *The Uses of Enchantment: The Meaning and Importance of Fairy Tales*[7] opens provocative vistas in the area of fantasy, of special interest to those who are enamored with C. S. Lewis and his *Narnia* stories or J. R. R. Tolkien and his *The Silmarillion* or the *Lord of the Rings* series. Other notables who repay perusal are O. Henry, Count Leo Tolstoy (and his famous story "Where Love Is, God Is"), Selma Lagerlov's "Christ Legends," Flannery O'Connor, Eudora Welty from the South, Peter DeVries, E. B. White

(*Charlotte's Web*), Annie Dillard, the great French storyteller Guy de Maupassant, and innumerable others.

Many preachers have been widely known for their storytelling, including D. L. Moody, Sam Jones who told stories very much in the Mark Twain style, Charles Haddon Spurgeon whose *John Ploughman's Talk* is an ingenious pictorial address to practical problems,[8] Henry Van Dyke, Phillips Brooks, and Billy Sunday, who although not having a booming, stentorian voice was exceedingly adept with the story. Crucial to storytelling, as in effective humor, is mastery of timing and the use of the critical pause. I have heard Billy Graham tell the story of the healing of the demon-possessed man of Gadara and can never forget its nuancing.

We are building here on the universal appeal of the story, and in particular the Hebrew genius for narrative, matched by the New Testament documents out of the same stream. Obviously, effective storytelling requires careful analysis of the story text— what has been called character and scene analysis. Jeanette Perkins Brown calls us to identify the introduction, the action, the conflict/suspense factors, the climax, the conclusion, and the relaxation.[9]

But can everyone become a storyteller? Certainly some people have unusual gifts, such as Ethel Barrett. If by storytelling we mean becoming an actor (in which the communicator seeks to become another person), the answer must be no. This involves theatrics, as John Harrell shows. But everyone can become a better storyteller—that is, remaining oneself but warming to more effective interpersonal relationships. Harrell helpfully demonstrates that the ancient Greek Pindar used narrative explosively because he never fully told every detail but left some matters to the imagination.[10] The abilities being utilized in storytelling are memory, imagination, and visualization. How to use the language of voice, motion, and gesture to foster and enhance imagination is also critical.[11]

"Once upon a time" opens the door to a voyage, to exploration, to transports in space and time. Telling rather than reading affords greater intimacy.[12] Ethel Barrett advocates giving a brief dramatization of an exciting portion of the story by way of introduction and thus grabbing attention. Using Bunyan's *The Holy War* as her paradigm, Barrett favors use of dialogue in the story (with different intonations), using either first, second, or third person, with first person being the most intimate.[13] Aunt Theresa has inclined toward the use of a single narrator. The employment of artifacts and visuals can be helpful, and Pellowski and others have used the candle ceremony, lighting the candle before starting to tell the story, and then extinguishing it when the story is over, to drop a kind of curtain of expectancy around the storytelling event. Pellowski also likes a personal introduction and beginning in *media res*—that is, at the last possible moment.[14]

Grant and Reed argue for actually holding the Bible as the story is told as a constant reminder that the story is from or based on the Word of God. Pivotal in their understanding of the art is to "see the action of the story yourself" and to build this through your reading, writing the components, rehearsing, and actually relating the action.[15] Henry James was exasperated by Anthony Trollope's habit of "reminding the reader that the story he was telling was only, after all, a make-believe." The biblical narrative, apart from the parabolic, is in point of fact true and should be presented as real and alive.

The hazards of translating the original story into slang and cultural equivalents are apparent[16] (the problem of narrative wobble, to be discussed subsequently). Marie Shedlock poses the following dangers in storytelling: (1) beware of introducing side issues; (2) be wary of altering the story; (3) don't use unfamiliar words; (4) beware of asking questions of your hearers—their answers may sidetrack you totally; (5) beware of over-illustration; (6) don't burden the hearers with too many details; (7) avoid over-explanation.[17] The person who would preach narrative with effect needs to work on telling a good story. General Kitchener learned his Bible geography from his mother's Bible storytelling. Right on!

PREACHING THE STORY

> Never water down the Word of God, preach it in its undiluted sternness; there must be unflinching loyalty to the Word of God; but when you come to personal dealing with your fellow men, remember who you are—not a special being made up in heaven, but a sinner saved by grace. (Oswald Chambers)

Since narrative bulks large in scriptural content, if the servant of the Word is to preach the whole counsel of God, the preacher will preach narrative. Preaching is the lifeblood of the Church. In what we properly call the great High-Priestly prayer of our Lord in John 17, Jesus prays as the one to whom authority is given and the one who gives eternal life. His work on earth involved revealing the Father. This disclosure of the Father was accomplished by giving the disciples "the words you gave me" (17:8). The Scriptures were critically paramount in what was taking place (v. 12). The word entrusted to the disciples would occasion hostility (v. 14), but that word is truth (v. 17). The epochal process envisioned is culminated when people "will believe in me through their message" (v. 20).

As a vital link in this living chain, the preacher today opens the Word of God in an age of moral anarchy, gross biblical illiteracy, and widespread confusion and great anxiety about the future. As Tom Brokaw described the seed-bed of the sixties, which has spawned much of our present mood, "A new form of popular religion flourished, the rock-and-roll church with nocturnal, narcissistic, mischievous, anti-authoritarian creed financed by great gobs of cash offered up by faithful acolytes."[18] Preparation for the preaching task involves attention to four indispensable areas:

Spiritual Preparation

> After all is said and done, the only way to know the Greek New Testament properly is by prayer. (J. B. Lightfoot)

> Unless he [the preacher] has spent the week with God and received divine communications, it would be better not to enter the pulpit or open his mouth on Sundays at all. (James Stalker)

Jesus prayed mightily for His own who were to be involved in the transmissive task: "Protect them by the power of your name . . . protect them from the evil one . . . sanctify them by the truth" (John 17:11, 15, 17). The biblical preacher is at the very forefront of the spiritual battle. No mastery of technique can compensate for spiritual unpreparedness. Someone has accurately said that the quality of our preaching depends on the quality of our praying. Luther argued that to pray well is to prepare well. Before we can prepare the message, we must prepare the messenger.

The recently published life of E. M. Bounds and the story of his "Great While Before Day Prayer Band" has opened helpful insight into the experience and ministry of a servant of Christ who has blessed us much with his writings.[19] His personal mottos were, "Hold fast to the old truths—double distilled" and "Have a high standard and hold to it" (such as plenary inspiration). He realized this meant he had to be "crazy for God," and he was much ostracized. He loved to quote Archbishop Leighton's summary of a holy life: (1) remember always the presence of God; (2) rejoice always in the will of God; (3) direct all to the glory of God.[20] This is where the preaching task properly begins.

Exegetical Preparation

> So then let us understand that God recommends to us the honour and the authority of His Word. As if He had said that we must receive in all humility everything contained in Holy Scripture, making ourselves teachable to what is contained in it. . . . Without exception, then, let everything contained in Holy Scripture be received with reverence. (John Calvin)[21]

In preaching narrative portions, as with any of the literary genres of the Bible, the preacher must begin by steeping and soaking his or her own mind deeply in the Scriptures and using every available tool for the preparation of the text. James Daane's formula is timeless: (1) select the text; (2) listen to the text; (3) scientifically study the text. Our purpose is to pick the lock on the safe and get at the valuables contained in it. In the very next chapter we shall grapple with the peculiar challenge of getting the meaning of many narrative pericopes, but the essential exegetical task is the same for any passage (exegesis meaning "to lead out").

The preacher who can use the Hebrew and the Greek should beware of their overuse. That is, biblical exposition is the art of selection. No one can preach exhaustively covering everything in a passage. The younger preacher invariably attempts too much. We need to delimit scope; or as Tim Stafford puts it so well, we must be willing to "kill our darlings." We must resist the temptation to go on fascinating but irrelevant excursions. In the development of the rhythm of preparation and delivery, the preacher develops "homiletical killer-instinct"—that is, the sense of what must be treated and dealt with in exegetical conscience, that which cannot be omitted in sharing the text. Conversely, there are secondary- and tertiary-level supportive materials that are part of the sub-text but may or may not be included in the exposition. Those who use only the English translation should employ every available tool for the excavation of the text.

An unusually helpful work is Douglas Stuart's *Old Testament Exegesis*, now in its second edition, revised and enlarged.[22] Genre-sensitive, this work also makes invaluable bibliographic suggestions. For the New Testament I would recommend Walter Liefeld's *From Text to Sermon: New Testament Exposition*.[23] The upshot of this plea is to not go to the commentaries too soon, depriving yourself of the excitement and thrill of personal discovery with the help of the Holy Spirit. Use the commentaries only to check your work and suggest possibilities you had not considered. Perhaps you have missed something very essential . . . and obvious!

Also most positive are pieces like Ronald Ward's *Hidden Meaning in the New Testament*[24] and updatings for our exegesis in D. A. Carson's *Exegetical Fallacies*[25] or suggestive monographs like E. K. Simpson's *Words Worth Weighing in the Greek New Testament*.[26] There is no substitute for meticulous exegetical work.

Theological Preparation

According to Luther, the Word of God always comes as *adversarius noster*, our adversary. It does not simply confirm and strengthen us in what we think we are and as what we wish to be taken for. (G. Ebeling)[27]

As the exegetical process continues, the meaning of the text in its context comes into focus more sharply and clearly, and our understanding of the thrust of the inspired writer crystallizes. Right at this emerging juncture, another body of data comes into necessary play. Our concern activates for *analogia Scripturae* (what the Scriptures as a whole teach; that is, the fruit of Biblical Theology) and for *analogia fidei* (what the Christian Church as a whole has understood this passage to teach, along with all of Scripture; that is, the fruit of Systematic and Historical Theology). Having little or no regard for this larger picture in preaching exposes us to the danger of highly idiosyncratic interpretation. It is highly unlikely that we shall discover a meaning that has not been seen heretofore in millennia of study. This is often the point where cultic interpretation and heresy originate.

Yet it is right here that we confront a mine-field of peril. Walter Kaiser has wisely warned us to interpret an earlier passage before we transport the fuller and richer later disclosure into that text.[28] That is to say, we shall lose the necessary concern for authorial intention in a given text if we are not cautious. Certainly we subscribe to the inner consistency of Holy Scripture; we do not believe there will be any contradiction between earlier and later divine revelation. But we must not read the latter into the earlier. The preacher, nonetheless, has the weighty responsibility of seeing his or her interpretation of a given text in the light of the whole.

The preacher is inevitably a theologian in this sense. Here we find ourselves at cross-purposes with the growing evangelical impatience with theology and doctrine. The "queen of the sciences" has been more and more consigned to be the scullery maid, as has been observed. We want relevance, not theological toil. We have already lamented in this chapter the increasing psychologization of the Christian message in our times. The abdication of theology with its insistence on the glorious, transcendent, Almighty God will lead to the humanizing horizontalization of Christianity.

The question is not whether we will be theological; the issue is whether we will have good theology or bad theology. Every statement about Jesus Christ is theological. In today's climate of "New Age" usage of biblical terms, when we hear the name "Jesus Christ" we need to ask, which Jesus Christ? The Word comes with judgment as well as mercy. Will we hear that message also?

The tendency in much narrative preaching is moralism— sweet advice, gentle nudgings toward more benevolent behavior, unctious elaborations of the obvious without any emphasis on the divine dynamisms. Note the emphasis in the epistles on the doctrinal and then the practical. We must avoid practical Pelagianism in our preaching of Bible characters. The widespread abandonment of theological concern in preaching is disastrous. The Gospel is good news, not good advice.

Homiletical Preparation

Two things are urgently required of us modern Christians: to see Jesus truly and to show Him just as we see Him. (A. B. Bruce)

Rather, we have renounced secret and shameful ways; we do not use deception, nor do we distort the Word of God. On the contrary, by setting forth the truth plainly we commend ourselves to every man's conscience in the sight of God. (2 Cor. 4:2)

At a pregnant moment the homiletical or preaching outline will emerge from the exegetical outline. We shall address at length the unique challenge of the form that narrative preaching takes in comparison and contrast with more didactic passages; but here we stress the principle that sermons must take form. Crafting the expository sermon involves a dedication to the crafting of such form as will not distort or change the truth of the text.

One of the 102 "Great Ideas" in Hutchens's and Adler's famous series is the idea of "form." In ancient Greek rhetoric, invention (the content) was followed by arrangement (the form). Intrinsic preparation is the preparation of the truth of the passage; extrinsic preparation is the fashioning of the form of the message. The manner is to the matter as powder is to the ball. What is said and how it is said exist symbiotically. If the content is vacuous, effective form can do little to help (we have but well-organized nothing). Yet, superb content can be utterly ruined by poor form. Form stands in relation to culture (and therefore we must exegete culture as well as the text). There is no one form, but there are more effective and less effective forms.

Function should be the determinant of good form. We do not preach the syntactical outline because the sermon is not a lecture. Nor is the sermon a literary essay with a highly "read" or "written" sound. Such highly polished surfaces are at odds with communicational effectiveness in our time. French laquer preaching became obsessed with fine points of style and technique, focusing on how it would rate on an oratorical Richter scale. Preaching is an oral event. Thus we seek form that accentuates the dialogical character of the preaching event, such as the skillful use of questions. Never has a generation of preachers faced more competition for attention than ours. We have to face it: if we bore our hearers, we lose them.

Reflection would indicate three factors in the matter of form: 1. The effective sermon form must convey *the meaning of the text*. This axiom is at the aorta of what expository preaching is. We seek to find what the text means and preach what the text says. The text must shape the sermon, whatever the literary genre of the text. There must be clear and careful correspondence between the thought development of the text and the emerging sermon. The sermon must have inner coherence (why is not logic a required course for preachers?).

Not every facet in a passage can be developed within the normal time restraints. No real exposition can be developed in fifteen or twenty minutes. We need at least thirty or thirty-five minutes for exposition. This necessitates careful and judicious selectivity and the steadfast resistance of our souls to "rabbit-trails." John Stuart Mill once observed: "On all great subjects something remains to be said." The Magellan sermon is out—we can't go around the whole world in the sermon. Better to say less and communicate more. As Ronald Ward used to say, remember that the sermon is a monograph, not an encyclopedia.

The form should seek to preserve proportionality. What looms large in the text should loom large in the sermon. What is subordinate in the sermon should be recessive in the sermon. Correspondence in mood should also characterize the sermon. The feeling tone in the sermon should match the controlling feeling tone in the text.

Compaction increases density, and many expository sermons have too high a density and are consequently heavy and sluggish. "Gridlock has gripped America," a news magazine trumpets. Sermon style can be as crowded as a Japanese commuter train. NBC's treatment of the 1988 Olympics was faulted because they tried to cover too much activity and did not satisfy the viewers with enough of any activity. In 1992 the coverage was much superior because there was greater concentration on fewer events. In all of this, however, we must recognize that the simplification of any truth exposes us to the danger of distortion. Putting it more simply is a tall order.

2. The effective sermon form should foster *a sense of movement*. As Clovis Chappell used to remark, "A good sermon needs to be like a journey: we begin, we travel, we arrive." In some marked sense the sermon needs to be sequential. The typical narrative passage catches us up in linear progression, and this becomes one of the interest-sustaining advantages of narrative preaching. If the trajectory of the sermon has a sense of unity, direction, and purpose, we shall sense movement. The crafting of the main points should help us avoid "plot clot," or the clogging of the arterials. Like golf shots to the green and the waves of the

sea to the shore, so the structure should ease us toward the climacteric. With carefully crafted transitions we increase the fluidity and liquidity of the "moves."

While overemphasis on the parts, the total triumph of the syllogistic model (against which stands the mass of narrative material in Scripture), and the neo-scholastic emphasis on structure are hidden reefs to be avoided, we know that we remember best what is organized. Classifying materials aids unity. As Aristotle put it: "Beauty depends on a certain sense of order and magnitude." Symmetry and balance are functions not only of the logical outline but of the emotional outline as well.[29]

Narrative poses some unique and special problems with conclusion and application, and we shall address these in upcoming chapters; but the present weakness in conclusion and application is lethal. Without some crescendo and final climax to "preach it home," the message wilts and withers just at the point where business needs to be transacted. Both content and form must assume responsibility at this critical juncture. This is, of course, the strategic value of the concluding contemporary focus illustration. H. Grady Davis is on the mark when he asserts: "We overestimate the power of assertion, and we underestimate the power of a narrative to communicate meaning and influence over the lives of our people."[30]

3. The effective sermon form must achieve *a meeting with the hearers*. This is the striking of "the preaching arc" described by Harold Freeman or "Between Two Worlds" as delineated by John Stott or "On the razor's edge–between the then and the now" as deployed by Joel Gregory. This is what A. B. Bruce has in mind when he speaks of the two things that are urgently required of us: first to be mastered by our biblical content, "to see Jesus truly"; then to put that message in appropriate and impactful form, "to show Him just as we see Him."

In this sense preaching is application. Our application must really commence in the introduction itself. Continuous application is generally to be preferred to compact application for expository preaching. A good blend of inductive and deductive elements is beneficial. The wise personalization of discourse is important. If we are concerned about interest factors, we need to remember that the word *interest* means "between us." Those who would be "the inheritors of Nathan's legacy" (using Bausch's phrase) need to know how to blend the "we" of identification and the "you" of confrontation.

And all of this with some passion and warmth and moral earnestness, recalling Robert Frost's good line that all poetry of substance begins with a lump in the throat. We are talking here about "fire in the belly" of the preacher—that irresistible and irrepressible burden and necessity to preach, when God's truth fills us so completely we will fairly burst to express it.

Variants and adaptations are particularly opportune with the narrative genre. By this I refer especially to the following:

1. *The use of artifacts and visuals* in the interest of greater pictorialization in preaching. Thomas Guthrie of Scotland and Peter Marshall in our country are examples of gifted pictorial preachers. We who are less gifted can use visuals to immense advantage.

2. *The development of a drama segment* to give a contemporary focus to the issues being authoritatively addressed from the scriptural portion for the day.

3. *The employment of dialogue* throughout the entire or most of the message to augment the point/counterpoint and give-and-take on the issues.

4. *The enhanced involvement of the congregation in first-person or dramatic monologue* is especially appealing to some, though admittedly difficult for others. Alton H. McEachern has shared some helpful theory and positive examples of the dramatic monologue. He urges beginners to start with segments rather than with full sermons to get a better feel of the technique.[31]

One of my favorite monologists is James Rose, formerly of Calvary Baptist Church in New York City. His unusually gripping first-person sermons, his vivid use of words and word pictures, and his overall surgical skill as a preacher merit attention and analysis.[32]

This is the ultimate in the adaptation of a form that can maximally benefit from the narrative genre. We shall analyze its pluses and minuses in a subsequent section.

What a beautiful coming together—the biblical story and the sermon!

II

OUR SKILLS

Not so he that hath applied his soul, and meditateth in the law of the Most High; He will seek out the wisdom of all the ancients, and will be occupied in prophecies. He will keep the discourse of the men of renown, and will enter in amidst the subtilties of parables. He will seek out the hidden meaning of proverbs, and be conversant in the dark sayings of parables.

FROM THE APOCRYPHAL BOOK ECCLESIASTICUS, 39:1-3

CHAPTER FOUR

Keying in on the Meaning
for Narrative Preaching

Come, search ye critics, and find a flaw; examine it from its
Genesis to its Revelation, and find an error. This is a vein of
pure gold, unalloyed by quartz or any earthy substance. This
is a star without a speck; a sun without a blot; a light without darkness; a moon without its paleness; a glory without
a dimness. O Bible! it cannot be said of any other book, that
it is perfect and pure; but of thee we can declare all wisdom
is gathered up in thee, without a particle of folly. This is the
Judge that ends the strife where wit and reason fail. This is
the book untainted by any error, but is pure, unalloyed, perfect truth.

CHARLES HADDON SPURGEON

Later Protestant orthodoxy did incalculable damage with its
doctrine of inspiration in which it did not accept the para-
dox that in scripture God's Word is given to us in the con-
cealment of true and authentic human words, when it
removed the salutary barrier between scripture and revelation, when it adopted pagan ideas and made the authors of
the Bible into amanuenses, pens, or flutes of the Holy Spirit,
and thus found in the Bible an open and directly given revelation, as though this were not a contradiction in terms.

KARL BARTH, IN THE GOTTINGEN DOGMATICS[1]

The appeal and lure of the extensive narrative sections of
Scripture is undeniable and perennial. Robert Coles of Harvard,
the doyen of children's religious and moral impulses in his moving *The Call of Stories*, shows how out of all the early storytelling
has emerged *The Story* that has shaped western civilization and
molded countless generations of humankind.[2] Homileticians and

theologians of the Left, having essentially surrendered the Bible to modernity, are scrambling frenetically to snatch something of significance from Scripture to fill the yawning abyss of pulpit emptiness. Thus has come the stampede toward preaching narrative and doing theology narratively. Evangelical and fundamental Christians find normative and objective truth in the narrative portions of Scripture, as in all the genres of inspired Holy Writ.

The primary and absorbing concern of the preacher of narrative (as in all of the Bible) is to discover the meaning of the passage. Where is the meaning to be found, and how is it to be found? This is the concern of hermeneutics (Hermes being the messenger of the gods in ancient Greece). Some in the field presently will contest whether or not there is meaning in the Bible for life today. I am not now speaking only of radicals of the deconstructionist and structuralist stripe. A critical watershed exists as to the nature of scriptural authority, bearing significantly on our whole quest for meaning. How we handle the Bible hinges largely on what we believe the Bible is. Karl Barth, retaining in large measure the higher-critical legacy of liberalism, refuses to identify Scripture and revelation. The words of the Bible, from his standpoint, can never be equated with the Word of God. His essential Kantianism consigns him in the final analysis to subjectivism and agnosticism.

The hermeneutical consequences of this epistemological judgment are to be seen in the thinking of Thomas G. Long of Princeton. In a recent article (as well as in his several books), Long blasts "the old way" of cracking the seal of a text and then applying the text through the sermon. What it *meant* is not to be seen as the clue to what it *means*, according to Long.[3] It is in the act of imagination on the part of the interpreter (cf. David Buttrick's "contemporary field of consciousness")[4] that we ascertain meaning, Long argues. He defends "the desirability of a certain kind of eisegesis." This is productive *eisegesis*, but this approach essentially jettisons biblical authority in favor of human authority. We shall argue in this chapter that the new hermeneutic is at the bottom line anthropocentric. Human imagination is slotted in improperly. In Long's scheme of things, the order is text-imagination-meaning-sermon. The orthodox and better order is text-meaning-imagination-sermon. Imagination generates the creative processing and packaging of biblical meaning. In this chapter we propose to trace how we obtain that meaning of the text.

The plethora of crazy interpretations in the long history of interpretation are used by critics to undercut the argument for plenary inspiration and inerrancy. Lewis and Demarest show that this is to mistake the difference between "what is given by inspiration and what is taken by illumination." As they insist: "No amount of interpretive abuse can change the the nature of the Biblical message as it was originally given."[5] So our determination and dedication must be to very careful and correct interpretation of the text of Scripture, which has special and unique wrinkles as far as the narrative sections are concerned. We shall want to painstakingly pick our way between the overdone allegorizing of the Alexandrians and their progeny on the one hand and the hyper-finicky, overly rationalistic friends who in the name of a wrong-headed, scientifically precise hermeneutic rule out virtually anything poetic or figurative or even the mildest of *sensus plenior*.

Most regrettably, we are seeing some serious fissures in the underlying foundation of biblical authority on the part of some avowed evangelicals. Some specific examination of a case in point is relevant to our concern about the meaning of narrative passages. I am referring to the work of Clark H. Pinnock, whose earlier works, such as *Set Forth Your Case*[6] and *Biblical Revelation*,[7] were solidly in the camp of those who stand for the orthodox and received doctrine of biblical infallibility. Restless with Christian exclusivism in a pluralistic world,[8] it is in *Tracking the Maze* that Pinnock lays bare the most disturbing and distressing aspects of his ever-moving, almost unpredictable theological journey.

Choosing to misunderstand and malign conservative evangelicalism from which he has come (what else is new?),[9] Pinnock downplays the importance of scriptural authority[10] and dismisses premillennialism and its pessimism.[11] Seeking some middle ground between liberalism and orthodoxy, Pinnock seizes upon "the epic story of salvation" as a kind of "newscast." While attempting to hold on to genuinely historical foundations for the Christian faith,[12] Pinnock tilts toward Barthianism as he talks about Scripture bearing witness to God and "pointing" to the story of salvation[13] and theology resting not on scriptural principle but "upon Jesus Christ and the Christian story."[14] But whence do we derive what we know and tell of Jesus Christ and the Christian story except from Scripture?

Pinnock unabashedly pits theology and doctrine against

"story-truth."[15] He exults in "the story" (this is critical for our purpose in this chapter) because the story is "a dynamic category, permitting much interpretation from many angles."[16] Orthodoxy is seen here as that which keeps the story alive; heresy is that which distorts the story. The question we must face here is, are we basically surrendering normative hermeneutics and objective truth? Is all revelation "story"? Are the Ten Commandments revelation?

The problem and plague of the conservative house of theology, according to Pinnock, is that it is "deductive and exegetical." Is that so bad? More is involved, and there are inductive elements to be sure, but where will we go if we surrender logic and exegesis? Are propositional revelation and propositional theology really our chief nemesis as Pinnock argues? If the problem of liberalism is that it is "a hall of mirrors," is not Pinnock himself vulnerable to what he describes as "addictive accommodationism" and dangerous "concessions to modernity" in cutting loose the "macrostory" from the conscientious exegesis of propositional revelation and normative theology?

Perhaps there is amnesia in the scholar and smoke in academia, to turn about the figures he uses. As early as in his *The Scripture Principle* (1984), Pinnock projects a belief in degrees of inspiration and advances the category of "legend" as appropriate for portions of Scripture such as Genesis 1–3, Jonah, Matthew 17:24-27 and 27:52, and Acts 19:11-12 and 28:1-6. Much to be preferred is the Pinnock who wrote *Biblical Revelation* in 1971 and there stoutly and steadfastly defends the integrity of the original autographs. Pinnock then stood for a "perspicuous, inerrant and noncontradictory Bible."[17] There he warned against a loose hermeneutic "which can destroy the meaning of inspiration altogether, and may be a cloak for a denial of biblical teachings."[18] A good place to stand!

We must now proceed to an examination of the hermeneutical dilemmas of the narrative genre.

THE TRENDS

Your word, O Lord, is eternal; it stands firm in the heavens.
(Ps. 119:89)

All your words are true; all your righteous laws are eternal.
(Ps. 119:160)

. . . give me understanding according to your word.
(Ps. 119:169b)

You have exalted above all things your name and your
word. (Ps. 138:2b)

To be behind an age that is drifting away from truth and godliness is the only safe, the only dutiful position.
(John Kennedy of Dingwall in Scotland)

Charles Colson has adeptly observed, "We really live in an
age where new barbarian hordes are overrunning our culture."
Carl F. H. Henry has spoken of the onset of "the new dark ages."
The societal and moral collapse of our times is in no small part
due to what the late Francis Schaeffer foresaw as a time of "con-
tentless mysticism" in the last part of the twentieth century.

The disparagement of objective truth, building on Kant's
agnosticism, sees truth as what we make of it. Morality reduces
to a matter of sheer preference. Within this view, preaching must
abandon discursive rhetoric (i.e., it must discard any sense of the
sermon as argument and the whole Cartesian grid as a sellout to
Hellenism).[19] Explanation of the text becomes anathema.
Commands are unacceptable because they are discursive and
informational. Hans Frei insists that "the very idea of a referent
for biblical narrative is an illusion."[20] For Gadamer and the "new
hermeneutic," meaning is logically distinct from the truth. This
hermeneutic cannot distinguish between orthodoxy and heresy.
These become meaningless terms.

For Kelsey it is the *pattern* of the Bible and not its content that
makes it normative. This is a functional view of truth that leaves
us without truth. With functional authority only, as we see in Karl
Barth, we have no absolutes. Vaihinger's paraphrase of Kant
shows us where we are: "The idea of Virgin Conception is another
expedient religious fiction—a beautiful, suggestive and useful
myth."[21] Modernity thus fulfills the sighing longing of Keats: "O
for a life of sensations rather than thoughts." But isn't this a
thought? So Stephen Crites observes: "One cannot derive universal inclusives from narrative." We are with Alfred North
Whitehead: "It is [now] more important that it be interesting than
that it be true." The attitude of anti-objectivity has prevailed.

Umberto Eco's *The Open Work* (1962) celebrates indetermi-

nacy in literary interpretation. Such an open text means that mis-
interpretation is impossible. Multiple interpretations are in the
saddle. As one astute commentator put it: "No view is wrong: it
is at best revealing, and revealing only of the speaker." Thus the
move is virtually totally away from the author and the author's
intention to the reader and his or her response. Truth is subjective. We are in the clutches of existential hermeneutics today.
Normativity is surrendered. Historical skepticism runs rampant.
How is the Lord Jesus Christ demonstrably different from others
called "christ-figures," such as Billy Budd, or Pietro Spina in
Bread and Wine, or the black priest in Alan Paton's *Cry Beloved
Country*, or the whiskey priest in Graham Greene's *The Power
and the Glory*?

Since no one ever reads the same book twice (a la Heraclitus),
inasmuch as we are constantly changing, it is argued, we can only
expect multiple meanings. It would be the height of futility to aim
at what the writer meant. We are really back to Schleiermacher's
notion that the key to understanding and interpreting a text is self-
understanding. Beyond doubt we face the issue of historical distance in interpreting Scripture. Lessing's ugly broad ditch is there.
But we shall argue vigorously here against anarchic plurality of
meanings in which the text is viewed as a handwoven blanket
with many threads,[22] as a kind of religious Rorschach ink blot test,
or a Thematic Apperception Test.

The quest for eternal truth seems to have vaporized in our
times. Interest in truth about the text or truth from the text may
yet survive in some circles, but what about the truth *of* the text?
We hear nowadays about "the simultaneous legitimacy of a number of meanings," and we are in chaos. The object is self-reinter-
pretation. Now who is capitulating to the Greeks?

Thiselton succinctly characterizes the "new hermeneutic":

1) we lose all emphasis on correct understanding
2) the emphasis is on poetry and metaphor displacing
   straight argument or discourse
3) we see the undervaluation of propositional truth and
   propositions
4) what's true for me is what is true.[23]

Dennis Nineham's *The Use and Abuse of the Bible* presents a
case study of one who bemoans the quest for norms as a false trail

and all Christian doctrine as a human construct.[24] His argument that we cannot understand people of more than 300 years ago is thoroughly demolished by Joe Houston's demonstration that many ancient writers (including Herodotus and Thucydides and biblical writers) were concerned with the difference between fact and "story."[25]

Thus when we are advised, "don't give the moral or explanation"[26] of a narrative pericope, we are aware at once where this stream is flowing. When we feel the pressure of Fred Craddock's push against interpretation and application, we know where we are.[27] We have gone through the dicer of the "new hermeneutic," and what ground do we have to resist Gloria Steinem's "I began to look inward for solutions" or Gore Vidal's blasphemous "full frontal assault on the New Testament" in his *Live from Golgotha*? What criteria do we have to challenge these "meanings"?

Even Charles L. Rice has to pull back here when he advises, "To ask for application is no more than to insist that we be in touch with men and women here and now."[28] There is meaning in texts, and therefore there can be application. Scripture can be understood (2 Cor. 3:14-16). If we do not desupernaturalize the Gospel with false presuppositions, we can have steadfast confidence in the person and work of the Holy Spirit who inspired writers then (2 Peter 1:21) and who illuminates readers now.

Thiselton is right on when he urges us to respect the rights of the text and let it speak! He writes: "The biblical text comes alive as a speech-act when correspondence occurs between the situation the biblical writers address and the situation of the modern reader or hearer."[29] Let us "humbly accept the word planted in [us], which can save [us]" (James 1:21b).

THE TASK

"Is there any word from the Lord?" (Jer. 37:17)

Let me understand the teaching of your precepts. (Ps. 119:27)

I trust in your word. (Ps. 119:42)

I will walk about in freedom, for I have sought out your precepts. (Ps. 119:45)

Before we can state anything of religious value about God, we must have some means of assuring ourselves that God is. . . . If we know this, then our statements have an objective as well as a subjective validity—they represent reality, and are not "judgments of value" only. (James Orr)

We have embarked upon our quest for the meaning of narrative passages on the premise that Scripture presents objective truth through divine revelation and inspiration. Without certain objective realities, as James Orr points out, subjective "judgments of value" are ephemeral, flimsy, and soon forgotten. The subjectification so in vogue today does not seem to realize this. According to the Old Testament, false prophets are "those who prophesy out of their own imagination" (Ezek. 13:2).

Woe is pronounced on "the foolish prophets who follow their own spirit and have seen nothing" (v. 3). Their preachments are "false visions and . . . lying divinations" (v. 9). They say, "Peace" when peace does not exist (v. 10). The issue here, as Fairbairn shows so clearly, is that "the whole was subjective merely without any objective reality."[30] The true prophet, by contrast, has the landmark, the fixed and given divine disclosure, as the basis of subjective experience. Fairbairn quotes old J. A. Bengel concerning this danger:

What some teach about the inward word, is likely to occasion much fearful evil. . . . Persons who are always dwelling upon that subject are impatient to get possession of the kernel without its fostering shell . . . in other words, they would have Christ without the Bible. But notwithstanding this favorite refinement, they are insensibly approximating to an opposite extreme, and they will arrive at it. For as it often happens that extremes meet, so are fanaticism and gross deism found at last to coincide; and mischiefs symptomatic of the one and of the other may already be seen occasionally in one and the same beclouded mind.

Some passages indeed quite readily yield their meaning inasmuch as we are expressly told what the passage teaches. Jesus Himself interpreted the parable of the sower (Matt. 13:18ff.) and the parable of the weeds (Matt. 13:36ff.). We can be in no doubt whatever as to the author's purpose in relating the first miracle of Jesus at the wedding feast in Cana (John 2:1-11). This is not a pericope intended to teach us about Jesus' approval of marriage, nor about believing prayer or obedient faith or creative power as such. All of these are elements involved in the sub-text, but the Apostle John tells us explicitly that the miracle was performed to reveal Christ's glory and to foster faith in Him (v. 11). The larger context is a gospel record intended to encourage faith (forms of *pisteuo* occurring ninety-eight times) in Jesus as the Christ, the Son of God (cf. John 20:30-31). We shall deal subsequently with the important matter of context. Some passages in Scripture, then, present little difficulty in grasping the essential meaning because Scripture itself tells us the meaning.

Every literary genre in Scripture poses some problematic passages with which the preacher excavating the text must seriously grapple. Some didactic passages in epistolary literature are quite as clear as those narrative texts just cited. Little doubt can exist as to the thrust of Romans 4:1-25 (justification by faith alone); or 1 Corinthians 15 (dealing with the resurrection of Christ and our own resurrection); or Hebrews 5:11–6:8 (while presenting some thorny issues for the exegete, nonetheless in the flow of the argument this essentially hortatory piece addresses Christian maturity, its nature, and its hindrances). The larger arc in many cases (or the commanding motif of the passage) is explicit. But even in didactic sections, what is the "big idea" in, for example, 1 Thessalonians 5:12-28? Can we import an inclusive like "characteristics of healthy Christians" to give us some organizing principle? Can we analyze the Beatitudes of Jesus or the fruit of the Spirit in Galatians 5 under some organizational rubrics? In preaching Colossians 1:1-14 are we to succumb to an outline as wooden as salutation, thanksgiving, and intercession? The components are not hard to interpret, but the overall thrust can be more elusive in any of the genres of Scripture.

As we have argued, the preacher's task is to find what Scripture means and then to preach what it says. Ours is not to *decide* what it means but to *discover* what it means. We are seeking, therefore, in each narrative passage what Walter Kaiser denominates "the central point of reference."[31] We would agree with what Frank Kermode shares—namely that "a text will offer, at some point a hint—an index, or emblem of the whole—as a guide to our reading of the whole (eindruckspunkt)."[32] In our next section we shall trace out the procedure by which this center of gravity in the passage is identified.

Some narrative passages seem to present little help as to meaning or significance. When some of David's mighty men heard the king long for water from the well of Bethlehem, three of them at great risk broke through enemy lines to fetch water, which David then threw on the ground (2 Sam. 23:13-17). How does this passage fit into the cycle? Is it an instance of heroism? Does it model loyalty? What does it tell us about David? What preaches here?

Differentiating between symbolic vision and actual happening is not easy throughout the book of Ezekiel. Instructed to lie on his left side 390 days (for Israel) and on his right side forty days (for Judah), the prophet is delivering a message about the impending siege and judgment of Jerusalem. The significance of the numbers is clear (particularly the forty and the total, 430; cf. Exodus 12:40-41). Fairbairn sees the whole episode as symbolic and in a vision, not as Ezekiel lying over a year on one side or another. His whole approach to interpreting the visions tends to spiritualize them (cf. Ezek. 40–48).[33] Beasley-Murray follows the Septuagintal reading and sees the numbers rather as literal and actual descriptions of the time of exile for Israel and Judah respectively.[34] Ralph Alexander sees Ezekiel as spending brief portions of the days lying before the people and the 430 days as 430 years extending to the time of the Maccabean rebellion.[35] Our task is to get to the meaning of the passage.

THE TECHNIQUE

The law of the Lord is perfect. . . . The statutes of the Lord are trustworthy. (Ps. 19:7)

The precepts of the Lord are right. . . . The commandments of the Lord are radiant. (Ps. 19:8)

The ordinances of the Lord are sure and altogether righteous. (Ps. 19:9b)

Your word is a lamp to my feet and a light for my path. (Ps. 119:105)

> We need to get back to basics. Christians must start with
> nurturing holiness and then preaching, then theology and
> then development of a Christian world view. (Os Guinness)

Since our objective is to instruct with the living preaching of
the Word of God, we face the primary necessity of wrestling with
a text and drawing out its meaning, the principle being enunciated. We cannot preach the passage and apply it without clear
insight into the author's intention in the passage. We need to
employ every tool available to us to draw out the meaning.
Believing in the perspicuity of Scripture, we are of the persuasion
that the Spirit-led student of Scripture can basically understand it
(cf. 1 John 2:27). As Augustine observed: the Scriptures are like a
river in which children can wade and elephants can swim. We can
never grasp the depths of Holy Writ, no matter how long and how
deeply we excavate.

The history of interpretation shows us grievous and egregious
errors in interpretation. The sign "All kinds of twisting and turning done here," hung outside a wood-working shop, would not
be inappropriate with respect to the work of some biblical interpreters. The Alexandrians or the allegorists lost much of
Scripture, making the three baskets of bread in Pharaoh's dream
the Holy Trinity, or the bride's hair in the Song of Solomon "the
mass of nations converted to Christianity," or the two silver coins
given by the good Samaritan to the innkeeper baptism and the
Lord's Supper, or the four barrels of water on Mt. Carmel the four
Gospels, or the ship in which Jesus and the disciples sailed the
Church of England and the other little ships nonconformity, or
Job's friends the heretics, his seven sons the twelve apostles, the
7,000 sheep God's faithful people, and the 3,000 hump-backed
camels the depraved Gentiles. Overuse of types has led some Bible
teachers into expounding twenty-five ways in which Eliezer,
Abraham's servant, represents the Holy Spirit in calling out the
Church, or in which pegs and nails in the tabernacle of Israel have
great theological significance. We shall speak more of typology,
but we want to note here that Hans Frei's notion of figural language potentially opens the door for an interpretive free-for-all as
dangerous as any the Church has ever seen.

While helpful hermeneutical guides such as the highly
regarded work by Milton Terry in the last century[36] and the

durable piece by Bernard Ramm from the middle of this century still have value,[37] Grant Osborne's compendious new *The Hermeneutical Spiral*[38] will command the field for some time. More in tune with the new hermeneutic is the volume by Duncan Ferguson[39] (though of questionable value, it is of use to sense the tensions in recent critical scholarship). But invaluable to us, especially for the very vexed and demanding job of application, is Elliott Johnson's recent *Expository Hermeneutics: An Introduction.*[40]

No one has been more helpful in the general technique of responsible interpretation than Alan M. Stibbs, who sets out the following basic guidelines:

1) Get at the true meaning of single words
2) Get at the use, syntax and idiom of the original language (with the help of commentary and concordance if your facility in the original is limited)
3) Get at the form of expression: literal, figurative, actual, metaphorical
4) Get at the character of the composition [what we have called genre recognition]
5) Aim to appreciate the allusions, figures, and expressions
6) Recognize literary customs, such as Hebrew parallelism in poetry
7) Do not be misled by chapter or other divisions
8) Seek to understand the particular significance of each passage
9) Beware of introducing conceptions foreign to the original text
10) Recognize the character of divine revelation as given in and through history, i.e., the original, literal historical meaning of Scripture is of fundamental importance.[41]

The crucial matter of context, whatever the length of the preaching portion, can never be emphasized sufficiently. Whether we have one verse or a whole chapter, we must not wrench any portion out of its context. The meaning of the parable of the workers in the vineyard becomes quite clear when this portion (Matt. 20:1-16) is seen in relation to Christ's conversation with Peter in response to Peter's question, "What then will there be for us?" (cf. Matt. 19:27-30). Similarly, our understanding of the meaning of our Lord's transfiguration is greatly enhanced when seen in the context of His words about "the Son of Man coming in his kingdom" (Matt. 16:28–17:8).

Modern narrative criticism can be helpful to the interpreter, as Osborne points out, particularly in showing us how the author communicates his message (which is theological). Such issues as the omniscience of the implied author and narrator, point of view in the narrative world, story time, plot and character analysis, and characterization of the personalities involved are all essential components in understanding the meaning of the narrative.[42] While it is our purpose to get back to the author's intention, we must recognize that the human author was not always aware of the full significance of his own inspired utterance (1 Peter 1:10-12). Thus we would argue here for a mild *sensus plenior* and the possibility of a biblical writer (as any other writer) having a primary and then a secondary meaning (for example, the Gospel of John is really built on a series of double meanings). This may all complicate the work of interpretation, but it does not mean subjectivism run riot.

Sometimes, as in one Sherlock Holmes mystery, the fact of significance is that the dog did not bark. What isn't said or the insignificant line may supply the key that opens the lock. Consideration of the whole narrative cycle is vital, and regard for patterns of repetition and arrangement can be helpful. I have elsewhere argued that selection of details and the shape of the climax frequently are giveaways as to the meaning of the narrative.[43]

THE TRUTHS

I am laid low in the dust; preserve my life according to your word. (Ps. 119:25)

My soul is weary with sorrow; strengthen me according to your word. (Ps. 119:28)

Every word of God is flawless. . . . Do not add to his words. (Prov. 30:5-6)

There is only one way of bridging that gulf between God and man; and that is that God Himself should speak. . . . Whoever has been satisfied with what we sometimes call natural revelation, it has not been those who have been left to it. (James Orr)

The eternal God has spoken. The Church of Christ is properly seen as a textual community existing "within the context of what Thomas Mann once called the 'quoted life,' that is, a life that conceptualizes its own existence in terms of authoritative texts."[44] We are a community of interpreters seeking the meaning of the Scripture as the basis for application to daily life and the issues in our times. A mind-set that is open to the truth, an essential mastery of the tools of interpretation, reference to the history of interpretation, and prayerful reliance upon the divine author of Scripture, the Holy Spirit, will bring us to better and better understanding of the passage. The fact that we can't know everything ("Now I know in part," 1 Cor. 13:12) doesn't mean that we can't know anything (note 1 Cor. 2:10-12).

Scripture is its own best interpreter, as we know from struggling with the meaning of "the keys of the kingdom" from the words of our Lord in Matthew 16:19. To what is Jesus referring when He speaks of the keys? Jesus in Luke 11:52 refers to "the key to knowledge," which can admit or exclude from an understanding of the truth. The key that opens a passage may not always be right at the door, but if we will look about with some diligence, we may well find the solution.

The late Donald Grey Barnhouse had an amazing ability from God to discern patterns of meaning in Scripture. He showed how Genesis 19 parallels and contrasts with Genesis 18, in the story of Abraham and Lot, his nephew. Abraham was in the tent and received the Lord and two angels; Lot in the place of honor at Sodom's gate received only the two angels. The inner attitudes of the two men are strikingly different. "Lot's communion was disturbed and distracted," while Abraham was a confidant of God.[45] The final pictures are most moving and anticipate the New Testament contrast between the spiritual and the carnal Christian. Such a rich and rewarding perception of truth came only after much disciplined study and application.

The distinguished Jewish scholar Robert Alter has given us an invaluable study entitled *The Art of Biblical Narrative*.[46] Unscathed by destructive higher criticism, Alter is a literary critic and affords us immense assistance in our analysis of biblical story. Emphasizing the connectives in biblical narrative, Alter tackles the tough 38th chapter of Genesis, the story of Judah and Tamar. Rather than viewing the passage as unrelated *excursus*, Alter shows how the story describes "the reversal of the iron law of primogeniture, about the election . . . of a younger son to carry on the line."[47] While earlier Judah led his brothers in treachery (Gen. 37:26-27), the focus is now shifting past Judah as a rascal to the Judah who will plead for his brother (Gen. 44:16-34) and ultimately to Judah as the line through whom Messiah would be born (Gen. 49:10). Alter is especially good on patterns of repetition that reinforce the central point of reference in the narrative (as in the story of Joseph and Potiphar's wife, Gen. 39:7-20). Beyond question, any serious student of narrative preaching must obtain Robert Alter and read him thoroughly (though Alter's volume on biblical poetry is widely considered to be inferior to his brilliant work on narrative).

Another example of meticulous and careful study (what we would call exegetical conscience) is the work of Donald Grey Barnhouse on the book of Hosea. The admittedly vexed issue as to whether or not God told Hosea to marry Gomer who would subsequently be unfaithful to him is faced head-on. Conjugal infidelity as a picture of spiritual unfaithfulness is a common theme in the prophets (cf. Ezek. 16, 23). Barnhouse is unusually skilled at telling the story with vividness and power. James Montgomery Boice's superlative exposition of Hosea 1–3 picks right up on Barnhouse's insights as the triumph of God's covenant love is seen in the restoration of Gomer as a foreshadowing of God's ultimate and final deliverance of His ancient covenant people (cf. Hos. 14:1-9).[48]

To beware of allegorizing biblical passages is important (as over against the dear brother who preached the five points of Calvinism out of the story of Mephibosheth, the son of Jonathan, with the lameness of Mephibosheth setting forth total depravity, etc.). Yet there is allegory in Scripture itself, and we are alerted to the necessity of genre recognition and careful exegesis of the form. Paul in a characteristically rabbinic mode uses the Sarah/Hagar story as an allegory (Gal. 4:21-30). Allegory, which is an extended metaphor, is also used by our Lord in his extended development of the vine and the branches in John 15.

Beyond question we have a biblically authorized basis for preaching the typical significance of Old Testament persons and institutions and events (cf. 1 Cor. 10:11 and the book of Hebrews).[49] Under the influence of Goppelt, we are facing with greater liberty the explicit types in the Old Testament such as Adam, the Flood, Melchizedek, the brazen serpent, manna, the Passover, and Jonah in the fish as a picture of Christ's resurrection. There are also implicit types that must be used with great caution and care, such as the cities of refuge in ancient Israel, the religious calendar of Israel, and the life of Joseph as a picture of the sufferings and the glory of Jesus Christ. How Christ is found in and preached from the Old Testament is a pressing issue for the expositor. The specific steps in the application of the narrative passage will be dealt with in an upcoming chapter.

Ezekiel's story presents a good case study in hermeneutical method. As the "mystic among the prophets," as one has put it, he is often neglected; but his prophecy is full of exquisitely beautiful and eminently preachable material. The prophet's call in Ezekiel 1:1–3:15 is a prime example of a highly imagistic passage that is difficult to preach. The key would seem to be in the datings at the outset of the passage. I would understand Ezekiel to be in his thirtieth year (1:1), in the fifth year of his exile in Babylon. Had he been home with his priestly family in Jerusalem, this would be the year he commenced priestly service. Now deeply disappointed, he is given a vision of the throne of the Lord (which according to rabbinic teaching was to be seen only in the land of Israel itself). But here coming down out of the north is the Lord God Himself on a throne mounted on wheels! The point of the extraordinary chariot is clearly mobility with a vengeance! Oh, that we might see the possibilities of the power and presence of God where we are.

Ezekiel's escorted inspection tour through the temple of Jerusalem in 591 B.C. opens a great opportunity to preach the searching scrutiny of the Lord as He sees the idolatrous incursions (Ezek. 8). The four stops show the hideous image of a heathen god infiltrating the temple; lewd and idolatrous representations within "the chambers of imagery," as this has been expressed; the investment of emotion in pagan lamentation; and the worship of the created object rather than the Creator. This book just teems with bold pictures replete with gripping truth.

The great revival in "death valley" full of dry bones (Ezek. 37) has a primary and clear relevance to Israel's future destiny, but a secondary application to the spiritual renewal of God's people in any age. The miracle stream of Ezekiel 47 (like the entire section) is millennial but full of powerful significance for the spiritual refreshing of the people of God. *How rich the Word of God is!*

While some might question whether or not the building of the tabernacle in the Old Testament is "a proper narrative event," I think it qualifies. Here is the early worship center of the newly liberated people of God. It is built on a pattern shown to Moses on Mount Sinai (Ex. 25:8-9; Heb. 8:3-6). Extensive instructions are given as to the materials and specifications of the components. Interestingly, the description begins from within the Holy of Holies—from the divine point-of-view. Many chapters in Exodus are devoted to a depiction of the entire procedure, the offerings that made it possible, the spiritual giftedness that brought it into being (Ex. 31); and then the actual process is outlined by which the vivid and colorful cultus functioned, with the priesthood led by the high priest and the whole sacrificial system.

Here is the story of the God who wanted to manifest His presence among His ancient people. This is one of the great visuals of the Old Testament, and the story is graphic. The use of models and visuals in the telling of the story is helpful. The actual logistics of construction are intriguing.[50] But clearly the very centrality of the tent of meeting in the middle of the camp speaks of the place that worship should have among the people of God. But even more striking is the clarity of the way of salvation.[51]

The white linen fence excludes (speaking of God's righteousness). Then through the one door via the brazen altar of sacrifice the worshiper comes. The laver further addresses spiritual defilement for the priests, and then the artifacts in both the Holy Place and the Holy of Holies set forth aspects of the divine provision. Thank God, the veil was torn in two at the time of the death of Jesus; and as believers we now have access, not only to the table of shewbread, the golden lampstand, and the altar of incense, but to the holiest of all through the blood of Christ (Heb. 10:19ff.). Here we see the way of salvation made clear as the essential principles of redemption are set forth in the rituals of cleansing and purification. Without overstressing the minutiae, here is an overture through the eye-gate that can tell the old, old story of Jesus and His love. The truth in shadow and substance is that which leads to life eternal ("Now this is eternal life: that they may know you, the only true God, and Jesus Christ, whom you have sent," John 17:3).

CHAPTER FIVE

Constructing the Narrative Sermon

After Jesus bad finished instructing his twelve disciples, he went on from there to teach and preach in the towns of Galilee.

MATT. 11:1

First of all it should be noted that the office of preaching is excellent, necessary, and agreeable to God, and that it is profitable to the preacher himself and useful to souls, and lastly that it is very difficult to reach perfection in preaching.

HUMBERT DE ROMANS, THIRTEENTH-CENTURY DOMINICAN

Give me the Bible and the Holy Ghost and I can go on preaching forever!

CHARLES HADDON SPURGEON

They were not serving themselves but you, when they spoke of the things that have now been told you by those who have preached the gospel to you by the Holy Spirit sent from heaven. Even angels long to look into these things.

1 PETER 1:12

In exegeting a passage, we get at what the inspired writer said; with the help of hermeneutics, we get at what the inspired writer meant. Up to this point we are within the province of the teacher who is, above all, concerned with a content to be understood. But now we move into the province of the preacher who is concerned, above all, with an object to be achieved. While teaching and preaching are used virtually synonymously in the New Testament, there are differences. All good preaching will have a teaching component, and all good teaching will have a preaching component. But the pulpit is not a lectern. Preaching is application. Indeed, application (bridging between the biblical word and the contemporary world) begins in the introduction of the sermon. We now turn to the packaging and processing of biblical meaning as encased in the narratives of Scripture for contemporary communication. Our objective is comprehension and application. The preacher is "bilingual" (to use Krister Stendahl's expression) in that the preacher must know the action of the ancient text and then how that action is reenacted in the present.

Bernard Manning's classic definition still stands: "Preaching is the manifestation of the incarnate Word, from the written Word, through the spoken word." As such, preaching is the lifeblood of the church, the fuel of worship, the agent for conversion (1 Peter 1:23ff.), the means of sanctification, the source of comfort and encouragement, and the impetus for service and ministry.

Thus when preaching is in decline, we're in big trouble. If preaching degenerates into an "unilluminating discussion of unreal problems in unintelligible language," as one writer put it, we can see the handwriting on the wall. We are facing horrendous obstacles in the communication of God's message today. Ours has been characterized as "the age of indifference," when, as the *Los Angeles Times-Mirror Center* says, the average person in the United States knows less, cares less, and reads the newspaper less. The average person is less informed and less interested; and the younger persons are tuning out. The answer of some in the news industry is to soften and glitz up until there is no real news at all.

Historically, discourse has shaped people and events, as Garry Wills shows in his captivating bestseller *Lincoln at Gettysburg*. This astute historian demonstrates how Lincoln's 272 words in his famous address and their vernacular rhythms are "the words which remade America." Three minutes of the fruit from Lincoln's verbal workshop led the audience and posterity back to the Declaration of Independence, the nation's founding document. Able in distinguishing alternatives, using his typical grammatical inversion, alluding to Scripture, Lincoln in his Gettysburg Address shows us orality at its potent best.[1] The sermon is likewise discourse that takes the written document and makes it an oral event. Or is the sermon done as a form?

The older linear narrative with its dependence on print media is being overshadowed by the "new-wave techniques" of the new storytellers, who like Oliver Stone in his movie *JFK* is "fully determined to have his own way with the pictures inside our heads." But the Bible does not take a backseat to anyone or anything when it comes to the power of its images; and while, as James Wall well observes, "This notion of a transcendent source to narrative is especially difficult to grasp in our era," yet "the Christian knows that stories are not bound by their linear shape" and that the living God as Creator and Redeemer "is the source of all that we are and will be."[2] The Bible is not a museum for antiquities but the highest drama of the intervening God.

Will we quash the explosive vitalities of the biblical message in order to conform to culture, or will we be intent on challenging culture to conform to the ineradicably supernatural Christ? As Professor LeCerf of Paris used to say: "When you preach, you do not know what you do: you wield lightning." We cannot yield the action to those who see New Testament events as "the creation of a theologically motivated tradition" and Jesus as no more than "a striking Galilean charismatic preacher." For then we have lost all control and factual referent, and then Jesus was possibly "the most ruthless of men," as Mark Van Doren maintained, or, as John Allegro argued, Jesus never existed but rather there was "an orgiastic magic mushroom cult," and the Apostle Paul is made out to be some kind of a homosexual Roman agent or informer. Then the book of Jonah may well be a short story on line with Kafka, Kierkegaard, or Borges. Such massive surrender to cultural relativity and subjectivity is not the way to go.

But ministerial sloth and ineptitude can likewise sink the ship. If the goddess of dullness is in the saddle, all is lost. Offhand remarks are not preaching. In a day when public confidence in the clergy has reached an all-time low, we must not try to shortcut the often agonizing labor of exegesis and sermonic preparation. There are those who hawk their wares but who would turn our messages into babbling displays of ignorance. One service offers "Sunday Sermons" that are "trusted year-after-year" by the world's busiest clergy. Another handbook promises "over 120 eloquent, inspirational sermons on scores of religious and secular subjects . . . ready to use or adapt." This is to sell our souls.

In a recent episode of *The Simpsons*, churchgoing was the subject. In this segment God appeared to Homer in a dream and ended up agreeing with Homer's reasons for skipping church: "Rev. Lovejoy's sermons are boring, and watching football is more satisfying."[3] As any attorney knows, if you bore the jury you will lose the case. We're at a critical juncture. Will we build the sermon on the powerful narratives of Scripture in such a way as to release the power and the majesty of the divine revelation, or will we darken counsel with words? What an awesome challenge for the lovers of the Word of God.

THE PROTOCOLS OF THE NARRATIVE SERMON

Today I must attend committee; tomorrow I must preach; someday I must die. Let us do each duty as it comes the best we can. (Principal Rainy)

God has spoken from His sanctuary. (Ps. 60:6)

One thing God has spoken, two things have I heard: that you, O God are strong, and that you, O Lord, are loving. (Ps. 62:11-12)

. . . to him who rides the ancient skies above, who thunders with mighty voice. (Ps. 68:33)

When Harry Emerson Fosdick led the charge away from biblical preaching ("the stereotyped routine in which old-fashioned expository preaching had fallen was impossible to me," he argued, referring to the elucidation of the scriptural text and its application with exhortation), he was abandoning the message with its power.[4] We have to stay close to the biblical text. Of the milieu in which the Welsh poet Dylan Thomas lived, his biographer says: "When Sunday came it was to the pulpit that they turned, Bible in hand, forefingers quivering toward Heaven, threatening damnation to those who flirted with temptations of the flesh, or the perils of Demon Drink."[5]

Dylan Thomas, tragic figure that he indeed was, constantly used biblical phrases. He testified: "The things that first made me love language and want to work in it and for it were nursery rhymes and folk tales, the Scottish ballads, a few lines of hymns, the most famous Bible stories and the rhythms of the Bible . . . the great rhythms that rolled over me from the Welsh pulpits; and I had read for myself from Job to Ecclesiastes, and the story of the New Testament is part of my life."[6] How can we cause these rhythms to surge from our pulpits? Sermons are more like babies being born, it has been observed, than like buildings being built. Preachers are more like weavers than sculptors. We want now to examine some of the protocols of narrative preaching, not all of which are unique to the preaching of narrative, but all of which are important.

Emphasize the Unity

Preaching in our time especially demands a coherence and a sequencing that will distinguish it from the mere stringing together of biblical texts. We have already emphasized the necessity of clearly identifying the central point of reference. Busy preachers are tempted to jettison this discipline, especially with narrative, supposing that the story line will carry the message. We need to give our people something of God and His grace to take home; but if we have not focused on what it is, by what sleight of hand will our congregants pick it up? What is the center of gravity to which all moves? Narrative unity presents a large challenge to every communicator.

Utilize the Diversity

One of the plagues of the contemporary pulpit is a lethal sameness and predictability. Growing in love for narrative and developing skills in handling it effectively opens broad new vistas. From the dramatic episodes of the book of Jonah with its haunting unanswered concluding question to the poignant letter of the Apostle Paul to Philemon (which lends itself so superbly to a dramatic monologue on Christian reconciliation), we have such a breadth and depth of resources. The birth narratives of our Lord and the passion and resurrection sections are so very familiar and call for special treatment in this study, but they invite us to break some new ground and blaze some new trails.

Respect the Complexity

The fact that we are not in heavy doctrinal and dialectical discussion in the narrative sections does not save us from arduous work and tough calls. The difficult double reference in the prophecy of the Virgin Birth (Isa. 7:10-16) or the similar patterns in the fascinating missionary itinerations of Paul and his companions are but two issues among so many. The chief purpose of the story of Jesus with the woman at the well of Sychar (one of seven of what we might call immortal interviews in the fourth gospel) is clearly that of the self-disclosure of the Messiah; yet we could not deny that in a secondary and tertiary sense we learn about personal evangelism and appreciate greatly the cameo on true, spiritual worship.

Explore the Novelty

In expounding a story we might wisely decide (particularly in longer passages) to begin in the middle of the story and in a series of flashbacks bring our hearers up to full speed. For example, in preaching a single sermon on the book of Ruth (in a series on the doctrine of divine providence), I chose to begin the story with 3:1ff. Experimentation with cinematic technique in storytelling can introduce some positive variation, such as cross-cutting (two simultaneous centers of action with a split-screen), or close-up, or jumpcut (used in the portrayal of dream action or fantasy). In other words, we should not always begin on square one with "Once upon a time." Feel something of the mystique of the storyteller and go for maximum effect.

Appreciate the Variety

We all have a large debt to the black preacher, who is essentially a storyteller. Henry H. Mitchell, called by James Forbes "the dean of imaging," has given us a significant book to help us here,[7] as has Gardner Taylor in his Yale Lectures.[8] Samples of their wares are indispensable. Perhaps many white preachers cannot duplicate the black preacher's skill, but we can learn much from those who do it so well. Missionary Brad Hill has given us an invaluable journal monograph on variations in style among African preachers. "The stories are never stale recitations. They are constantly modified, tuned, and reshaped to emphasize different points."

Among the variants are (1) the diminishing-spiral model, in which the story is repeated in an increasingly compact way and turns its angle slightly so as to catch the glint of a new point; (2) the pin-cushion model, in which the preacher has one major point and comes to it again and again in a variety of ways; (3) the sunburst model, in which the central text seems to explode, sending its shrapnel whizzing into the audience; (4) an adapted linear-progression model that works through the text but repeats the basic idea at each juncture.[9]

Remember the Gallery

Walter Wangerin, that steadfast apostle of evocative language and a master storyteller, frequently reminds us: remember the children. To keep our imagery and descriptions honest and clear, the narrative preacher should always think in terms of children and their understanding.

THE PROCESSING OF THE NARRATIVE SERMON

> The writer seeks to change blood into ink; the preacher seeks to change ink into blood. (Charles L. Bartow)

> I wait for form. (Robert Frost)

> I need a design. (A character in *Oliver Sacks*)

> But thanks be to God that, though you used to be slaves to sin, you wholeheartedly obeyed the form of teaching to which you were entrusted. (Rom. 6:17)

The human brain is programmed to seek patterns. There are patterns of truth in Scripture. Literary devices such as repetition, chiastic structure, inclusio, parallelism, alliteration, assonance, paronomasia (beyond the name), and other types of rhetorical ornamentation are used in the writings of Scripture. In moving, then, from the written form to the oral event of preaching, we need to formulate a "rhetorical strategy."[10] Homiletics has tended to wallow in our civilization's reaction against structure, but there is evidence of a move back toward structure and the sense that we need it.[11] We see this, for example, in the crossback from open form to formal poetry.

The Greek rhetoricians spoke of discourse as being composed of invention (content), arrangement, delivery, and memory. Over twenty of the Yale Lectures have been devoted to the matter of form and structure. The real question is not really, shall we have form, but what kind of form shall we have? Frederick Buechner, in reacting to the question as to whether storytelling could be overdone, insightfully commented: "Oh yes. When I hear the phrase 'storytelling' my hackles rise. I heard one preacher announce that he was going to give a 'story sermon,' and it was one of the worst experiences of my life. He told, as if set in the old West, the story of the Prodigal Son, making every allegorical point so apparent."[12] We are talking "rhetorical strategy" here.

In a more didactic or epistolary passage, we divide the text to correspond with our diagramming of the structure of the passage and edit the statement of the mains for oral communication (e.g., moving the principial action into the present tense, avoiding proper names except for the name of God, etc.). The *lucido ordo* (lucid order) of a narrative passage has too often been simply to divide the story syllogistically and preach it like any other text. If there is to be a variant it would probably turn out like:

> Tell the story.
> Give the meaning.
> Share the application.

So the interest factor is high during the story (hopefully) but then sags in what may be quite a moralistic concluding movement.

While we do not use a syntactical outline for narrative, it is essential that we divide the text in preparing the sermon. The divisions are what Clyde Fant calls "thought blocks" and what I am calling here "narrative blocks." We need to identify the significant sequential chunks of story. I will be arguing that we should use good running or continuous application rather than compact application at the end, and that this application be skillfully woven into each narrative block. The narrative blocks of the David and Goliath story would be:

I. Goliath intimidates the children of Israel, 1 Samuel 17:1-11.
II. David comes and is concerned about the situation, 1 Samuel 17:12-30.
III. David is extraordinarily pressed into facing Goliath, 1 Samuel 17:31-44.

IV. David triumphs over Goliath by the power of God,
1 Samuel 17:45-58.

This is a long passage in the preaching of which the preacher should vividly tell parts of the story and actually read critical sections. It would not be necessary to state the mains lest we become overly atomistic and too structured, and so dampen the power of the story line. Two objectives sometimes place us on the horns of a dilemma: we want to keep the story line going, and we want to be sure not to miss the meaning and application of the story.

This is not to say that we should never divide the text and enumerate the main points. However, little can be said in favor of ever enumerating the subpoints in any sermon. We only seem to be making matters too complex. In a sermon on spiritual decision-making from Numbers 13–14, the story of the children of Israel at Kadesh-Barnea, we might divide the sermon as follows:

I. A decision is required.
II. A decision is rendered.
III. A decision is regretted.

After all, the dramatic action of a play is not violated by dividing the action into two or three acts with intermissions in between the acts.

Where, however, we have a small piece of text (a true micro-text), such as the parable of the pearl of great price (Matt. 13:45), the narrative bind is relatively simple and short but deeply moving. When we have a large piece of text (truly a macro-text), we might be advised to craft with some care and clearly state what our main points are. If we are preaching the entire book of Esther in a single sermon, underscoring the gracious providential care God affords His people, we need the sharpened focus a series of mains offers. I have used the following outline to encompass the action of Esther with the wording of principial mains taken from elsewhere in Scripture:

I. "God makes the wrath of men to praise him"—the schemes of Haman *et al.*
II. "God works in all things for good"—God miraculously counteracts Haman.

III. "God will perfect that which concerns us"—the glorious outcome.

Or take Jesus in the home of Mary and Martha in Bethany, as recorded in Luke 10:38-42. This text is not made of putty, allowing us to preach a range of ten different items. Jesus condemned Martha and commended Mary on one criterion: the matter of priorities. So we could preach in the flow of the passage on "The Tyranny of Trifles," or we might choose on "the one thing" and divide the text thus:

I. Priority—"at Jesus' feet" (cf. Luke 10:39 and John 11:32; 12:3).
II. Irritability—dragged in different directions—much serving.
III. Commendability—"Mary has chosen what is better."

The procedure for constructing the narrative sermon is similar, then, to any literary genre of Scripture except that more options are offered. Once having gained a perspective on "the big idea" or "the central point of reference," the craftsman can use a "rhetorical strategy" that builds on Act I, Act II divisions in the text, or on a more standard outline (especially a ladder or seek-and-find type of outline that builds suspense climactically), or on no identification of mains as the sermon moves through the narrative blocks.

Frequently narrative blends with poetry or didactic or apocalyptic. In the early chapters of Zechariah we have moving narrative that elucidates the purification of the servant of the Lord (chapter 3) and the empowerment of the servant of the Lord (chapter 4). We might outline chapter 3 as follows:

I. The Lord's servant is accused.
II. The Lord's servant is cleansed.
III. The Lord's servant is clothed.
IV. The Lord's servant is recommissioned.

The center of gravity in chapter 4 is clearly 4:6, where the principle of the indispensable power of the Holy Spirit is declared. Here I would be inclined to let the forcefulness of the imagery of the lampstand, the golden bowl, and the oil over against the pervasive sense of failure and futility carry the message, without forging a statement of the mains. However, in chapter 6, with the chariots and horsemen of God being somewhat more abstruse, I would incline to principalize three mains:

I. God knows (the surveillance of God).
II. God cares (the responsiveness of God).
III. God acts (the deliverance of God).

The material is so rich, and a plethora of alternatives in structure is available.

THE PROBLEMS OF THE NARRATIVE SERMON

My preaching almost always displeases me. For I am eager after something better, of which I often have an inward enjoyment before I set about expressing my thoughts in audible words. (Augustine, in *De Catechizandis Rudibus*)

Although I am old and experienced, I am afraid every time I preach. (Martin Luther)

Don't just throw the seed at the people! Grind it into flour, bake it into bread, and slice it for them! (Charles Haddon Spurgeon)

Preaching at every step and stage is hard work; it has always been hard work, and it is not getting any easier. Bible distribution is up 17 percent over a previous year, but people do not seem to be reading their Bibles. In point of fact, they are not reading much of anything. People may still buy books, but few are reading them. Industry experts say that soon there will be only technical works and airport books (books bought for a plane trip and left behind). The videocracy in which we live is subject to electronic tyranny, and this has immense implication for the preaching task. For example, 47 percent of the American people say they believe in special creation a la Genesis, but how informed and how deep is that conviction?

Central biblical motifs linger in contemporary consciousness, as when President Clinton invoked the idea of "a new covenant," or when Menachem Begin used the ancient biblical orders of Galilee, Judea, and Samaria, or when Martin Luther King employed the Mt.

Nebo vision of the land in his famous "I've been to the mountain-top . . . and I've seen the promised land" speech. Much biblical scholarship in our time has become so specialized that we are reminded of restaurant critics who spend all their time analyzing menus.

Yet the narrative sections of Scripture are especially inviting in a visual society. In literary fashion today we have the minimalists and the maximalists, and I would want to urge biblical preachers to become maximalists in the sense that we give assiduous attention to the most efficient exploitation of our materials. We need to be part of the diamond-cutting school of preaching. Some preachers are masters of incoherence, and their sermons flow like glue. May the Spirit of God enliven our preaching. Think of it! When Jesus urged, "Consider the lilies of the field," He was speaking as the One who designed and created the lilies and all of the flora and fauna. This is the highest reality! Lest we become too spastic in today's communications climate, we need to recognize with Randall Balmer that "the most effective oratorical style in contemporary politics is strongly influenced by the evangelical Protestant tradition"; but this means preaching, not a high-church tradition of liturgy and sacrament.[13]

Some of the problems and snares to be avoided can be pinpointed as follows:

Narrative Wobble

Wobble is the inclusion of incongruous and inappropriate embellishment in the story. In a well-intentioned effort to make the action of the ancient story relevant and germane, we are sometimes tempted to add a telephone call or the newspaper article to the biblical story, and we thus deflect the movement of the narrative with the implausible. In one of his plays Shakespeare gave ancient Bohemia a seaport. This is a narrative wobble. Walter Van Tilburg Clark in *The Track of the Camp* makes mountain lions do what they are not capable of doing: hunt human beings and break the necks of a bull and three steers in a flurry. We shall subsequently speak to the enlargement and expansion of creative skill in the use of narrative, but this should never involve putting a Mercedes or Porsche in a biblical story. Such action causes the listener to blink and jeopardizes the movement of the story line.

In his invaluable suggestions on storytelling, Eugene Lowry urges us to "attend to every 'insignificant' line."[14] (In this regard, don't miss Luke 15:26 in the parable of the prodigal son, where the elder brother calls one of the servants to ask him what was going on.) Small details are important. Accuracy and care should be sought in every representation. We should remember that a whole school of interpreting history has arisen (particularly in France) that emphasizes the relevance of the everyday details and aspects of life for understanding history.[15] Lowry also wisely pushes us to look between the lines, probe prior dynamics, utilize the senses, etc. But in doing so, beware of narrative wobble. Observe the reticence and omissions in the story of David and Bathsheba. Sternberg is right in calling attention to the fact that "biblical narratives are notorious for their sparsity of detail."[16]

Narrative Thickness
We must be wary of the danger of giving too much detail (and thus making the story lag) or excessive theological abstraction in the continuous application. Wallace Stegner has pointed to "the economy and precision which have marked the short story since James Joyce and in a sense since Poe." We need an awareness of theological construct and to recall, as J.I. Packer puts it, that the Puritans preached Bible characters doctrinally. But the story is action, and we want some narrative zip, some narrative propane. We should seek to avoid the heavier, too weighty background bypaths or doctrinal *excursi*.[17]

Narrative Clutter
We must watch out for failing to zero in on the critical focus of the action by being distracted with the sheer welter of that action. Too many subplots give us a Dickensian complexity. An "iris-out" is an older film technique by which "the director begins with a wide shot and then slowly closes the camera to a small circle of light which concentrates the viewer's attention on a single detail."[18] Here is where disciplined attention to patterns of repetition, two-step progression, questions, framing, and episodes in patterns of three (as in Mark's gospel) is important. Biblical narrators are not so much like Huck Finn or Holden Caulfield; our telling is more like *War and Peace* and Homer's *Odyssey*.[19]

THE PRODUCTION OF THE NARRATIVE SERMON

God is the poet of the world, with tender patience leading it by His vision of truth, beauty and goodness. (Alfred North Whitehead)

The world is charged with the grandeur of God. It will flame out, like shining from shook foil. (Gerard Manley Hopkins)

Pablo Casals when 90 was still practicing his cello 4-5 hours a day and was asked why he worked so hard at his age. He replied: "Because I think I am making some progress." (Quoted by Lewis Smedes in *A Pretty Good Person*)

The world of biblical narrative is an exciting but somewhat formidable realm for the contemporary biblical preacher. In the circles in which I have served we have always loved the narrative sections and dealt with them, but customarily with the same cookie cutter as all the rest of our sermons. John Broadus in his classic and still influential text on preaching (into its fourth major revision) has never discussed the narrative genre. He shows how narration in history and biblical biography is part of the explanation of texts, but this is a very modest attempt.[20] This is generally true of homiletical works up to the present.

When evangelicals begin to sniff around some of the newer expressions by the homileticians of the Left in hopes of some helpful hints and guidance, we are immediately put off by a sweeping dismissal of "the traditional, conceptual approach" that fails to work and "capture the interest of listeners."[21] It is hard to accept this anti-conceptual bias, and I suspect it is ultimately epistemologically suicidal. The essential pattern in all narrative is:

I. Put the heroes up a tree.
II. Throw stones at them, or get a bear growling at the foot of the tree.
III. Get the heroes down from the tree again.

Polti may be right that there are thirty-six basic dramatic plots, and every story is a variant of one of them. But each of them is a concept. We can have more than simply a concept, and in effective preaching we *must* have more, though minimally there must be conceptualization.

A new generation of younger evangelical scholars is rejuvenating vast sections of text by their emphasis on the "narrative artistry" achieved by textual and structural patterning. They are indebted to many pioneering scholars such as Jacob Licht, who spoke insightfully of the biblical storytellers: "Their excellence is a matter of common experience, not of aesthetic theory."[22] Licht moves away from the old-style analysis of the floating axhead story (2 Kings 6:1-7), which was content to see tree-cutting (6:1-4) and miracle (6:5-7). Licht built the story on a much more appealing pattern:

> Early calm
> Tensive action
> Later calm

Licht's study of the "roaring" repetition in Daniel 3, the four calls to Samuel in 1 Samuel 3:3-10, the twice triple pattern in 2 Kings 1:2-17, the three unsuccessful/one successful in Judges 16:4-22, the Egyptian plagues repetition, the many repetitions in the Balaam cycle, Joseph's brothers (first visit, intermezzo, second visit) is well worth undertaking.[23]

A sparkling instance of the positive recent work of younger evangelicals is J. Paul Tanner's "The Gideon Narrative as the Focal Point of Judges." Tanner impressively argues that there are seven major narrative blocks in Judges and that the twenty episodes in the Gideon story are the turning-point in the book. Using the technique that is called "episode bonding," Tanner demonstrates how Gideon's inner struggle for the certainty of his calling and the solidity of his faith encapsulates the heart of the message of the whole book. The resolution of Gideon's fear is explored through the concentric arrangement of six episodes "as though the very structure reflects the reversal going on within Gideon."[24] The very structure of the scriptural account embodies aspects of the author's inspired message. How well I recall taking Esther McIlveen's characterization of Gideon as "the hesitant hero"[25] and preaching eight messages over the inner wrestling of this dear man. I found them personally helpful to me and most applicable to heterogeneous congregations at home and abroad.

Similarly splendid literary analysis has been done by Eugene Merrill and Reg Grant on the lovely book of Ruth. The latter sees the plot in Ruth moving from tragedy through anti-romance and then through comedy to romance.[26] This type of analysis is extremely productive for preaching. Somewhat earlier John A. Martin gave us studies of the structure, literary quality, text, and theology of 1 and 2 Samuel. The underlying premise in all of these studies is that there is more than mere history here and the basis for some devotional observations. Martin finds "the reversal-of-fortune" to be the major narrative tool in these two books.[27] This is to say that the important persons are shown to be unimportant, and the unimportant persons turn out to be important, and God is the prime mover!

But at what point do the desire and drive to principalize the text move beyond bounds? Recently I took the Luke 4:14-30 pericope and preached a sermon entitled "The Snare of Spiritual Familiarity." The point of this danger seems to rise out of Luke's analysis of our Lord's rejection by the hometown folks of Nazareth after His appearance in their synagogue. Manifestly a problem exists here (cf. Matt. 13:58; Mark 6:5). Dr. Luke seems to be saying that unbelief arose out of an overfamiliarity that blunted their perceptive faculties. I drew three main points in the telling of the story:

I. Familiarity can rob us of the worship of God (the synagogue service, like any service, can become habitual and perfunctory; cf. Isa. 6).
II. Familiarity can rob us of the Word of God (how easily the Word of God can become marginalized—did they notice what Jesus did not read?).
III. Familiarity can rob us of the wondrous Christ of God Himself (they were put off because He seemed just like the peasants they were).

This sermon is an effort to get at the teaching of this passage and at the reason for its inclusion in Luke's story at this juncture. The preacher faces the fact that this is a negative instance. (We must remember we cannot delimit positively; e.g., the Decalogue). In this case I struck three clear mains to assure the clarity of my argument. I believe this is exposition of Scripture using an essentially narrative passage. The sermon certainly applied Scripture.

In the final analysis the kind of preaching in which we are interested is that kind of preaching owned by the Holy Spirit in the conviction and conversion of men and women, such as is described in a recent novel by the British writer A. N. Wilson, by no means a committed Christian himself:

Then Father Cuthbert told them "the old, old story of Jesus and His love," but here was preaching with a difference. Many there were who confessed and called themselves Christians who believed that our Lord performed miracles 1800 years ago. "But go, show John again the things which ye do hear and see in this reign of Victoria—how the blind receive their sight, and the lame walk, the deaf hear, the dead," he gulped and his high voice rose yet higher and then broke into a sob, "the dead are raised up, and the dear poor have the gospel preached to them. . . ."

. . . he [Lionel Nettleship] realized that he had never accepted Jesus Christ, God and Man, as his personal Savior. He had never opened his heart to Jesus and let Him in, to change and purify his whole life. And now during the singing of the hymn he did so, and he felt his whole being suffused with a glow which he knew to be the sure token of our Lord's presence with him.[28]

CHAPTER SIX

Crafting the Components of the Narrative Sermon

We evangelicals are Bible people.

G. CAMPBELL MORGAN

To me the work of preaching is the highest and greatest and most glorious calling to which anyone can ever be called.

D. MARTYN LLOYD-JONES

The most urgent need in the Christian Church today is true preaching.

D. MARTYN LLOYD-JONES

"He commanded us to preach to the people and to testify that he is the one whom God appointed as judge of the living and the dead. All the prophets testify about him that everyone who believes in him receives forgiveness of sins through his name."

THE APOSTLE PETER, IN ACTS 10:42-43

We come now to putting together the parts and pieces of discourse. In some respects the narrative sermon will have its unique considerations, but in other aspects it will resemble general homiletical practice. I am assuming by this point that the preacher has seriously engaged the text. If we have bypassed serious exegesis, we have nothing to process or package homiletically. The elaboration of the trivial still yields only the trivial. We must possess the substance of Scripture if we are going to have something to say.

The landscape of preaching in North American churches suggests strongly that we are in something of a retreat from biblical substance. One ministerial candidate was turned down because he preached more than eighteen minutes. No significant or serious exposition can be done in less than thirty minutes. People sit for hours in the cinema, in front of the television, and at athletic events. The fact is, we are in a time such as St. Paul describes: "For the time will come when men will not put up with sound doctrine. Instead, to suit their own desires, they will gather around them a great number of teachers to say what their itching ears want to hear. They will turn their ears away from the truth and turn aside to myths" (2 Tim. 4:3-4).

"Management talk" and "vacuous therapeutic talk" are but sawdust for the soul. We must open the Word of God. A veteran missionary well argued, "If there is any denial of the sufficiency of God's Word (the Scriptures of the Old and New Testaments) as the only rule of faith and practice, there is to that degree a declaration on the part of man of his independence of God." We are dealing here with the basic theological issue of our time.

Our commanding presupposition here is that of the intentionality and total reliability of the biblical text. With regard to narrative in Scripture, I am insisting that narrative is deliberately crafted, and this received text has a normative claim. Cleverness and brilliance will not suffice. We've got to have the message of Scripture. In Samuel Beckett's "Krapp's Last Tape" (1958), we hear tell of an old man listening to a thirty-year-old tape of his younger self and and agonizing over the discovery that then and now he has "nothing to say." This is the solemn possibility that should drive every preacher back to the Word of God.

An American preacher was preaching in England and unctiously extrapolated on the idea that "Faith is both abstract and concrete." The interpreter for the deaf congregation signed to her audience, "So far he hasn't said anything; when he does, I'll let you know." The call here is for the most rigorous exegetical conscience. We can't preach on the cross of Christ from Genesis 48:14 ("And crossing his arms, he put his left hand on Manasseh's head, even though Manasseh was the firstborn").

My fear is that the highly pressurized North American preacher will do exactly what Thomas Sowell warns all of us about in many areas of life and endeavor. He tells the story about the French police chasing a criminal into a building in Paris. Their first thought was that they would surround the building. But when they realized the building was quite large and had many more exits than they had policemen, they surrounded the building next door, which was smaller and had fewer exits. We must not move away from what the Bible says, whatever may be our frustration level.

The problem is not with the powerful Word of God. Our problem may be in our crafting of the sermon. This we shall proceed to discuss. Possibly the problem is dead delivery. The fact may be that our preaching is about as exciting as watching paint dry. Instead of using the sharp sword of the Word, we may be using an egg-beater and are fluffing up the surface but never getting beneath it. Gyratory energy can never be a substitute for succulent facts. But tacking some pretty piece of text onto the outskirts of things dooms us to irrelevance. We must attempt more than tiny scratches on the paintwork. Airbrushing of images in a good-natured haze will not carry the responsibility of the Christian pulpit amid the ideological rubble of the 1990s. Some have the uncanny ability to make the most exciting matter gray. This is the issue we shall address directly in this chapter.

Here we are talking about pouring refreshing, cold water into a cup (the cup is our packaging, our structure). We have pointed out how Harry Emerson Fosdick tragically led a previous generation away from biblical content. The "life-situation" preachers (such as Charles F. Kemp) followed and left millions starving spiritually.[1] Now voices calling many to a similar crusade for "reaching people" in our time expose us to grave new danger.

Three levels of communication must obsess the preacher: (1) the meaning level: here is our commitment to the text—this is essentially information; (2) the feeling level: this is making it moving—this is purposeful inspiration; (3) the obedience/verdict level: this is the "so what?" question—the issue of application for life today, here and now.

One of the great preaching models out of the last century must be Charles Simeon, whose fifty-four-year ministry at Holy Trinity Church in Cambridge moved a generation for Christ and shaped evangelical Anglicanism in England. Of his 2,500 published sermons, Simeon wrote (in his preface to *Horae Homileticae*) that he wanted to judge every sermon he preached in terms of three questions: (1) Does it humble the sinner? (2) Does it exalt the Savior? (3) Does it promote holiness? If any sermon he preached did not address these criteria, he believed that sermon should be "condemned without mercy." May God help us run the flag to this pole for Christ's glory!

THE INTRODUCTION TO THE NARRATIVE SERMON

They were absolutely still. All the faces were turned, like radii of a circumference, toward the central point: the silhouette of a man at the heart of that circle . . . drawn to him as to a magnet, standing there and gesticulating. A storyteller (*el hablador*). (Mario Vargas Llosa)[2]

"He who has ears, let him hear." (Matt. 13:9)

Who has believed our message and to whom has the arm of the Lord been revealed? (Isa. 53:1)

The first task of the preacher in our contemporary climate for communication is to get the attention of the hearers. The story is told of the old farmer who sold a mule with the assurance that the mule would work hard if spoken to sweetly. Not long afterwards the new owner complained that the mule would not work, even when spoken to nicely. The old farmer promptly took a stick and hit the mule between the ears. The mule staggered but began to plow. The new owner was perplexed. The old farmer explained, "It doesn't do any good to talk to him until you get his attention." The preacher must get the attention of the hearers.

The good cause is not well served by simply getting attention, perhaps through a humorous story or some clever aside. We want to get the attention of our hearers in relation to the subject to be preached. So many are the distractions and diversions in the modern situation for preaching that it is probably true that if we don't get the attention of our hearers in the first two minutes, we can forget about any hoped-for results. We do not have time for throw-away lines. At the same time, if we come out of the balcony on a guy wire with a rose in our mouth, we have not obtained the attention of our audience for the subject; we have only succeeded in making a ridiculous spectacle of ourselves and in point of fact trivializing the Gospel.

The introduction should initiate dialogue in preaching. Preaching is far more dialogical than some concede, but we need to foster even more dialogue. We live in the day of the interactive movie and the improvisational stage. We need to strike an immediate point of contemporary contact with our audience. We need to cultivate a style and manner of delivery that build effective rapport with our hearers. The narrative preacher in the storytelling mode has an obvious and an immediate advantage. We can start right into the story, or we can ask some lead questions right out of the chute that begin the work of application.

So perhaps a message on Elijah out of 1 Kings 19 could begin: "Have you been feeling lower than a snake's vest button lately? Are circumstances and situations in your life getting you down? I met a man the other day who told me that he was so far down, he had to reach up to touch bottom. He said he was so low in his spirits that a mosquito would have to bend over to bite him. Elijah, the servant of God, was feeling like that . . ."

Avoiding unnecessary breaks and transitions and seeking a simple, straight-line introduction, the preacher wants to interweave the point of contemporary contact with textual materials and get going. Nowadays the introduction should be about 10 percent of the length of the entire sermon. The hazardous moves of the sermon, like those of an airplane, are the taking off and the landing. Blessed is the sermon that takes off like a 727 or 737 and not like a 747. We need to get up and started, reach our destination, and then get down.

At this point the very significant discussion of induction vs. deduction in preaching is apropos. The inductive approach (the scientific method) begins with specific instances and observable data and moves then to the generalization or the universals with appropriate tentativity. The deductive method begins with a universal or a "given" and then moves syllogistically and necessarily to the specific or immediate application. A reaction against deductive preaching has set in (consistent with the anti-authoritative mood of our time that would challenge any universals). Fred Craddock has argued persuasively for the inductive approach, and the conservative Ralph Lewis has gone so far as to say that the inductive method was the method of Jesus and that all great preaching is inductive. Much of this is silly talk.[3]

As soon as the text is read and we seek to explicate and apply it, we have abandoned the possibility of pure induction. The conclusion is before us from the very outset. The scandal of scriptural authority cannot be obviated. Yet, I would argue that good preaching is always a blending of both deductive and inductive elements. Start where the people are and then lead them into a treasure-hunt through the text. "Art is allowing the one seeing or hearing it to enter into a new experience," as one writer put it. Begin the sermon on Hosea 1 with a prayer such as Hosea and Gomer's children might well have prayed: "Dear God, please bring Mommy home tonight."

The storyteller holds off a little. McLuhan sought to show that the cool approach invites participation. Dag Hammerskjold advised: don't stay by the keyhole; break in or pass by. The opening sentence should be carefully crafted. Edward Bulwer-Lytton's attention-grabbing opening sentence in one of his novels is: "It was a dark and stormy night."

As Gertrude Stein counseled a young writer who was timidly pouring tea for her guests: "When you pour, young man, pour boldly!" Think how the Gospel of John begins, or Dickens's *A Tale of Two Cities*, or Tolstoy's *War and Peace*, or Herman Melville's *Moby Dick*. Proust began a work: "For a long time I used to go to bed early." Study what makes a good narrative launch.[4]

The whole matter of the mood and tone for beginning is focused when we remember how important what just precedes the sermon really is. So Fred Watts observes: "The better the singing, the better the preaching; if you want dull preaching, just have dull singing." We need to think through carefully this critical transition into the preaching. We have heard, "when E. F. Hutton speaks, everyone listens." I doubt this is a factual statement, but to the degree that it is true, why is it true? And, are people listening to us?

THE PROGRESSION IN THE NARRATIVE SERMON

Show me something in the Bible I don't teach and I will start teaching it; and something I do teach which is not in the Bible, and I will cease. (Bishop Jewel)

If the thing is not in the Bible, deducible from the Bible or in manifest harmony with the Bible, we should have none of it. (Bishop J. C. Ryle)

I am ready to confess that I regard this question of form, and true division, as being so important that when I have failed

to find the desired division to my satisfaction with a given
text, rather than preach on it in this unsatisfactory state
I have put it aside and taken another text. (D. Martyn Lloyd-
Jones)

Making clear divisions in the text is important for marking
progress through the text and in the sermon. Our hearers do not
have the customary written paragraph and section demarcations
that the preacher has in his notes or in the script. Even though the
narrative sermon is not always so fastidious in the matter of
phrasing and enumerating the statement of the mains, as we have
seen, we must never sidestep the clear identification of the narrative blocks. As John Claude (1619-87), the French Protestant
homiletician who influenced Charles Simeon so markedly, argued,
the division of discourse "should be restrained to a small number
of parts: they should never exceed four or five at the most: the
most admired sermons have only two or three parts." In the interests of fostering a sense of movement and progression toward the
climacteric, three principles should be observed.

Demand Selection

The key to effective biblical exposition is selectivity. If we are
determined to be exhaustive, we shall be exhausting. John Stuart
Mill used to say that on all great subjects, something remains to
be said. The preacher cannot cover everything. Too many points
blur the main point. Some preachers become heavy and flow like
glue because they refuse to limit their scope. The resulting message is high-density. Too much is crowded in, and the product is
in danger of sinking from its own weight. It will certainly not
achieve significant elevation.

As mentioned earlier, in the 1988 Olympic games, American
network television tried to show too much and ended up showing nothing very satisfying. During the 1992 games, by way of
contrast, a more satisfying and protracted focus was in evidence.
We must resist tantalizing bypaths and tangents. We are talking
about cutting back on subordinate support structures, not about
dismantling the coordinates of the text. This is not an easy discipline for professional talkers.

Insist on Translation

Tense and mode in preaching are critical for the sense of progression. Grady Davis is classic in his recommendation that we preach "in the present tense."[5] Transpose not only the mains into the present or future, but let the whole discourse reverberate with the sense that "Today this Scripture is fulfilled!" John Updike, the contemporary novelist, usually begins his stories with a personal recollection (quite inductively)[6] and moves into the present tense, a device that he had seen in Joyce Carey's *Mister Johnson*. Damon Runyon also wrote in the present tense. To speak overly much in the past tense weighs down discourse. We can readily use the perfect tense ("Christ has died"), giving the sense of continuing effect in the present from the completed act in the past. "How delicious the present tense is," one talented writer rhapsodizes, and we could not be more in agreement.

Work on Transition

Centrifugal progression will be severely inhibited by jagged and jerky transitions. Deftly crafted transitions that are finished and polished facilitate moving from one narrative block to another. The power of the story line in narrative is a great asset for the preacher. We have something special going for us. Why should we expose the Word of the Lord to carelessly honed transitions that can endanger the move altogether? We must not lose momentum. We do not want to preach down. The law of entropy can apply to sermons; we can tend to wind down, to become more random and diffuse. In terms of the emotional outline, we want to move to climax. Too often we have started the sermon with a bang, but our prose style has gone flat. Rather should we want to sustain the glowing filaments in the sermon. The question here is really, will our sermon be like a Concorde flight or a beached whale?

For example, examination of Genesis 13 presents us with a pericope in the Abraham cycle. Obviously the chapter continues on with the series of separations that Abraham was called upon to effect, beginning with the call of God when he was yet in Ur of the Chaldees (Gen. 12:1ff.). We are dealing here with what we might call "The Parting of the Ways," or "God-induced Good-byes." The spiritual believer cannot stay at the level of the carnal believer.

The division of the text is called for lest we ramble and unravel in a careless and heedless manner. The mains could be stated explicitly or be developed implicitly with the use of three narrative blocks, skillfully applied with good bridging "from then to now." I probably lean toward enumeration in this instance because the story line is not very dramatic or graphic:

I. Tension, 13:1-7.
    Abram got out of Egypt, but it was hard to get Egypt out of Abram and his company. Lot was a follower. Abram prayed (13:4), but no mention is made of Lot praying. Prosperity brought conflict. The situation was dangerous because of Canaanites and Perizzites living in the land.

II. Decision, 13:8-13.
    Abram is generous; Lot is greedy (note, "like the land of Egypt")—the parting.

III. Compensation, 13:14-18.
    God is no man's debtor—Abram as a person of faith.

Every possible factor catalyzing progression should be utilized.

While careful running application is being crafted with each narrative block, the third block lends wings to bridging to Christian life and experience today as God's fidelity to His covenant promises is traced to its parallel with us here and now. Powerful climacteric can be achieved by showing how the Apostle Paul through the Holy Spirit in writing to the Corinthians opens up the breathtaking vistas and reaches of what the believer enjoys in Christ—"all things are yours, whether Paul or Apollos or Cephas or the world or life or death or the present or the future— all are yours, and you are of Christ, and Christ is of God" (1 Cor. 3:21-23). Demonstrate and illustrate the principle in the terms of contemporary experience and you've preached the truth home!

THE ILLUSTRATIONS FOR THE NARRATIVE SERMON

So here I am . . .
Trying to learn to use words, and every attempt
Is a wholly new start, and a different kind of failure
Because one has only learnt to get the better of words
For the thing one no longer has to say, or the way in which
One is no longer disposed to say it. And so each venture
Is a new beginning, a raid on the inarticulate

With shabby equipment always deteriorating
In the general mess of imprecision of feeling,
Undisciplined squads of emotion.

T. S. ELIOT, IN EAST COKER

If anyone speaks, he should do it as one speaking the very words of God. (1 Peter 4:11a)

The now classic phrase of the late William Sangster on "finding the elusive illustration" resonates with all preachers.[7] If we are trapped in the text, we have not really preached. We have to strike "the preaching arc" from orthodoxy to orthopraxy. We need the apt metaphor, the contemporary positive focus illustration. God Himself is a great illustrator, and the Bible abounds with imagery and didactic story.

Some use illustration too much, to be sure, and some use it not enough. Martyn Lloyd-Jones used the words "abomination" and "prostitution" in relation to crafting illustration, but he used more illustration (particularly biblical and historical) than perhaps he realized. Donald Grey Barnhouse was a master of illustration, and his several books of illustrations are among the very few I would ever recommend. Spurgeon's actual illustrations are not usable today. They have a musty, dated sense about them. There are what we would have to call "pictorial preachers," whose immense giftedness is very clear in this area, such as Peter Marshall and the old Scot of Edinburgh, Thomas Guthrie. I feel for those preachers who would have to say, as Denis Donoghue often said, "I have never been able to tell a story."

As we have tried to demonstrate, storytelling skills can be enhanced. Learning a sense of timing in telling humorous stories should be cultivated by more than afterdinner and banquet speakers. I remember the hours my father spent with the books of the humorist Irwin S. Cobb, who was indeed a master storyteller. The narrative sermon needs illustrative work, but less than the usual didactic type sermon, and illustration of a somewhat different kind.

The purpose of illustration is to give us help with the more right-brained aspect of preaching. The illustration is a kind of instant replay of the thought being developed. Since illustration is a kind of story, the preacher would be well-advised to read a short story every week. Illustration not only helps to make clear the point being made (for those who are having a problem understanding it), but it is calculated to lift the interest level (for those who feel bored). We're wanting to spice up and spruce up discourse. Joseph Conrad wrote that his ambition in his stories was "to make you hear, to make you feel—it is above all, to make you see." This is the passion of the biblical expositor, and illustration is critical.

Several critics have described the mass of political discourse as having no music, no cadence. But Jesse Jackson is one speaker who understands the power of anecdote. Vivid description helps us escape blandness. Although he may well have overdone it, the late Robert G. Lee of Memphis never let us forget "a chunk of cloud bank, buttered with the nightwind." Plato's cave people were chained to a wall and saw only flickering images. They thought the images were the reality, denying the existence of the entire universe outside the walls of the cave. Actually in the use of illustration we are seeking to bring the people out of the constrictive cave and into the real world outside. We want to do more than turn over abstract ideas. We are concerned with translating biblical concept and precept into real-life experience. Jesus Christ is both word and person.

We are eager for illustrations that are driven from the inside of a point out rather than from the outside in; that is to say, we want to tell stories from the inside out. We must avoid telling a story within a story or we shall generate only confusion. We should not use stories that need explanation because that defeats our purpose. The story should be true and not strain credibility unless we clearly indicate it is imaginative. Some old sugar-sticks that have reappeared in ten forms should be retired. Occasionally an illustration is so overpowering that it blows us out of the water and we can't remember the point it made.

Obviously, the narrative sermon is pictorial. We may well use a story in the introduction to capture attention and then come back to finish it up in the conclusion (*inclusio*), especially if the story is an instance out of life today. The most vividly narrated story out of Bible times still needs contemporary impact to be convincing. We can strand people in the story unless we translate the principle into shoe leather for today. Does the essential action still happen? A series of negative instances (as, for example, in the lives of King Saul or King Solomon) need to show a positive contemporary focus or application.

Contemporary situations must ever be before us. Read the sermons of Charles H. Spurgeon and see how he uses a mine disaster or the death of a member of the royal family or some British foreign engagement or escapade. He had great skill in engaging his hearers and then socking it to them with Scripture. Jay Adams has given us an invaluable monograph on Spurgeon's use of sense appeal in his preaching.[8]

Clearly, the timely illustration is invaluable for the preacher; and while no retrieval system is perfect, the preacher needs to be stashing good illustrative material away non-stop. Good illustrations do away with our defenses like snowballs in a furnace. Biblical illustrations are important in the mix, although an increasing biblical illiteracy limits their use. We must be wary of overusing any category. Too much talk about football or the family dog is unwise. A good mix of illustrations is important. David Buttrick is leery of the personal instance, but I feel that careful use of such is important. It is good to tell one on ourselves and to be vulnerable without being masochistic.[9]

History and geography yield good illustrations, although we should beware of the "Wellington and Nelson" stories—i.e., too much of Victorian England or the Victorian pulpit, which may mean much to some of us but are scarcely recognized by many of today's audiences. Someone has well said that "everyone's life is full of stories." We must be careful in telling about people we have met and deathbeds we have attended. We can end our counseling ministry quickly in this way. Emerson bemoaned a preacher he had heard who "had no word intimating that he had ever laughed or wept, was married or in love, had been commended, or cheated or chagrined. . . . The capital secret of his profession, namely, to convert life into truth, he had not yet learned . . . the true preacher is one who deals out to his people life passed through the fire of his thought."[10]

Overdoing the personal reference or making the pulpit a confessional for a psychological strip-tease in the name of honesty can place too heavy a burden on our listeners who have come for help and encouragement. This tendency also ignores how implicitly transparent every communicator is, as every thoughtful listener knows. It has been pointed out that Beatrix Potter's animals predictably escape from claustrophobic domestic environments similar to that imposed on Beatrix by her own repressive parents. J. M. Barrie's Peter Pan never achieved maturity, and E. B. White's Stuart Little was a mouse born into a human family. Much is said about the author or the preacher in what is written and said, and therefore one must beware of personal overload that makes preaching overly autobiographical.

Two medium-length or longer illustrations are never advised, but especially in narrative. Several short illustrative parries can be used when they are on the same line of thought, as in David Frost's "The World's Worst Decisions," among which he nominated those who told the young Einstein that he showed "no promise," or those who decided *Star Wars* wasn't worth producing, or those who told the new rock group called the Beatles that "groups with guitars are on the way out," etc. In a message centering on spiritual decision-making, the negative instance can adeptly be turned to the positive—to make the *right* decision!

THE CONCLUSION TO THE NARRATIVE SERMON

My greatest burden is not my weak physical frame, nor my relative afflictions, nor the attacks made upon me, though from all of these I have suffered. It has been hidden in my heart . . . the burden of eternity. (J. A. Bengel)

"Choose for yourselves this day whom you will serve." (Josh. 24:15)

"How long will you waver between two opinions?" (1 Kings 18:21)

"Therefore everyone who hears these words of mine and puts them into practice is like a wise man who built his house on the rock." (Matt. 7:24)

When the people heard this they were cut to the heart and said to Peter and the other apostles, "Brothers, what shall we do?" (Acts 2:37)

The average sermon starts more strongly than it concludes. The conclusions in narrative sermons need a jump-start, like most conclusions in the North American pulpit. Application and conclusion continue to be the weakest aspects of the contemporary sermon. Even some sermons that might register 8.0 on the oratorical Richter scale and mount up with soaring Ciceronian phrases do a fade-out that no oratorical sledgehammer can rescue. Prose that once hyperventilated is now in collapse, gasping for breath. Other messages fall quietly in the void.[11]

No less a person than Aristotle in his *Rhetoric* holds that the purpose of discourse is persuasion. Our objective is quite baldly "the affecting of decisions." We need to know what to say toward that end and how to say it. According to Aristotle, the conclusion (the epilogue or the peroration) has four parts, all essential: the credibility of the communicator; effective presentation of the facts; the excitement of the emotions; and reminder of the facts (*recapitulatio*).[12] Recap of the mains is seldom helpful for today; it is best to recap as we go along and not take valuable time in the conclusion for what should have been accomplished as the sermon moved along. But let it fly in the conclusion! We speak of a symphonic Aristotelian climax. By this we do not mean loud. The most effective concluding mood may be in fact *diminuendo*.

The critical importance of a strong concluding movement is seen in all modes of communication. One book critic observed: "The first half of this big book makes racy reading. The second, containing a lot of factitious material about what happened later, somewhat diminishes what would otherwise have been a much sharper and salutary jab at our forgetfulness of recent history." To preach down is to undercut the appeal and the invitation as we finish.

Sermons can be like the end of Samuel Johnson's *Rasselas*, a conclusion in which nothing is concluded. We are talking about an unenviable terminal flatulence, but every preacher has experienced it, and it is dreadful! I am aware of the true happening when an old preacher actually fell asleep while preaching. E. M. Forster showed how easily a novel can go dead in the last third. So while we say, "Blessed is the preacher who can get airborne without too much runway," we also say, "Blessed is the preacher whose train of thought has a caboose." The conclusion needs careful preparation and honing. Ernest Hemingway rewrote the ending for *A Farewell to Arms* sixty times.

This means we seek to build toward a crescendo, moving with what Willem Zurdeeg called "convictional language" under the power and unction of the Holy Spirit. We recognize that it is the Holy Spirit moving in, with, and under the Word of God who convicts of sin, converts the sinner, and comforts the saints. Pulpit pyrotechnics can't do it. Sextus Parker in Anthony Trollope's *The Prime Minister* made bold to assert: "I'd give myself a chance to go to heaven, I think." Hesitation or equivocation at this point is fatal.

We must remember that what we are applying and concluding in the sermon is the central point of reference, the "big idea," the proposition. Perhaps our failure to focus on the single driving thrust of the text is responsible for our inability to bring it together at the end. Perhaps this is why we "pile on" at the end instead of rounding off with a clear and compelling finale. The duplex conclusion poses grave danger—everybody gets off the hook.

Beyond doubt Thiselton's insight assists us in seeing what we have going for us in a well-crafted conclusion. Says Thiselton in *The Two Horizons*: "The biblical text comes alive as a speech-act when correspondence occurs between the situation the biblical writers address and the situation of the modern reader or hearer."[13] Here is the perennial practicality of the Word of God (cf. 2 Tim. 3:16-17). Think of how the Scriptures conclude—with the book of Revelation sharing the ultimate outcomes. As Reinhold Niebuhr put it, "History is to have a worthy conclusion." Or as a simple but dear old brother put it, "Jesus is going to win!" The conclusion brings us to God's answer in Christ. What is more uplifting or encouraging? If God says we must, that means by His help we can. Here is the conclusion of the matter.

Some are especially gifted to use probing and searching questions. Perhaps *inclusio* is possible, coming back to the opening story and joining the motif again. Very often a contemporary positive focus illustration shows the principle operative and embodied in the lives of people today. Perhaps some brief, direct poetic lines or a hymn stanza can be used. These should not be read but memorized and declaimed sensitively and skillfully. Here is where some training in oral interpretation would help those preachers who veer toward mono-mood. We shall speak of delivery skills in the next chapter. Reading long quotes or extracts is always dangerous, but in the closing movement of the sermon this is in fact a millstone around the sermon.

Perhaps a word of personal testimony by the preacher will

personalize the message suitably. While mingling first and second persons throughout discourse, in the conclusion we definitely want to move it to "you." Spurgeon used to say that we have not really preached until we have said "you," and Nathan would have said nothing to David had he not trumpeted, "You are the man!" What an awesome aspect of preaching—when we place the capstone on the exposition of Holy Scripture with exquisite care and much prayer and say with all our heart, *Amen. May it be so!*

CHAPTER SEVEN

Communicating the Narrative Sermon

I assume that the preaching really is preaching, not reading an essay, not filling up time. He is there living, palpitating, bringing to bear on the people the stored-up power of his whole life, focussing into that moment the thinking of a life-time, pouring out on them the tide of emotion called forth by the situation and by the time which may be a time of decision for those who hear, rousing them by the flood of passion for their well-being, a passion that has grown with his growth and strengthened with his strength, and has now become a rushing tide that sweeps the people into conclusions which shall affect them to eternal issues. . . . If we come forth fresh from fellowship with Christ, our people cannot but feel the glow and power which must be ours if we have been with Jesus. We may not be conscious of it ourselves, but others shall know it. Moses wist not that his face shone, but the people knew it.

PROFESSOR JAMES IVERACH, ABERDEEN, SCOTLAND, 1839-1922

He preaches as though Elijah had descended to earth in his fiery chariot.

AUTHOR UNKNOWN

My message and my preaching were not with wise and persuasive words, but with a demonstration of the Spirit's power, so that your faith might not rest on men's wisdom, but on God's power.

1 COR. 2:4-5

Up to this point we have dealt largely with the substance and shape of the narrative sermon. Now our concern moves to the sharing of it with listeners in our time. We are moving from the design of the sermon to the delivery of the sermon and the factors

involved. No matter how rich the content and accurate the interpretation, the truth must be communicated. As said a classic
preacher of yesteryear, "In preaching, manner is to matter as powder is to the ball." How we say it can overshadow what we say.

That we are wholly dependent on the person and work of the
Holy Spirit does not obviate careful preparation of the sermon
any more than concern for clear delivery of the message. We want
people to respond to the message. Our communication involves
persuasion, reasoning, warning, admonishing, begging, reprov-
ing, urging. David Hesselgrave quotes Berlo to the effect that
"Our basic purpose in communication is to become an affecting
agent, to affect others . . . and to become a determining agent, to
have a vote in how things are. In short, we communicate to influence—to affect with intent."[1]

While we can become too dependent on classical rhetoric, this
legacy can be one of "multiple rhetorics" and can supply invaluable aid and assistance in our task. What David Hesselgrave has
to say about communicating cross-culturally is increasingly relevant for the North American preacher. More and more ours is a
pluralistic society. We are really contextualizing our message for
the widening spectrum of our hearers. Proper contextualization
involves carefully guarded biblical definition, then wise selection,
then accurate adaptation, and finally application.

More and more in our culture "truth is whatever gets the
most applause." The "drip effect" of violent images in the media
immunizes and desensitizes young people especially. The "anything goes" approach to life today is critiqued by the astute Philip
Rieff along with the "radical contemporaneity" outlook as the
tragic "failure of memory." This is barbarism. Bemoaning the
emergence of "psychological man," Rieff, of the University of
Pennsylvania and author of *The Triumph of the Therapeutic*,
laments our becoming a shameless people and that Christians
have become so tame and that, as a consequence, "churches are
empty of life, if not people."[2] No one has critiqued this more tren-
chantly than Mortimer Adler, whose conversion to Christianity in
recent years is such an extraordinary work of God. In a recent
book Adler rebukes Joseph Campbell's "unrestricted pluralism"
in which there is only poetic truth. As over against Harvey Cox
(in *Many Mansions*), who clearly has no understanding of the

logic of truth, or Hans Kung, for whom "the question of truth is fatal," Adler insists on logical and factual truth.[3]

To see how far our culture has drifted from its moorings in the Judeo-Christian ethic and has moved relentlessly on toward decomposition and disintegration, we have only to read a conclusion of C. S. Lewis and realize how frightfully out-of-date it seems in our present communications climate. I refer to his conviction, "There is no getting away from it: the Christian rule is 'Either marriage, with complete faithfulness to your partner, or else total abstinence.'" William Willimon is really right on in raising the question, "Preaching: Entertainment or Exposition?" Since exposition makes demands and has something serious to say, it is out of step in our world today.[4] We want privilege without commitment. Seventy percent of those surveyed in a Gallup poll indicated they looked to the Bible for guidance in determining conduct, but 70 percent also said, "there are few moral absolutes; what is right or wrong usually varies from situation to situation." In other words, the influence of the Enlightenment and the sexual revolution is now reaching the masses (and, sadly, even the clergy).

In this setting, then, we seek to persuade men and women of the truth of the Gospel of Christ. We must call attention to the work of Mack and Robbins, which draws from the form-critical scholarship of Martin Dibelius the pattern of editorial persuasion known as "*chreia*" in ancient rhetoric. The Synoptic writers— Matthew, Mark, and Luke—used the basic techniques of Greco-Roman schoolmen in their argumentation.[5] Let us likewise draw on Marshall McLuhan, difficult as he is to understand. McLuhan, a devout pre-Vatican II Roman Catholic from the prairie provinces of Canada, predicted that the "information glut" in our information age would lead us to "a future of generalized functional illiteracy, historical and cultural amnesia and spiritual impoverishment."[6] We need all the resources that ingenuity and divine providence can afford us for preaching in times such as ours.

Balanced and wise, Calvin Miller in elaborating his philosophy of preaching pleads that we need both precepts and storytelling. Indeed he says, "Precepts then are the skeletal systems upon which we hang our stories of faith." He urges on us the power of narrative for our day, quoting Augustine: "If the hearers need teaching, tell the truth by means of narrative."[7] Which undoubtedly means that even in preaching the more didactic sections of Scripture, we should give great care to illustration and imaging of the abstract concept. I cite in this regard the late Donald Grey Barnhouse's ingenious stick drawings and visuals on the great doctrines of the Bible. I often used those materials in seeking to make "justification by faith alone" come alive for Bible instruction classes of eighth and ninth graders.[8]

The challenge that we face then, to use William Fitch's marvelous imagery, is "preaching amid smog." Indeed, the day of preaching is not done. Preaching is a miracle, as Fitch says.[9] But what is involved in the effective communication of the biblical narrative or any Scripture in today's world?

CONCEPTUALIZATION

> Let us be certain, brethren, that the Lord hath more truth and light yet to break forth out of His holy Word. (Rev. John Robinson, July 21, 1620)

> Proper words in proper places make the true definition of a style. (Jonathan Swift)

> Speech which fails to convey a plain meaning will fail to do just what speech has to do. (Aristotle)

> "He who listens to you listens to me; he who rejects you rejects me." (Luke 10:16)

All consideration of communication must begin with the conceptualization of content. Content is primary. In his worthwhile study *Elements of Style for Preaching*, William Kooienga shows how Augustine in the first extensive treatment of preaching wrestles with how Scripture is to be understood (hermeneutics) and then goes on to deal with how Scripture as understood is to be communicated (homiletics).[10] Said Augustine: "Wisdom is more important than eloquence."[11]

If, as Peter Ramus pointed out, rhetoric is "the art of speaking well," we must reinforce our insistence that the narrative sermon must say what the text of Scripture says. We need clear ideas clothed with evocative language in appropriate style. This is what makes the present-day move away from the objective text of Scripture so disturbing. One recent sampling of Protestants disclosed that 83 percent regard the Bible as the revealed Word of God, but 40 percent "never or hardly ever" read the Bible. No matter how high a view of the inspiration and authority of the Bible we may hold, if we do not really draw on the Word, we are profiting nothing.

God has promised to bless His Word. Although His ways and thoughts are in an absolute sense ineffable, the word from His mouth (like the rain and snow and seed) "will not return to me empty, but will accomplish what I desire and achieve the purpose for which I sent it" (Isa. 55:10-11). This Word is "living and active" (Heb. 4:12). We don't have to push a river. I am not insinuating that some magical or quasi-automatic result accrues from the sounding of biblical sentences. We are not like the Sikhs of India who venerate and worship their holy book, the Granth, and in their holy places read it continuously in shifts of readers (the pathis). Auxiliary lamps and candles are in readiness in case of power failure. Comprehension is minimal and application superfluous.[12]

This is what makes the present penchant for the idea that a text is what the reader makes of it so profoundly disturbing. To be freed from the responsibility of searching out the author's real meaning is a tragic cul de sac. Facing reality in a superficial culture is not easy, especially when the working axiom seems to be, "It's dangerous to talk substance." The strategy of selling in our society has become the bypassing of the consumer's analytic processes. In his last essay Norman Cousins spoke of "The Communication Collapse," which he saw as the disastrous failure to "develop respect for thought processes."[13] To mold and shape thought, the preacher must think clearly and use good and true words.

Those who hope for a share in a will listen carefully. The accused in a trial listens carefully to the reading of the verdict. We have a message that addresses the despair, the hopelessness, the anxiety, and the listlessness of modern life. As Dr. Johnson once observed, "Depend on it; when a man knows he is going to be hanged in a month, it concentrates his mind wonderfully." The issues are so urgent and of such eternal significance.

The need for clear conceptualization in communication is

illustrated in a story told by John Allen Paulos: "Martha and a big dog are standing at a bus stop. Waldo approaches them and asks if her dog bites. She assures him that her dog is friendly and doesn't bite, whereupon Waldo pets the dog. The dog bites his arms and legs and thoroughly mauls Waldo who screams at Martha, 'I thought you said your dog doesn't bite.' Martha responds quite innocently, 'Oh, that's not my dog.'"[14] The unthinking use of suppositions and premises can land us in all kinds of trouble.

Recently Luciano Pavarotti was unprepared when he sang Verdi's *Don Carlo*. Notwithstanding his great gifts and talent, he didn't pull it off and was roundly hissed and booed. We can't take shortcuts in preparing the text for preaching either. There is no quick, easy, or effortless method.

There is no substitute for personal exposure and experience. Commentary-clotted sermons, to use Calvin Miller's phrase, will have difficulty getting off the pad into significant elevation. I was much struck by this lately as I read an article about the late Warner Sallman's "Head of Christ," which has circulation in various forms beyond one billion copies. As I read the discussion about conflicting versions of the origin of the painting and how Sallman "dehistoricized the image and placed it within the realm of private devotion" (thus affirming the traditional, paternalistic order),[15] I realized that the author of the article had never known Warner Sallman as I knew him.

A subsequent correspondent on the issue interpreted the painting as showing "a Docetic Christ . . . who never suffered and died . . . who makes few or no demands upon the believer." A theologian responded by characterizing Sallman's "Head of Christ" as "the most graphic indictment of popular American Protestantism—of our individualistic, pietistic, ahistoric, sentimental, superstitious travesty of the gospel."[16]

These persons have every right to assert what they see in the picture, but to have known Sallman as I have is to know how wide of the mark their observations really are. The preparation of the text for preaching requires our knowing its divine author and grappling with the purpose and intention of the human and divine authors in the text.

EMOTION

[The preacher of the Word as over against the great orators

of history] lights his torch at all their fires, and then has a torch lit not by their flaring lamps, but at the sun, which sun is Christ. The preacher has all they had, and more, gloriously more! No interest vital to the world which he does not touch. He stands at the center of a circle whose entire rim is fire. Glory envelops him. He is a prisoner of majesty. A dumb man would stumble into luminous speech on such themes as the gospel grapples with. We dare not be ineloquent when we have themes which do as Aaron's rod did, burst forth into perfumed bloom. We must not be insipid. There is not a dull page in all this age-long story of the redeeming of the race. The minor prophets leap into eloquence which silence Demosthenes; and the major prophets take the thunders for a trumpet on which to blow their universal summons; and the apostles stand in the highway where the peoples throng and exact a tribute of hearing from the unconcerned; and the evangelists forget bookkeeping and fishing, in eloquence which time has not had the effrontery to dim. (Bishop William A. Quayle)

That which comes from the heart goes to the heart. (William Wordsworth)

If you would make others feel, you must feel yourself . . . the heavenly flame must be kindled first in your own bosom, that by this law of sympathy it may radiate thence into the souls of your hearers. (Robert Dabney)

One day Boswell was questioning Samuel Johnson about sermonizers. Boswell: "A clergyman whose name I do not recall asked: 'Were not Dodd's sermons addressed to the passions?'" To which Johnson replied: "They were nothing, Sir, be they addressed to what they may." Dr. Johnson was quite critical, as we know, but he was on to something when he said of Samuel Richardson's novels, "If you were reading for the plot, you'd hang yourself." The preacher must have the goods to deliver, but the preacher must also help the hearers "feel" the importance of what is shared.

We are addressing here the mission of emotion in preaching. Two issues come to the fore: (1) the *existence* of deep feeling, and (2) the *expression* of deep feeling. If the truth is not deeply felt, the speaker has no business in the pulpit. We do recognize that there are those who feel deeply but who find it difficult to express that feeling. I am talking about more than gyratory energy in preaching. I am speaking about passion, such as constrained Jeremiah to exclaim, "But if I say, 'I will not mention him or speak any more in his name,' his word is in my heart like a burning fire, shut up in my bones. I am weary of holding it in; indeed, I cannot" (Jer. 20:9).

The essential inner ignition rises out of an authentic experience of the living God. Freeing up the more inhibited preacher to flow represents a considerable challenge. Work in oral interpretation, dramatic art, and impromptu speech can help. We're not talking about something excessive or "put on." We can draw too much attention to ourselves and away from the truth in that way. Narrative preachers are especially vulnerable to this danger. Of a certain orchestral maestro it was said: "Dispassionately virtuosic, infuriatingly glib, lacking in genuine sentiment, and disfigured by preening pulpit mannerisms of a sort that force the presence of the conductor on the audience's attention."

But the fact remains, as Karl Barth put it so powerfully, "If there is no great agony in our hearts, there will be no great words on our lips." Augustine long ago insisted: "Rhetoricians require passion in one who pleads a case." Soren Kierkegaard was right when he said, "there is no lack of information in a Christian land—something else is lacking." We must do more than state the truth. Ours is a feeling age, and many feel affectively starved. Is it not ironic, then, that many evangelicals in an overreaction to emotional excess in bygone years have become so rationalistic? The absence of emotion is no badge of achievement in the pulpit; it is a disastrous forfeiture.

Trying to preach without passion is not preaching at all. Our emotions are part of what we are. Emotional bypass is an ill-advised strategy. Stories and narrative are means of emotional intensification and must not be used exploitively or manipulatively. A series of articles in the *Chicago Tribune* on our litigious society pointed out that "Stirring Jurors' Emotions Becomes the Key," as the headline ran. Another headline in the series said, "Jurors' Emotions Play Large Role in Verdict." This is not surprising, but what is surprising is that so many preachers seek to downplay feelings and tone.

A prominent pioneer in advertising creativity has well

observed: "Creativity is just doing what other people don't." His philosophy emphasizes "the primacy of emotion in advertising creation and in salesmanship."[17] Every product has its rational arguments. The danger of emotional backfire exists if people sense phoniness. Even little children recognize a phony. The principle operative here is simple and basic. It is called "the bucket principle." If we want blessing and refreshment to slosh on our people, then our own buckets have to be full. We cannot give them what we don't have ourselves.

The "discursive" level of reality has to do with the actual words that we say; the "presentational" level of reality has to do with what's between the lines, what is heard with the third ear, what is conveyed beyond the words themselves. Something is wrong at the "presentational" level when a person speaks flatly; the music doesn't go with the words. There is lack of congruence. Some sermons are like the psalmist's description of the Almighty on a chilly day: "He casteth forth his ice like morsels: who is able to abide his frost?" To talk about fire as if you were sitting on a cake of ice is incongruence of a difficult order.

A. N. Wilson's recent biography of C. S. Lewis speaks of "the immediacy of his rough-hewn style." We feel truth as well as perceive it in C .S. Lewis, and fascinatingly his conversion released a great literary flow in his life.[18] So I am urging here something other than and more than incendiary rhetoric—a kind of narrative crackle. This is more than an oratorical tour de force–this is molten lava. It's like rain on mown grass; it's language creaking and groaning under the weight of a great heart. It's avoiding that of which Shakespeare spoke:

> *Those who, moving others, are themselves as stone,*
> *Unmoved, cold and to temptation slow.*

Citing the climactic outburst at the end of Romans 9, 10, and 11, Martyn Lloyd-Jones makes as strong a case as anyone for preaching that is more than Matthew Arnold's "tinged with emotion," preaching that has deep and moving pathos and emotion. Writes Lloyd-Jones: "My contention is that when a man really understands this truth which he claims to believe he must be moved by it. If he is not, he does not belong to that company, that category which includes the great Apostle himself. But it has become the fashion to dislike emotion."[19] And this is of particular importance when we preach the narrative sections of Scripture, because nothing reaches and teaches our emotions as much as do stories.

CONVICTION

When E. F. Hutton speaks, everyone listens. (A popular commercial)

To be dead in earnest is to be eloquent. (An old axiom)

I could not tell what he was driving at, except that he seemed desirous not to offend the congregation. (Henry Wadsworth Longfellow)

"My people come to you, as they usually do, and sit before you to listen to your words, but they do not put them into practice. With their mouths they express devotion, but their hearts are greedy for unjust gain. Indeed, to them you are nothing more than one who sings love songs with a beautiful voice and plays an instrument well, for they hear your words but do not put them into practice." (Ezek. 33:31-32)

The nightmare of every preacher of the Word is that he should be merely a flute player, an entertainer, a stimulus to aesthetic enjoyment, and not a prophet upon whom is the hand of God (Ezek. 33:22). Shall we just titillate our hearers, or shall we be the instruments clothed with the Spirit of God who are used to change and transform human life and experience? We are talking here of spiritual unction (which we shall treat in the next section), and we are also dealing with elenctics, the solemn and searching sense of conviction and call to repentance (cf. Jude 14-15; Rev. 3:19; John 16:8; 1 Tim. 5:20; Matt. 18:15—in all of which the verb *elengchein* is used).[20] In opening the biblical narrative text, what are the human factors that make for the divine/human confrontation at the deepest and most significant levels of being?

In all of the professions there is a call today for greater and more sensitive communicational skills (we are looking for skills, not tricks). Modern persons are awash with more information than they know what to do with. We have witnessed the advent of high-speed, broadband telecommunications, massive databases, and multimedia. What our culture needs is not more pur-veyors of information but tellers, those who will explain what the facts mean, those who will explicate and educate. People are searching for answers in a confusing world. What are the human skills involved in effective declaration?

The late Kyle Haselden in pleading for the urgency of preach-ing lamented that so many preachers "whose chief tool is the spo-ken word have in general less skill and less training in oral communication than men and women in a host of other profes-sions . . . we assume that whatever voice we have and whatever skills in expression are native to us—are good enough."

But if our interest is in "performative discourse," we must take into account the oral nature of preaching in a visual age. While Calvin was troubled by some oratorical devices, he felt strongly that the preacher should not be lifeless but lively. He favored preaching extempore—i.e., preparing massively, but not following a manuscript sentence by sentence. He would concur with the Berne Preacher Act of 1667: "They must not read the same in front of the congregation from notes or paper, which is a mockery to have to watch and takes away all fruit and grace from the preacher in the eyes of the listeners."[21]

Every preacher ought to prepare a manuscript regularly to keep tabs on patterns that may be developing; but reading the ser-mon is totally out of sync with what is needed for direct appeal today. We need oral, not written, voice inflection. We need pur-poseful eye contact. This enhances the dialogical component, just as does the skillful use of questions. The eye is a critical organ of speech. H. H. Farmer was of the persuasion that "the direct encounter with the will is hampered when the sermon is read." If he is only 33 percent correct, how can we hold on to our paper in preaching? We need free delivery. Paper is not a good conductor of heat. We need that careful preparation and familiarization that permit us to think paragraphically from an "orascript." We need to wean ourselves gradually from overdependence on written materials. This is true of all preaching but is especially pressing for the preaching of narrative.

Attention to proxemics (matters of distance, elevation, obstruc-tions, and lighting), as well as kinesics (grooming, posture, facial gesture, and hand use), are imperative. Relaxation techniques for better word formation and projection and the cultivation of variation in delivery are subjects on which basic speech books can be of immense practical help. The volumes by Paul Sangster, B. B. Baxter, Jay Adams, and Duane Litfin are all written from the viewpoint of the Christian communicator. A special piece is that by Reid Buckley, brother of William F. Buckley, entitled *Speaking in Public*.[22] The author is interested in fostering the use of "juicy vowels" and "hard rock candy tooth cracking consonants." The reason for stressing such matters is the one similarity between preaching and television performance, as a news anchorwoman pointed out: "People get only one chance to understand what you are saying—it's not as if they can re-read a page—so you use whatever facial expressions and body language you need to make it more understandable." In the pulpit we share that situation.

The preacher must be always on the prowl for more effective words and descriptives, remembering that *Language Is Sermonic*, as the title of a book by the late Richard M. Weaver reminds us.[23] The nature of words and language, avoidance of logical fallacies, and the ethical issues involved in persuasion are all very pressing for the preacher.[24] We have such a message to deliver that we should seek excellence and effectiveness in every human skill needed to do the job, knowing that it must all be owned by the Holy Spirit or it will fall down.

UNCTION

Preaching is a great mystery. (D. Martyn Lloyd-Jones)

"The Spirit of the Lord is on me, because he has anointed me to preach good news to the poor." (Luke 4:18)

But you have an anointing from the Holy One, and all of you know the truth. . . . As for you, the anointing you received from him remains in you, and you do not need anyone to teach you. But as his anointing teaches you about all things and as that anointing is real, not counterfeit—just as it has taught you, remain in him. (1 John 2:20, 27)

The Second Helvetic Confession boldly asserts that *"Praedicatio verbi dei est verbum dei"* ("The preaching of the Word of God is the Word of God"); i.e., to the degree that preaching says what the Word of God says, that preaching is the

Word of God. The neglect of serious study of the Word and the distraction and diversion of the preacher by a mass of impressive trivia amount to criminal neglect. One leading purveyor of preacher-helps explains why in his judgment preachers need the canned outlines and illustrations he offers: "Some ministers are running pre-schools, building campaigns, or are active in community affairs. There just isn't time anymore for a clergyman to do an adequate job preparing a sermon."[25] We must regard this abdication of responsibility and duty both tragic and culpable.

Are we in danger of desupernaturalizing the preaching process? At every step and stage from germination to proclamation "we are God's fellow workers" (1 Cor. 3:9a). The divine author of Holy Scripture is our guide and teacher. We are in constant consultation with the author of our text! And even when our preparation is thorough and completed, done with exegetical conscience and accuracy, we now face the actual act of preaching itself. Preaching would be unacceptably audacious and presumptuous beyond words for the offspring of Adam and Eve apart from the unction/anointing of the Holy Spirit. This is a totally unique aspect of preaching—our entire and absolute dependence on the Holy Spirit for everything involved in preaching—before, during, and after the sermon event itself.

In the Old Testament we read of many anointings, including the anointing of Aaron and his sons entering priestly ministration with both blood and oil (Ex. 29:21). *Messiah* means literally "the anointed one," for He was anointed "with the oil of joy" (Heb. 1:9). Jesus was "anointed with the Holy Spirit and power" (Acts 10:38). The Greek word *chrisma* and the Old Latin and Vulgate *unctio* would seem to connote a supernatural empowerment and protection. John in his first epistle (2:20, 27), in speaking of the antichrists and the coming of *the* Antichrist, describes "the anointing" or "unction" that will safeguard and strengthen believers in a day of danger and difficulty.[26]

Generically this anointing is for all believers, but derivatively this anointing of the Spirit confers divine ownership on the preached Word and the sense of afflatus on the preacher. E. M. Bounds has put it this way:

> This unction comes to the preacher not in the study but in the closet. It is heaven's distillation in answer to prayer. It is

the sweetest exhalation of the Holy Spirit. It impregnates, suffuses, softens, percolates, cuts and soothes. It carries the Word like dynamite, like salt, like sugar; makes the Word a soother, an arranger, a revealer, a searcher; makes the hearer a culprit or a saint, makes him weep like a child and live like a giant; opens his heart and his purse as gently, yet as strongly as the spring opens the leaves.[27]

This is what is meant when we read of how "they preached the gospel to you by the Holy Spirit sent from heaven" (1 Peter 1:12). This is the "working of his power" (Eph. 3:7).

When preaching a more didactic passage with clearer doctrinal substance, I have generally felt more confident and stronger than when I ventured into narrative. I find tremendous thrust in the nature of story itself, but I struggle often with confident application. Is narrative preaching destined to be "lighter" and of less weight? Will this be frothy and ephemeral? At this point I need the vigorous reaffirmation of "unction" for the preaching of every literary genre of Scripture because it is needed every bit as much here and will be lavishly given by the Holy One.

Of John Brown, who preached in Haddington with powerful effect for thirty-six years, David Hume, the empiricist and skeptic, commented: "He preached as though the Son of God stood at his elbow." One hearer recalled:

I well remember a searching sermon he preached from the word, "What went ye out for to see? A reed shaken with the wind." Although at that time I had no experimental acquaintance with the truth as it is in Jesus, yet his grave appearance in the pulpit, his solemn, weighty and majestic manner of speaking, used to affect me very much. Certainly his preaching was close, and his address to the conscience pungent. Like his Lord and Master, he spoke with authority and hallowed pathos, having tasted of the sweetness and felt the power of what he believed.[28]

This was the preaching of an orphan boy with no schooling whatever, who had traveled for five years as a peddler. This is divine unction.

The *sealing* of the Holy Spirit would seem to have to do with the assurance of salvation; the *fullness* of the Holy Spirit with character and service; the *anointing* of the Holy Spirit with proper knowledge and insight with an aim to utterance. Of Basil of Nazianzen it was written: "His words were thunder, his life lightning." Isn't this what Paul prayed for when he pleaded, "Finally, brothers, pray for us that the message of the Lord may spread rapidly and be honored" (2 Thess. 3:1)? This is what Gardiner Spring, for sixty-two years the pastor of the Brick Presbyterian Church in New York City, called "sacred excitement."

Two more recent studies have emphasized this spiritual dimension in the preaching task after many years of having virtually nothing in print on the subject. Dennis Kinlaw's seminal *Preaching in the Spirit*[29] warmly and wisely speaks of "the inner explosion" of the truth of God in our own hearts as prefatory to preaching. Our peril is that our preaching will be "like dried peas on a tin roof." Kinlaw skillfully shows us that "we are the capacity. He is the supply." Oh, that our preaching were not in the sand of the flesh, but in the oil of the Holy Ghost!

The other significant study constitutes the Beecher Lectures for 1986 by the black homiletician and preacher James Forbes and is entitled *The Holy Spirit and Preaching*. Forbes differentiates between a spirited preacher and being a Spirit-filled preacher.[30] He quotes James Earl Massey on this point: "The anointed preaching carries the hearers beyond the limited benefit of the preacher's personality and rhetorical abilities."[31] Forbes is especially helpful in encouraging us to appropriate the anointing in the process of our own spiritual formation and spiritual growth.

Faith, as Luther used to say, is an acoustical affair. This is where preaching comes into the picture. In expounding the text, the preacher is plainly and simply seeking to be a persuader. Intuitively the preacher is endeavoring to persuade,[32] and this is only to replicate the pattern in the book of Acts and throughout the New Testament (cf. Acts 13:43; 18:4; 19:8; 26:28; 28:23). What is involved here?

We must concur with the young Winston Churchill in an essay he wrote in India at the age of twenty-three: "The key to a speaker's impact on his audience is sincerity . . . to convince them, he must believe." This is good as far as it goes. But for the Christian communicator, there must be this above all: the sovereign ownership of the Holy Spirit on the preacher and the preaching. Thus the preacher must preach the crucified Christ in a crucified manner. Or as John Bunyan classically depicts the preacher: "his back to the world, his face toward heaven, and a Book in his hand."

III

OUR SUBJECTS

The greatest treasure ever found—GOLD! For 131 years one of the world's richest treasures—perhaps a billion dollars in fine gold—lay lost and out of reach in the frigid, lightless depths of the Atlantic, entombed in the wreck of a once elegant 19th century steamer, the S.S. Central America. Until recently the riches of the Central America lay 8000 feet below the surface. Then in 1985 an unlikely trio from Ohio began a cautious but brilliant search . . . recovering enough gold to make everyone involved fabulously rich.

LIFE MAGAZINE, MARCH 1992, P. 32FF.

The ordinances of the Lord are sure and altogether righteous. They are more precious than gold, than much pure gold.

PS. 19:9B-10A

CHAPTER EIGHT

The Unique Charms
of the Parables

It will take all our learning to make things plain.

ARCHBISHOP USSHER

Jesus spoke all these things to the crowd in parables; he did
not say anything to them without using a parable. So was
fulfilled what was spoken through the prophet: "I will open
my mouth in parables, I will utter things hidden since the creation of the world."

MATT. 13:34-35

My heart grew hot within me, and as I meditated, the fire
burned; then I spoke with my tongue.

Ps. 39:3

Parables are tiny lumps of coal squeezed into diamonds, con-
densed metaphors that catch the rays of something ultimate
and glint it at our lives.

WALTER WINK

We turn now from the bulk of biblical narrative to some special kinds of narrative in order to sharpen our focus on both the
opportunity and the challenge of preaching narrative in our time.
The parables of the Bible are a unique and special kind of narrative. We have ordinarily spoken of parables as earthly stories with
heavenly meanings. More exactly, as Archibald Hunter defines it,
a parable is "a comparison drawn from nature or human life, and
intended to illuminate some spiritual truth, on the assumption
that what is valid in one sphere is valid also in the other." The
Hebrew word for parable is *mashal*, which means "be like." The

143

Greek word *parabole* means placing one thing alongside another for purposes of comparison. Certain more technical matters about parables and their interpretation will be considered later in this chapter.

The use of parable addresses the need to move abstract truth and principle into the more concrete and practical. Peters and Waterman have shown in relation to business and industry that "We are more influenced by stories (vignettes that are whole and make sense in themselves) than by data."[1] The parable is a part of what John Brokhof calls the "symphony of similitudes" found in Scripture, which include the simile, the analogy, the metaphor, the allegory, and the parable.[2]

The Old Testament uses parables somewhat sparingly, though we recall the skillful use of the parable by Nathan the prophet as he confronted King David. The parable is more than an illustration. It is a type of indirect discourse, but it brings to bear a serious principle. Isaiah's "Song of the Vineyard" (Isa. 5) and Jeremiah's story of Israel as the bride (Jer. 2) are both parabolic, as is Jeremiah's beautiful and winsome story of the marred vessel remade (Jer. 18:1ff.). Abimelech, son of Gideon, used the story of "The King Tree" (cf. Judg. 9) to make his point. The parable is an old and venerable and more eastern technique and yet very powerful in today's climate for communication.[3]

Jesus Christ as the Master-Teacher used parables with extraordinary skill. He came preaching and teaching. The two words are used virtually interchangeably in the Gospels, but we would hold out for a slightly different nuancing between them (although we cannot go nearly as far as C. H. Dodd in distinguishing them). Nonetheless, all good preaching has much teaching, and all good teaching has some real preaching in it. About 35 percent of Jesus' teaching was in parables (He used between fifty and seventy parables), depending on how broad a definition is used.

Sometimes in our concern to show that Jesus is so much more than a teacher, we have neglected to emphasize what a great teacher He was. Nicodemus, "Israel's teacher," came to Him and addressed Him deferentially as "Rabbi," or "teacher" (John 3:2). Jesus taught with authority (Matt. 7:29), with wisdom (Mark 6:2), and with a simple directness, at the heart of which was the brilliance of His parables. No one has more helpfully pinpointed the masterful excellence of the pedagogy of Jesus than Professor

Herman H. Horne of New York University in his superb treatment entitled *Jesus—the Master Teacher*. Horne showed how Jesus was a master at establishing contact with his auditors and in securing and sustaining their attention.[4] But a large part of His effectiveness was in the use of parables.

Two recent books have effectively summoned the church and its ministers to recover the teaching office. This note could not be more pleasing to those exercised about more and better expository preaching in our time. While in his advocacy of "a vital teaching ministry" Richard Osmer speaks more directly to the mainline churches, he has an important emphasis for all of us. Drawing upon Calvin's theory and practice and upon James Fowler's theory of faith development, Osmer makes a significant and bold proposal for the revitalization of teaching in the Church. As Calvin faced the assaults of humanism in his day, he strongly emphasized strengthening the ordained teaching office (Calvin himself was never ordained), but also catechetical instruction in the schools and in the context of the family. Osmer's healthy and salutary emphasis on seeking to bolster and enrich teaching in the local church brings us right back to Jesus and His methods of teaching, foremost of which is the parable.[5]

Not as weighty as Osmer, though more direct and usable, is Williamson and Allen's *The Teaching Minister*, again largely addressed to the gaping vacuum in mainline denominations but very relevant to evangelicals who seem to be becoming more and more like the mainline denominations in many respects. The essential argument is that all clergy, including administrators and psychotherapists, must see themselves essentially as teachers of the Christian faith.

Since the latest statistics show that mainline giving is up and for the first time evangelical giving is down (indicating that it is taking more dedication to remain mainline with evangelical popularity on the increase), we should be well advised to listen to what these authors have to say by way of antidote to the downward curve of mainline enterprise. The thesis of the book is that the mainline church must recover authentic teaching in order to address "the crisis of belief" in the churches. The problem has been "secularization from within."[6] The clergy must rediscover their identity as pastor-teachers (Eph. 4:11). The teaching office has its biblical antecedents. Think of the prophetic teaching of

Hosea or Amos or Zechariah. Reflect on the vivid use of metaphor and story.

The sermon is seen by these authors as a teaching event, but they strongly and wisely insist that everything in ministry and in the church should teach. Is not this a crucial part of the Great Commission (Matt. 28:18-20)? All of this necessitates our probing deeply into the teaching of Jesus, and most particularly the prominence of parables in his teaching.

AN INVENTORY OF THE PARABLES

> Dr. E. V. Rieu: "My personal reason for this [translation of the four Gospels] was my own intense desire to satisfy myself as to the authenticity and the spiritual content of the Gospels."
>
> Dr. J. B. Phillips: "Did you get the feeling that the whole material is extraordinarily alive? . . . I got the feeling that the whole thing was alive even while one was translating."
>
> Dr. E. V. Rieu: "I got the deepest feeling that I possibly could have expected. It—changed me; my work changed me. And I came to the conclusion that these words bear the seal of—the Son of Man and God. And they're the Magna Carta of the human spirit."
>
> Dr. J. B. Phillips: "I found it particularly thrilling to hear a man who is a scholar of the first rank as well as a man of wisdom and experience openly admitting that these words written long ago were alive with power. They bore to him, as to me, the ring of truth." (J. B.Phillips, *Ring of Truth*)

The word "parable" is actually used by the gospel writers quite broadly to include simple similes and metaphors. Parable and allegory are much alike, although we would be inclined to feel that the extended use of the metaphor of the vine and the branches in John 15 (which becomes virtually an allegory) should not be included in a listing of the parables.

There is value and advantage in using a simple classification of the parables of Jesus in order that we might appreciate something of the range and sweep of this remarkable body of teaching material. No one has used a better categorization, in my judgment, than James Montgomery Boice,[7] to whom I am principally indebted for the basic skeleton of the following:

I. PARABLES OF SALVATION.
   A. The lost sheep, the lost coin, the two lost sons, Luke 15.
   B. Workers in the vineyard, Matthew 20:1-16.
   C. "Come to the banquet . . . everything is now ready," Matthew 22:1-14; Luke 14:15-24.
   D. The narrow door of salvation, Luke 13:22-30.
   E. The Pharisee and the tax-collector, Luke 18:9-14.
   F. The conflict of the old and the new:
      1. Children of the bridechamber, Matthew 9:14-15; Mark 2:18-20; Luke 5:33-35.
      2. The new patch and the old garment, Matthew 9:16; Mark 2:21; Luke 5:36.
      3. Old wineskins and new wine, Matthew 9:17; Mark 2:22; Luke 5:37-39.
      4. Treasures old and new, Matthew 13:51-52.
II. PARABLES OF THE CHRISTIAN LIFE.
   A. A tale of two sons, Matthew 21:28-32.
   B. Two stories about lamps, Luke 8:16-18; 11:33-36.
   C. The good Samaritan, Luke 10:25-37.
   D. On not giving up in prayer, Luke 11:5-13; 18:1-8.
   E. On being thankful, Luke 7:36-50.
   F. The chief seats and humility, Luke 14:7-11.
   G. The bondservant and what we do for God, Luke 17:7-10.
III. PARABLES OF WISDOM AND FOLLY.
   A. Five foolish women and their friends, Matthew 25:1-13.
   B. The rich fool, Luke 12:13-21.
   C. A shrewd man of the world, Luke 16:1-9.
   D. Wise and foolish builders, Matthew 7:24-27; Luke 6:46-49.
   E. Conditions of discipleship:
      1. The empty house, Matthew 12:43-45; Luke 11:24-26.
      2. The unfinished tower, Luke 14:28-30.
      3. The rash warfare, Luke 14:31-33.
IV. PARABLES OF THE KINGDOM.
   A. The seed growing silently, Mark 4:26-29.
   B. The sower and the seed, Matthew 13:3-8, 18-23; Mark 4:3-8, 14-20; Luke 8:5-8, 11-15.
   C. The tares and the wheat, Matthew 13:24-30, 36-43.
   D. The mustard seed, Matthew 13:31-32; Mark 4:30-32; Luke 13:18-19.
   E. The leaven, Matthew 13:33; Luke 13:20-21.

F. The treasure in the field, Matthew 13:44.
G. The pearl of great price, Matthew 13:45-46.
H. The draw-net, Matthew 13:47-50.
V. PARABLES OF JUDGMENT.
A. The wretched man's wretched end, Matthew 18:21-35.
B. The wicked trustees, Matthew 21:33-46.
C. Unprofitable servants and unprofitable goats, Matthew 25:14-46.
D. The rich man and Lazarus, Luke 16:19-31. (Although I list this passage here, I incline to think it is probably not a parable since it uses a proper name and shows other non-parabolic signs.)
E. The wedding garment, Matthew 22:11-14.
F. The barren fig tree, Luke 13:6-9.

Probably an extended series preaching straight through the parables is ill-advised, even though there is a striking variety in the subjects discussed. Most of us will come to parables in their larger setting as we preach through one of the Gospels (*lectio continua*). In this way we are more prone to see the parable in its natural context. On the other hand, a brief course of sermons on "The Parables of Grace" or one of the above-entitled categories presents a good change of pace both for preacher and congregation.

According to our Lord, when interrogated as to "Why do you speak to the people in parables?" He used parables both to reveal and to conceal (Matt. 13:10-17). The use of smoked glass to view an eclipse shows how it is necessary to conceal in order to reveal. Some of the hearers of Jesus were set to reject whatever He said. He therefore concealed the truth through the use of parables for all such; but those who knew Him, saw and heard (Matt. 13:16).

THE HISTORY OF THE INTERPRETATION OF THE PARABLES

He taught them by parables, under which were hid mysterious senses, which shined through their veil, like a bright sun through an eye closed with a thin eyelid. (Jeremy Taylor)

His disciples came to him and said: "Explain to us the parable . . ." (Matt. 13:36b)

If you utter worthy, not worthless, words, you will be my spokesman. (Jer. 15:19)

Let the one who has my word speak it faithfully. . . . "Is not my word like fire," declares the Lord, "and like a hammer that breaks a rock in pieces?" (Jer. 23:28-29)

Incredible atrocities can be seen in the history of interpreting the Scripture. Hermeneutical mayhem! I refer not only to the undermining of the authority of the Word by "the systematic exercise of a critical disposition to reduce the Word of God to literary-theological construction, instead of seeing it as the revelation of our creator and redeemer."[8] The presuppositions and commitment of historical criticism are now being examined and admitted, and the damage of the essential secularity of historical criticism is now being recognized. As one scholar concedes, "It [historical criticism] is the realization of the Enlightenment project in the realm of biblical scholarship."[9]

But even among confessing conservatives we hear how Matthew has embellished his source and written a gospel that mixes history with midrashic theological embellishment. Thus whether Jesus actually said it or did it fades into irrelevant insignificance. But have we not lost control of the text just about as much when a respected conservative preacher asserts that Genesis 45:25-28 (relating how Jacob's heart revived when he saw the wagons that his long-lost Joseph sent full of supplies from Egypt) is the most "suitable portion of the Old Testament upon which to preach a resurrection message"? Really, is it the purpose of the Genesis text to teach us about the resurrection of Christ? This is unacceptable liberty with the text.

Grant Osborne observes that parables and apocalyptic passages are "the most written about yet hermeneutically abused portions of Scripture."[10] For many centuries the allegorization of the parables was widespread. This was done to follow the Greeks (who allegorized Homer mercilessly). Philo, the Jew of Alexandria, attempted to reconcile the Old Testament with Greek philosophy through allegorization. To Origen, Abel and Noah were the first workers in the parable of the workers in the vineyard (Matt. 20:1-16); those at the third hour were the patriarchs; the ninth-hour laborers were the prophets; and the eleventh-hour men were the

Christians. Similarly, in the parable of the lost son (Luke 15), Irenaeus argued, the fatted calf was the crucified Savior. We have already seen that indeed there are allegories in the New Testament (cf. Paul in Gal. 4). But clearly we cannot make the stories of Jesus walk on all fours like this. These are "encounter mechanisms" and "speech events" that cannot properly be handled with a hermeneutic that leaves us so totally at the whim of subjectivity. Augustine's elaborate allegorization of the parable of the good Samaritan (which gave vent to a most enjoyable ingenuity, as A. T. Hunter has pointed out) allowed the powerful truth of the parable to slip away in the complex welter of far-fetched interpretation. For Augustine, the man who fell among thieves is Adam, Jerusalem is the heavenly city, and Jericho is the moon, which signifies our mortality; the priest and Levite are Old Testament religion, which cannot help; the good Samaritan is Jesus; the innkeeper is the Apostle Paul, and the inn is the Church; the extra coins are seen as counsel for celibacy.

Certainly there were voices historically that protested this excess, and among them was most notably Chrysostom, who insisted that we should "always consider the parable as an organic whole, meant to make one point." Luther, it has been asserted, combined "the clear insights of Chrysostom with the errors of Origen." Calvin rejected the "idle fooleries" of the allegorizing Fathers. Archbishop Trench's book (1841) is still in wide use, but he seemed to learn little from Calvin. It was Adolf Julicher at the end of the last century who struck the big blow for the idea of a single main point in the parables. This single point is moral and ethical, and that's it.

While building on Julicher, C. H. Dodd and Joachim Jeremias insisted that the parables be seen in their first-century setting of Jesus' ministry as the eschatological break-through of the powers of the age to come.[11] So every aspect of the parable and all of its details (and some may even be allegorical, as in Matthew 21:33-45) must be considered and weighed and seen as part of the meaningful whole. In the parable of the wicked husbandman, surely we see aspects of Messiah's coming and the contemporary rejection, along with the succession of the Gentiles. But Grotius goes too far when he sees the gathering of the stones as the expulsion of the Canaanites, and Bengel is off when he insists the tower is the temple in Isaiah 5:1-7.

Milton Terry lays out the basic interpretive procedure as well as anyone:

1) determine the occasion and the aim of the parable
2) analyze the subject matter and the imagery
3) develop the several parts and make the central truth prominent.[12]

This is to say that we want to grapple with the setting, the story itself, and then its significance. We shall illustrate the issues quite specifically in the next section.

The parable is both argument and narrative. The parable calls for response. We are projecting something different than in a lecture or a research paper. The parable is an imaginative appeal that is intended to strike sparks and inflame the human imagination. How can this be done more imaginatively by today's preachers? Jesus was an absolute master at it. How can we do better and more effective work? This is the question to which we now turn.

OUR STRATEGY WITH THE PARABLES

A parable is art harnessed for service and conflict.
(C. J. Cadoux)

If you only followed the parables you yourself would become parables and with that rid of all your daily cares.
(Franz Kafka)

We did not follow cleverly invented stories when we told you about the power and coming of our Lord Jesus Christ, but we were eyewitnesses of his majesty. (2 Peter 1:16)

"You [God] have hidden these things from the wise and learned, and revealed them to little children . . . learn from me, for I am gentle and humble in heart, and you will find rest for your souls." (Matt. 11:25b, 29b)

The parables of Jesus are "God's picturebook," to use the translation of the original German title of Helmut Thielicke's classic book of sermons on the parables. If, as Linnemann projects, our Lord had an active ministry of about 1,000 days over the three years described in the Gospels, and if He averaged two hours a day preaching, two hours a day instructing the disciples, and half an hour performing signs and wonders, this would mean that He preached over 2,000 hours, instructed the disciples 2,000 hours, and spent 500 hours doing signs and wonders.

The parables do not stand by themselves. They are replete with doctrinal implication, but they are chiefly illustrative of principles Jesus states. They are part of the whole fabric of His teaching. While the propitiatory, substitutionary atonement of our Lord is implied in the prayer of the publican (Luke 18:13), we do not really find teaching on the transactional nature of the atonement in the parables. Liberals tended to see the whole plan of salvation in microscopic focus in the parable of the prodigal son, but this is to expect too much of the stories Jesus told. We need to consider the pervasive themes of the teaching of Jesus, such as G. Campbell Morgan classically delineated as being about the Father, Himself as the Son, the Holy Spirit, the kingdom of God, humankind and sin, redemption and the way of salvation, human responsibility and sanctity.[13] We must never wrench the parables loose from their larger context in the Gospels.

The preacher's strategy with the parables must be to seek the theme in the parable and preach that. Even a coach of professional basketball speaks of seeking a theme for the new season—i.e., the unifying and cohesive focus out of which emerges the plan of action. Parabolic communication is more right-brained and for the heart, and it will occasionally exasperate the more analytic-type individuals. The parable is art.

Henri J. M. Nouwen, an immensely creative and prolific writer in our time, movingly describes how he was enthralled with a poster copy of Rembrandt's "The Return of the Prodigal Son," to the point that he embarked upon a spiritual journey.[14] He was so much in the grip of this representation that he made a trip to St. Petersburg in Russia where the original hangs and with no small difficulty visited the painting again and again. Out of this absorbing concentration on the themes of this immortal tale came his book of meditations on fathers, brothers, and sons, which is well worth reading. This is the kind of inner ignition we need in order to make these ancient stories come alive!

The peril we must avoid is preaching out of the parables instead of preaching the parables. Spinning pleasant and even profitable discourse by matters suggested in the parable is drastically different from preaching the story Jesus told in relation to the point Jesus intended to make. Luke 15 is a good instance in point.

Clearly the three parables Jesus tells in this chapter relate to the critical attitude of the Pharisees and scribes toward our Lord and what one preacher called "The Pharisees' Life of Christ"— namely, "This man welcomes sinners and eats with them" (Luke 15:2). Each of the parables reflects the joy of finding what was lost, the joy to which the religious leaders were strangers. The stories relate to the heart of God and what it means for the lost to come home again.

To be sure, in the parable of the lost sheep we are additionally impressed with the wandering of the sinner as we consider the lost sheep (15:3-7). The poor, silly, stupid little sheep pictures all of us as sinners, so prone to get lost, to bump into walls, to land on our backs and be unable to get up. This is familiar imagery from all of Scripture. The woman and the lost coin shows us the worth of the sinner (15:8-10) because this was undoubtedly her dowry, and she was tragically and painfully bereft of something very precious.

Actually in the third parable we come to the climax with a picture of the welcome for the sinner in the Father's warm outreach of love and restoration. We have in fact two lost sons here, one son who was lost at a distance but who returned, and another son who was lost near at home (the religious establishment to be sure) and who groused and grumbled ungratefully outside the feast. George Morrison of the Wellington Church in Glasgow is one of my favorite preachers, and his sermons are well worth reading. But his thoughtful sermon on "The Two Petitions of the Prodigal" is a prime example of the danger of preaching out of a parable rather than preaching the parable. Morrison's mains are brilliant:

I.   "Father, give me."
II.   "Father, make me."

The sermon powerfully developed two contrasting attitudes. The change in attitude is unquestionably found in the text, but the sermon bypasses the thrust of what Jesus is clearly driving at.

Far preferable, and my nomination for the best preaching on this parable, would be Helmut Thielicke's sermons in his book

The Waiting Father. He says explicitly, "The ultimate theme of this story, therefore, is not the prodigal son, but the Father who finds us. The ultimate theme is not the faithlessness of men, but the faithfulness of God."[15]

This proposed strategy does not imply we are to feel hamstrung in bridging from the text of the story to our contemporary situation. The parable of the rich fool (Luke 12:16-21) addresses our Lord's concern for "all kinds of greed" (v. 15) and is painfully relevant. When leading corporate figures in our day seriously argue that "greed is good," we need to press our analysis of the attitude of the man God called a fool. Surely we see narcissism and selfism in the first-personal pronouns, which moves the farmer to a gross materialism in his dedication to build bigger barns. The abandon to hedonism ("Take life easy; eat, drink and be merry," v. 19) inevitably follows. The application is so relevant as to be almost unbearably painful. In an age when instant enjoyment seems to be our goal and when deferral of gratification is unacceptable, we would be culpably guilty of dereliction of duty were we to pull our punches. We feel the pull sometimes between the prophetic and the pastoral, but we must not become "pillow prophets" in such a day as ours.

In his superb work on the parables, A. M. Hunter expresses pleasure in Soren Kierkegaard's sermon on Luke 18:9-14, in which he focuses on the true penitence of the tax collector as including: (1) being alone with God; (2) looking downwards; and (3) being aware of his danger.[16] This captures part of the parable, to be sure; but since the purpose of the parable is indicated by Dr. Luke in introducing it ("To some who were confident of their own righteousness and looked down on everybody else, Jesus told this parable," v. 9), I would feel better with more of a dialectical sense contrasting the two persons who went up to pray. This can be done in two sharply contrasting mains or in a series of contrasts running through the mains. Our theme must be the theme of Jesus in any event.

OUR AFFLUENCY IN THE PARABLES

When the Sabbath came, he began to teach in the synagogue, and many who heard him were amazed. (Mark 6:2)

When Jesus had finished saying these things, the crowds were amazed at his teaching, because he taught as one who had

154

authority, and not as their teachers of the law.
(Matt. 7:28-29)

So Jesus said, "When you have lifted up the Son of Man, then you will know who I am and that I do nothing on my own but speak just what the Father has taught me." (John 8:28)

It is sometimes given to us, this lovely emptiness, and then the Holy Spirit can fill it. (Madeleine L'Engle)

The Bible has been a greater influence on the course of English literature than all other forces put together. (William Lyon Phelps)

The immense and burgeoning literature on the parables causes us to be awash in a veritable embarrassment of riches. And here we have what we must recognize is a medium "far more powerful than abstract essays and sermons, expressing symbolically that which escapes the narrow bounds of literal, direct discourse."[17]

We have already seen enough of the danger in this particular genre, however, to alert us lest we become hermeneutical libertines and take too much liberty with the text. For example, J. Cheryl Exum in her *Fragmented Women: Feminine Subversions of Biblical Narrative*, fretting over what she feels is the androcentric nature of biblical narrative, proceeds to reconstruct and recast the ancient text entirely with feminine versions. We may face the same peril in coming to the Scriptures for our own purposes.

On the other hand, learning what a parable teaches can be "more like a shock to the nervous system than it is like a piece of information to be stored in the head," as McFague puts it.[18] We are invited into the experience, as in the parable of the wedding feast (Matt. 22:1-10; Luke 14:15-24). In the parable of the sower and the seeds (Matt. 13:1-9; Mark 4:1-9; Luke 8:4-8) we certainly have a vivid description of the severity of the setbacks that the sower experienced and yet the assurance of an abundant final harvest, all of which is calculated to press us to take the necessary risks in the work of God. The Word is powerful notwithstanding all (Matt. 13:8).

While not concurring in every interpretation, we still look to

George Buttrick's *The Parables of Jesus* as a classic and creative guide to interpretation. His analysis of the parable of the children at play (Luke 7:31-35; Matt. 11:16-19) and the parable of the wise and foolish builders (Matt. 7:24-27; Luke 6:46-49) under the rubric, "Earnestness to Translate Hearing into Doing" is timeless. His discussion of "The Rejected Overtures of God" (Matt. 21:33-45; Mark 12:1-11; Luke 20:9-18) is refreshing and new.[19] With all of our reservations on Professor William Barclay's attitude toward aspects of the miraculous in the Gospels, he is always helpful in applying and illustrating the parables, and his little handbook on the parables is invaluable.[20] He encourages simplicity along with textual integrity.

Among more recent resources is the compendious commentary on the parables by Bernard Brandon Scott, entitled *Hear Then the Parable*. This treatment stands in the mainstream of contemporary literary criticism and must be used with care at points; but it is nonetheless a veritable "encyclopedia" of background and interpretive material. He divides the parables into three sections: (1) Family, Village, City and Beyond; (2) Masters and Servants; and (3) Home and Farm. At once we sense the emphasis on the re-creation of "the originating structure" and then its reapplication in our time. His titles are arresting (which in itself opens up an important area of challenge for the preacher), such as his entitling the sermon on the parable of the leaven "One Rotten Apple," or giving the parables on the fig tree (the full parable of Luke 13:6-9 as well as the minimal narrative of Mark 13:28, Matt. 24:32, Luke 21:29-30) the title "A Garden of Delights." This study will be a basic referent for many years to come.[21]

Earlier classical work by A. B. Bruce, Marcus Dods, Ada Habershon, Benjamin Keach (the second pastor of the Metropolitan Tabernacle in London), and William Taylor should not be overlooked. G. Campbell Morgan is always worthwhile, although often brief. More recent work by Kenneth E. Bailey and Robert Stein is proving suggestive. Halford E. Luccock is bold and imaginative on the parables, as on everything else. Simon Kistemaker is meticulous on the text and right to the point on essential backgrounds (as, for instance, in his choice sermon on the ten virgins, Matt. 25:1-13, where information on ancient Middle-Eastern marriage customs is necessary in order to appreciate aspects of textual interpretation). In more specialized areas one should not overlook a volume like Arthur Pink's *The Prophetic Parables of Matthew Thirteen*. But this plethora of resources should not conspire to deprive the preacher of the opportunity to sit down, read and re-read the text, listen to the text, and let its powerful truth grip his own soul.

Some older sermons may be worthwhile—for example, Brownlow North's classic series of messages on the rich man and Lazarus (Luke 16:19-31), which he inclines (as do I) to take as history rather than parable, but of which he says, "Be it history or parable, however, the lessons taught us are the same."[22] Some superb more recent preaching on the parables would be Frederick Houk Borsch's *Many Things in Parables: Extravagant Stories of New Community*.[23] Especially tantalizing are three volumes by Robert Farrar Capon, the Episcopalian, on *The Parables of Grace*, *The Parables of Judgment*, and *The Parables of the Kingdom*.[24] His work is provocative. A little lighter, but rewarding in contemporary application, would be Lloyd Ogilvie's *Autobiography of God*, and also volumes by David Hubbard, Dan Seagren, and David Redding.[25] An intensely creative and very different approach by Rogahn and Schoedel matches Christ's words from the cross with a parable (and with more of a Lutheran flavor).[26]

And where do we come out sermonically, having gone through the hermeneutical and homiletical hoops we have described? In an extended series of messages on "Sacred Secrets," the mysteries of the New Testament, I attempted to preach with some thoroughness "the mysteries of the kingdom" out of Matthew 13. I took one sermon on each of the four kinds of soil of which our Lord spoke. Some of my titles in the series indicate my direction and strategization:

Seed by the wayside and the birds:
"When the Devil Goes to Church."

Seed on the stony ground:
"On the Religious Roller Coaster."

Seed among the weeds:
"A Saga of Spiritual Strangulation."

Seed on good ground:
"The Fruit-bearing Friends of Jesus."

On the wheat and tares:
"Spiritual Subversion."

On the leaven:
"The Ecology of Evil." (I take leaven as the picture of
the permeation of evil, having also seen yeast under a
microscope.)

In preaching a series a while back on "The Probing Parables
of Jesus," I began with a study of the two men in the story of Jesus
in Matthew 7:24-29, using the theme "The Only Firm Foundation
in a Wobbly World." The basic progression in the passage was as
follows:

I.   Similarity: both men built fine houses, perhaps used the
     same architect.
II. Severity: the difference was not apparent until the storms
     came.
III. Stability: the wise man dug deep and laid the foundation
     on rock.

I tingle all over in the thrill of the relevance of these stories of
Jesus for life and experience in our time. In these forty pieces we
range over the themes of human ecstasy and human tragedy—and
always within the context of the superabounding grace of God.
Let's go to it! "Preach the Word!"

CHAPTER NINE

The Sensitive Nuances of the Miracle-Stories

When Jesus had finished these parables, he moved on from there. Coming to his home town, he began teaching the people in their synagogue, and they were amazed. "Where did this man get this wisdom and these miraculous powers?"

MATT. 13:53-54

Jesus' life was a blaze of miracle.

KARL ADAM

The possibility of miracle, then, is indissolubly joined with "theism."

J. GRESHAM MACHEN

A Christ who being Son of God, and seeking to become Saviour of men, [and] wrought no miracle, would be less intelligible and credible than the Jesus whom the Gospel records so consistently present to us.

A. E. GARVIE

Mystery is a great embarrassment to the modern mind.

FLANNERY O'CONNOR

Another special kind of narrative material is to be seen in the many miracle-stories of the Old and New Testaments. The miracle-stories were to be told and retold to succeeding generations (Ex. 10:1-2) as primary attestation to the greatness and glory of God. C. S. Lewis defined miracle as "an interference with nature by supernatural power." Yet, this is to see miracle from the standpoint of our finite knowledge of the universe. Perhaps there are higher laws unknown to us and unobservable by our scientific method according to which miracles are performed. Modern science has become less dogmatic about its dicta concerning the universe overall, as Max Planck's quantum physics, Lloyd Morgan's emergent evolution, and Heisenberg's principle of indeterminacy clearly demonstrate. So perhaps we shall incline toward Everett F. Harrison's definition: "A miracle is an event in the external world wrought by the immediate power of God to accredit a message or a messenger."

We moderns seem to be acutely embarrassed by the category of *miracle*. Renan only reflected the arrogant anthropocentrism of the Enlightenment when he insisted that "miracles don't happen." But this is to assume we are omniscient, because how can we assert anything about what takes place on the other side of the moon or in one of the black holes of outer space or even somewhere else on earth? Fascinatingly, the aridity and sterility of the rationalistic closed-universe approach have left many oppressed in the secularistic box, and we must now speak of the post-secular world. As many as 60 million Americans have some tie with the New Age Movement at some point. This is to say that many people are searching for what is beyond the scientific method in supernatural categories, whether this is in astrology, channeling, crystals, tarot cards, or whatever. We must not suppose that our sharing of the God of the impossible is in quite the same venue as was the case even twenty-five years ago.

On the other hand, there are those who want to make the miraculous normative for the Christian life in somewhat the same spirit as Jesus rebuked when He spoke of those in a "wicked and adulterous generation" who were always looking for a miraculous sign. The sign was to be indeed the consummate sign of Jonah, the bodily resurrection of Jesus Christ (Matt. 16:4). Indeed, miracle-working is never the chief criterion of verification, but rather obedience to the truth of God (cf. Deut. 13:1ff.; 2 Thess. 2:9ff.; Rev. 13).

If we lay aside temporarily (for treatment at a later point) the mighty manifestations of the power of God in the creation narratives and in the apocalyptic and prophetic portions of Scripture, we notice that there are concentrations of miracles in several grand epochs of sacred history. God's sovereign hand interposes at His will at any time (as in Abraham and Sarah's life, or in

David's experience, or in the times of Daniel). But ordinarily the extraordinary catena of miracle, as at the time of the exodus from Egypt, is quite singular in the Old Testament. What we see in the ministry of Christ and the apostles (up into the book of Acts) is also quite a unique outpouring. This is no argument for cessationism (such as Sir Robert Anderson advocates in *The Silence of God* or B. B. Warfield espouses in *Counterfeit Miracles*, which seems to limit God's sovereign freedom without scriptural support). The ship in which the Apostle Paul took his voyage was spared total disaster, and the apostle did survive the viper on Malta and heal the father of Publius (cf. Acts 28:1-9). But these were, it would appear, not commonplace or normative (cf. John 10:40-42).

Our focus here will be on the miracles performed by our Lord Jesus Christ and how we understand and preach them, saving some of the very powerful and in some cases vexed miracle-stories of the Old Testament for a subsequent chapter. At this point we are arguing that Karl Barth was right in insisting that "There is an indissoluble connection of proclamation, miracle and faith." The miracle-stories are an integral part of the New Testament presentation of who Jesus Christ is and what His ministry on earth was.

The insipid Jesus of the stained-glass windows, the "gentle Jesus, meek and mild" of liberalism, is but a reflection, as George Tyrell protested, of the modern theologian, but not of the Christ of the Bible. Albert Schweitzer, while grievously in error on the deity of Christ, did see that apocalyptic could not be sliced out of the gospel representation of Jesus. We cannot just siphon off what we find objectionable and think we have done justice to the documents. Similarly, J. Gresham Machen brilliantly showed how Jesus without the miracles is not the Jesus of the New Testament.[1] We cannot desupernaturalize Jesus or sanitize the Gospels of miracles and suppose for a moment that we still have Christianity. Machen went on in an epochal feat of scholarship to establish that the narratives that give us the Virgin Birth are inseparably a part of the biblical records.[2] This was done with such skill and finesse that none less than Walter Lippmann, the highly regarded social commentator, paid him high tribute.[3]

The empiricism of David Hume, which sought and for many achieved the demolition of the miraculous, failed to take into account the once-for-allness of the bodily resurrection of Jesus Christ. When I came to believe that God raised Jesus from the dead on the third day, the problem of the miracles was resolved. As Trench well put it:

> The miracle is not a greater manifestation of God's power than those ordinary and ever-repeated processes, but it is a different manifestation. By those others God is speaking at all times and to all the world; they are a vast unbroken revelation of Him (Romans 1:20). Yet from the very circumstance that nature is thus speaking evermore to all, that this speaking is diffused over all time, addressed to all men, that its sound has gone out into all lands, from the very constancy and universality of this language, it may fail to make itself heard . . . but in the miracle wrought in the sight of some certain men and claiming their special attention, there is a speaking to them in particular . . . it is plain that God has now a peculiar word message to which He is bidding them to listen.[4]

We now turn to the miracles.

THE EXEGETICAL ISSUES

> Jesus did many other miraculous signs in the presence of his disciples, which are not recorded in this book. But these are written that you may believe that Jesus is the Christ, the Son of God, and that by believing you may have life in his name. (John 20:30-31)

> Healing and so on are not unimportant. They are like signs on a highway that warn us: "Look out for a coming curve!" We should see the danger without a special sign, but sometimes we are inattentive. In the same way, God sometimes has to use unusual (miraculous) means to approach us because we are too foolish to listen to Him, to trust in Him and His word without them. (Eduard Schweizer)

> God anointed Jesus of Nazareth with the Holy Spirit and power . . . he went around doing good and healing all who were under the power of the devil, because God was with him. (Acts 10:38)

As C. S. Lewis well said, Christianity is "the story of a great miracle." As we have seen, the miracle-stories of the Gospels are not incidental or unimportant parts of the New Testament narrative. In Mark's portrait of Jesus as the Divine Servant we have nineteen miracles. In Mark 1–10, 200 of the 425 verses deal with the miracles of Jesus (47 percent), and in the whole of Mark's gospel 209 verses deal with the miracles (or 31 percent). This concentrated cluster of miracles during the ministry of the Lord Jesus could be classified as follows:

I. NATURE MIRACLES—OVER NATURE.
    A. The water turned to wine, John 2:1-11.
    B. The first miraculous catch of fish, Luke 5:1-7.
    C. The stilling of the storm, Matthew 8:23-27; Mark 4:36-41; Luke 8:22-25.
    D. Walking on the water, Matthew 14:22-32; Mark 6:45-51; John 6:16-21.
    E. Finding the tribute money in the fish's mouth, Matthew 17:24-27.
    F. The cursing of the fig tree, Matthew 21:18-22; Mark 11:12-14, 20-24.
    G. The second miraculous catch of fish, John 21:1-11.

II. MIRACLES OF BODILY HEALINGS—
    OVER THE DERANGEMENT OF NATURE.
    A. The nobleman's son at Capernaum, John 4:46-54.
    B. Peter's mother-in-law, Matthew 8:14-18; Mark 1:29-34; Luke 4:38-41.
    C. The first cleansing of a leper, Matthew 8:1-4; Mark 1:40-42; Luke 5:12-14.
    D. The paralytic man, Matthew 9:1-8; Mark 2:3-12; Luke 5:18-26.
    E. The impotent man by the pool, John 5:1-15.
    F. The man with the withered hand, Matthew 12:9-14; Mark 3:1-6; Luke 6:6-11.
    G. The palsied servant of the centurion, Matthew 8:5-13; Luke 7:1-10.
    H. The woman with the issue of blood, Matthew 9:20-22; Mark 5:25-34; Luke 8:43-48.
    I. Two blind men, Matthew 9:27-31.
    J. The deaf and dumb man, Matthew 15:29-31; Mark 7:31-37.

K. The blind man at Bethsaida, Mark 8:22-26.

L. The ten lepers, Luke 17:11-19.

M.The man born blind, John 9.

N.The woman with a spirit of infirmity, Luke 13:10-17.

O.The man afflicted with dropsy, Luke 14:1-6.

P. Two blind men near Jericho, Matthew 20:29-34; Mark 10:46-52.

Q.The restoration of the severed ear of Malchus, Luke 22:50-51.

III. THE HEALING OF THOSE POSSESSED WITH DEMONS—OVER THE SUPERNATURAL.

General references: Matthew 4:24; 8:16; Mark 1:32, 34, 39.

A. The man in the synagogue at Capernaum, Mark 1:23-28; Luke 4:33-37.

B. The man both blind and dumb, Matthew 12:22-30 (cf. Mark 3:22-30); Luke 11:14-23.

C. Two possessed with demons at Gadara, Matthew 8:28-34; Mark 5:1-20; Luke 8:26-39.

D.A dumb man, Matthew 9:32-34.

E. The daughter of the Syrophoenician woman, Matthew 15:21-28; Mark 7:24-30.

F. The boy after the Transfiguration, Matthew 17:14-21; Mark 9:14-29; Luke 9:37-43.

IV. THE TWO MIRACLES INVOLVING THE MULTIPLICATION OF FOOD.

A. Feeding of 5,000, Matthew 14:15-21; Mark 6:30-44; Luke 9:10-17; John 6:1-14.

B. Feeding of 4,000, Matthew 15:32-39; Mark 8:1-9.

V. THE THREE RAISINGS FROM THE DEAD.

A. The son of the widow at Nain, Luke 7:11-17.

B. The daughter of Jairus, Matthew 9:18-19, 23-26; Mark 5:21-24, 35-43; Luke 8:40-42, 49-56.

C. Lazarus, John 11.[5]

The chief exegetical problem for the preacher is, of course, the Synoptic problem. On the one hand we must avoid the extreme position of Osiander who posited four different feedings of the 5,000 because of slight textual variants, and on the other hand those who conclude that there was only one feeding of the multitude and that there are hopeless contradictions, such as the

5,000/4,000 difference and different words employed for the containers used for the leftovers.

Clearly the Apostle John, writing under the guidance of the Holy Spirit, was selective in choosing the seven miracles in his portrait of Jesus. Skeptics will ask why John alone relates the raising up of Lazarus (John 11), which is clearly the pivotal event leading toward the arrest and death of Jesus. The apologist is obligated to supply one plausible explanation for an apparent difficulty, and we must say that were the Synoptic writers to put this in writing, the life of Lazarus possibly and others would have been endangered. John, writing at the end of the century, however, could tell the whole story because none of the principals would still be alive by that time. This could not be proved one way or another, but it is a plausible explanation.

The texts are quite straightforward and beg for clear and compelling exposition, but there are special challenges.

THE APOLOGETICAL ISSUES

> I wonder if there really are miracles. (Michael in Maeve Binchy's novel, *Firefly Summer*)

> "Believe me when I say that I am in the Father and the Father is in me; or at least believe on the evidence of the miracles themselves." (John 14:11)

> "He said to him, 'If they do not listen to Moses and the prophets, they will not be convinced even if someone rises from the dead.'" (Luke 16:31)

> Immediately the boy's father exclaimed, "I do believe; help me overcome my unbelief." (Mark 9:24)

Our Lord Jesus faced massive unbelief and granite indifference, even in the face of the highly focused witness and testimony He presented through the miracles He performed during His ministry. He even sent the lepers whom He cleansed directly to the religious establishment in Jerusalem, according to the instructions of Moses (cf. Lev. 13 with Matt. 8:1-4).

Hence we cannot really be surprised or shocked at the pervasive skepticism and cynicism in modern culture in the wake of the

Enlightenment. Many persons, educated and uneducated, would essentially subscribe to Professor Randel Helms's argument that the gospel accounts are "imaginative literature"—what he calls "the supreme fictions of our culture, works of art deliberately composed as the culmination of a long literary and oral tradition."[6] He traces the story of the resurrection of Lazarus to the Egyptian myth of the resurrection of Isiris by the god Horus. He denies that the gospel accounts are about "the historical Jesus" but gives little evidence of serious biblical scholarship. Yet he articulates the view of many that the miracle-stories of the Gospels are of a piece with the wonder-tales of antiquity and are to be understood as the inevitable concomitant of a highly superstitious pre-scientific age.

Such entrenched unbelief was only to be expected, but what stuns us and startles us is the degree to which these anti-supernaturalistic biases have seeped into ostensibly Christian circles, both academic and ecclesiastical; they have become a veritable torrent. Many scholars and preachers seem embarrassed by the supernatural generally, and the miracles most specifically. Anton Fridrichsen of Uppsala tried to argue that there was a sense of awkwardness even in New Testament times with reference to magic and an overly thaumaturgical emphasis.[7] This adamant resistance to the miraculous is seen in the influential work by Gerd Theissen entitled *The Miracle Stories of the Early Christian Tradition.*[8] Reflections of this common approach are to be seen in *The Interpreter's Bible,* and flowing over even into the popular commentaries by Professor William Barclay of Glasgow, whose prejudice against the miracles is seen in his reluctance with regard to the virgin birth of Jesus and his espousal of the "little brown paper bag theory" in relation to the feeding of the crowd.

The view of many is voiced by Reginald Fuller, who held that "Modern man is prepared to accept the healings of Jesus as due to His power of suggestion: the nature miracles . . . he can only dismiss as pious legend."[9] The preacher of the miracle-stories is smack up against what often seems to be intransigent resistance. Fuller's Bultmannian rejection of the miracles turns into a tirade against the "intellectual dishonesty" of anyone who believes in the miracles. If one mistakenly supposes this plague of unbelief is quarantined to the miracles, he quickly learns that it stems from or entails a seriously defective Christology. If the miracles are ontologically impossible, then so is the supernatural Christ impossible. All has been lost.

A far more reasoned position has been argued by Alan Richardson in his older but still well worthwhile *The Miracle-Stories of the Gospels*. Moving from a premise that "The miracle-stories form an essential and inseparable part of the Gospel tradition," Richardson shows that the only viable alternative to the view of the Evangelists "is a complete scepticism concerning the possibility of our knowledge of Jesus at all."[10] He stands here with C. H. Dodd who recognized that "the miracles taken together carry the suggestion of a life once lived which inaugurated a supernatural experience for men." The miracles of Jesus are the signs of the age to come that has broken into this present evil age.

The more recent work of Colin Brown has most helpfully addressed the apologetical issues that contemporary preachers must face. Out of a careful study of the words for miracle in Scripture, Brown shows that the miracles accredit Jesus because they are the works of God (cf. John 5:36; Acts 2:22; etc.).[11] We must see the miracles as a personal witness, a pedagogical witness (teaching about repentance, forgiveness, and responsibility for sin; cf. John 15:24), and a prophetic witness. Jesus showed His power by healing the paralytic in order that folks might realize He had power to forgive sin (Luke 5:24). C. S. Lewis is suggestive of this pastorally in his *Miracles*, just as he is in *The Problem of Pain*.

At this point it is well to bear in mind the character and nature of the miracles of Jesus, as set apart from other miraculous claims:

1. The miracles of Jesus are eminently reasonable (cf. the miracles related in the books of the Apocrypha and the Pseudepigrapha).
2. The miracles of Jesus are useful.
3. Jesus refused to just show His power (for example, with King Herod).
4. The miracles of Jesus were spread over many spheres.
5. The miracles of Jesus were openly performed.
6. The actual miracles were never denied by the contemporaries of Jesus.
7. The miracles of Jesus were enacted instantaneously (except for the healing of the blind man, Mark 8:22-26).
8. The results were complete and permanent.

9. The miracles seem to be fewer and fewer toward the end of His ministry.
10. The miracle narratives are records characterized by restraint and total naturalness.
11. The miracles of Jesus are not duplicated by modern science.[12]

Really at issue here is biblical supernaturalism itself. Voltaire said he would rather disbelieve his own eyes than 1,000 others'. The issue: *supernaturalism*.

THE PASTORAL ISSUES

His very miracles have convinced us of His deity. (Gregory of Nyssa, in the fourth century)

"I have testimony weightier than that of John. For the very work that the Father has given me to finish, and which I am doing, testifies that the Father has sent me." (John 5:36)

Always be prepared to give an answer to everyone who asks you to give the reason for the hope that you have. But do this with gentleness and respect. (1 Peter 3:15b)

The apostles said to the Lord, "Increase our faith." (Luke 17:5)

We have seen how dog-like devotion to scientism is responsible for a thinly disguised skepticism with regard to aspects of the miraculous as set forth in the Gospels.[13] We face this suspicion on the part of some as soon as we turn to a gospel pericope centering on a miracle of our Lord. But we face another pastoral problem with others who feel that the miracle-stories are normative for the Christian Church, and were we properly spiritual we would be reproducing the miracles week by week in our local congregations or ministries.

We have already pointed out that the scriptural record itself features epochs of concentrated outbursts of the miraculous. In his *Power Evangelism*, John Wimber argues for the normative continuation of "signs and wonders" as corroboration for evangelism throughout this age.[14] God may be pleased in this or that situation to give some accrediting miracle in His sovereign overlordship (as where Gospel rains are falling for the first time, for instance); but we have no basis in Scripture or history to make this normative. I concur with Colin Brown's assessment: "The church has no specific ongoing mandate from Jesus to heal that is recorded in authentic Scripture."[15]

Warfield and the cessationists go beyond what exegesis demonstrates in their contention that there have been no bona fide miracles of healing since the first century. This limits God. But Warfield's classic work does warn us of the existence of the fraudulent in the area of healing.[16] God warned Israel through Moses of the stringent tests needed to discern whether or not a worker of miracles was from God or not. There is evil supernaturalism. The magicians of Egypt were able to duplicate the miraculous plagues up to a point. Satan is able to enthrall through "counterfeit miracles, signs and wonders" (2 Thess. 2:9). The book of Revelation describes the deception achieved by the Beast out of the Earth and his cohort, the False Prophet, through "great and miraculous signs" (Rev. 13:13ff.).

So we must seek to discern the spirits (cf. 1 John 4:1ff.) and not be swept along by the claims of every healer who comes along. There is something in all of us that panders after the spectacular and unusual. Much on Christian radio and television essentially fosters a kind of prosperity, health-and-wealth gospel that holds out prospects far beyond what Scripture describes. This is why Warfield's approach, though extreme in its outcome, is salutary. There have been tricks and chicanery aplenty. Every pastor knows how difficult it is to help those who suddenly became convinced that God will heal them, and when He does not, there is often much wreckage of faith strewn over the landscape. Great caution needs to be exercised in relation to demons and exorcism as well. When we preach on passages dealing with these things, we must give clear exposition along with warnings and exhortations.[17] We must be wary of a pan-satanism that sees every problem and pathology as demonic. There is such a thing as mental illness, as well as demonic possession and oppression. Wisdom calls us to face the issues of our times head-on with scriptural and sane discourse.

Another serious pastoral problem arises in preaching the miracle-stories of Jesus. I remember preaching about the healing of the nobleman's son out of John 4:43-54 some time ago. I developed what I described as (1) the quest of faith; (2) the test of faith;

and (3) the rest of faith, the father's remarkable trust in the Lord's word to him. After the service a brokenhearted mother came up to thank me for the sermon but also to ask, "Why didn't the Lord heal my little boy?" I had not succeeded in showing that Jesus does not always heal and that in point of fact even in the most rabid circles in which healing is emphasized, the mortality rate is still quite close to 100 percent.

Although all blessings—past, present, and future—are mediated through the merits of Christ's shed blood, I do not see on the basis of Scripture that it can be argued that Christ's death has procured full physical health for all believers now. This is a hurtful teaching. Isaiah 53:4 is clearly fulfilled principally in the empathetic ministry of Jesus (cf. Matt. 8:16-17); "by his wounds you have been healed" has primary reference to the forgiveness of sin (1 Peter 2:24).

Although unbelief can block and obstruct the mighty works of Jesus (Matt. 13:58; Mark 6:5-6), it would be criminal to imply that if only we have enough faith God will heal entirely and totally. The fact is that our sovereign God said "no" to Paul's prayer (2 Cor. 12:8-9). Also, Paul prescribed something medicinal for Timothy (1 Tim. 5:23), and he left Trophimus sick at Miletus (2 Tim. 4:20b). In some gigantic healing rallies I have attended, and in some television programs I have watched, there was no expression of submission to the will of God. There must be place for "the prayer of relinquishment." Many have been burned out and devastated in atmospheres where people ordered God to embark on this course or that. It is not a cop-out to pray, "Your will be done." Even our divine Savior and Lord uttered that prayer (Matt. 26:39ff.).

God may be pleased to use the skills of a gifted physician. God may be pleased to grant a special touch (I have seen it and experienced it). But full healing and final healing will not come until we get to heaven and are like Christ. That even healers wear glasses and hearing aids and have tooth decay is no negative reflection on them unless they claim full physical health for all believers now. These are often painful and perplexing issues for the pastor to deal with. The raising of Lazarus is probably not the best text for a young man's funeral, but the principle enunciated by Jesus in John 11:25-26 is very preachable.

THE STRUCTURAL ISSUES

"Is anything too hard for the Lord?" (Gen. 18:14)

"For nothing is impossible with God." (Luke 1:37)

Therefore, if anyone is in Christ, he is a new creation; the old has gone, the new has come! (2 Cor. 5:17)

He who was seated on the throne said, "I am making everything new!" Then he said, "Write this down, for these words are trustworthy and true." (Rev. 21:5)

In the actual birthing and building of expository sermons on the miracles of our Lord, we face some special structural challenges. Since the sermon on the miracle-stories fits so neatly into the problem-solution type outline, we must beware of a kind of predictable sameness. Perhaps we are examining the challenge of Jesus to demons, disease, and death in Mark 5 and seek to do so in three sermons. D. L. Moody called this chapter "the high water mark of the gospels." Or let us say we are preaching on the seven select miracles in John's Gospel, each establishing in a different sphere the accrediting power and glory of the Son of God. Distinct and different as each instance is, we could easily fall into an oppressive rut.

Two outstanding preachers who almost always used a two-point outline were F. W. Robertson and Walter Maier of "The Lutheran Hour." Careful study of their sermons demonstrates this peculiar vulnerability of the two-point preacher. Our working premise in preaching must always be "variety within the bounds of propriety." We shall have some positive suggestions subsequently on variant patterns.

Preaching a miracle in textual isolation is dangerous. We see this in analyzing the healing of the blind man at Bethsaida (Mark 8:22-26). Certainly Jesus healed the blind man because He had compassion on him. But there is, as we have insisted, evidential and pedagogical value in the pericope of healing. Giving physical sight to the blind man is seen as suggestive concerning the need of the disciples of Jesus for spiritual sight. In Mark 8:18 Jesus asks, "Do you have eyes but fail to see?" and underscores the dimness of their spiritual perception. After the healing of the blind man, Jesus gives an eye examination to the disciples, including Peter.

Peter sees and confesses that Jesus is the Christ, but he is not clear in his perception of the necessity of the Cross (Mark 8:32-33).

In preaching this particular pericope, our narrative blocks would have to deal with the prelude to the healing (Jesus takes the blind man out of the village—those who would see must come apart from the unbelieving aggregate); with the process of the healing (in this miracle Jesus chooses to work in successive stages—the first touch leaving the man with partial clarity and vestiges of systematic distortion); and with the power of the healing (wherein Christ effected drastic change—"and he saw everything clearly"). The reiterated caution of Christ to "tell no one" or "don't go into the village" reinforces our conviction that there is a grave danger in relation to healing. We humans can fixate so quickly on healings in the external world and miss the spiritual implications.

The greatest miracle in my life has been the miracle of my conversion. The eternal salvation of an undying soul must be the grand miracle in the life of any Christian. Conversion brings wholeness and newness of life. The miracle-stories of the Gospels give us the opportunity to preach life-change through Christ, whether it be the lepers Jesus cleansed, the paralytic Jesus raised up, the blind to whom He gave sight, or whatever. Some years ago I preached a series of Sunday morning expositions on "Conversion Reconsidered," and several of the key texts opened up were miracle-stories.

A sermon on the demon-possessed man in Gadara (Mark 5:1-20) gives us an opportunity to clarify many points and insist on the ontological reality of the demonic and yet to warn against a growing pan-satanism in many circles that sees all problems as demonic. Clearly the emphasis here needs to be on the power of Christ over all the minions of evil, the basic moves in the narrative being: (1) a human being fettered; (2) a human being freed up; and (3) a human being fulfilled ("sitting there, dressed and in his right mind," v. 15). Similarly the woman with the issue of blood gives us the sequence of trapped, trembling, transformed.

We need to seize these great texts as vivid demonstrations of Christ's power to change even the most hopeless cases. Contemporary focus illustrations that share conversion stories of life-change need to be included. The sermon on the paralytic lowered by four friends into the presence of Jesus (Luke 5:17-26) should not really focus on the consecrated couch carriers but on the clearly basic issues of the forgiveness of sins (v. 20) and the authority of Jesus (v. 24). The feeding of the 5,000 should not concentrate on the little boy's lunch or the baskets left over but on Jesus (John 6:1-14). An outline I have used is:

I. Jesus feels for people.
II. Jesus feeds people.
III. Jesus fills people.

While the focus needs to be consistently on the person of the Lord Jesus, we can achieve this by using the sub-text to advantage, as in the case of the man with the withered hand (Mark 3:1-6), in whom we see a fascinating progression: from cripple to miracle to vehicle (the new possibilities in using his hand). The healing of the Syrophoenician woman's child (Mark 7:25-30) introduces the seeming indifference and unbearable silence of the Lord. The healing of the man born blind (John 9) is a long passage, and the seams of the text are hard to detect; yet we do see different kinds of blindness and sight through that passage.

Our concern needs to be to find fresh and creative approaches to these familiar passages, and yet to remain absolutely true to the intent of the passages.[18] After hearing about an Hawaiian volcano a little boy commented after touching a piece of lava, "It's still warm!" We should want our messages to be as was said of one preacher: "When he preached on Noah's ark, you could hear the rain on the roof."

CHAPTER TEN

The Powerful Scenes of Christ's Birth, Life, Passion, and Resurrection

Jesus stands before us not simply as a mighty miracle-worker or the zealous social reformer but supremely as the bearer of good tidings from God to men.

FRANK COLQUOHON

Preaching is both implicit in the Gospel and essential to the life of faith.

GERHARD EBELING

To the New Testament writers, preaching stands as the event through which God works.

HADDON ROBINSON

Paul was preaching the good news about Jesus and the resurrection.

ACTS 17:18B

For we do not preach ourselves, but Jesus Christ as Lord.

2 COR. 4:5A

The center and core of Christian proclamation are the person and work of the Lord Jesus Christ. The Holy Spirit is dedicated to the exaltation of Christ as the fulfillment of the promises of God (John 15:26; 16:13-15; 2 Cor. 1:20). Christ is to be seen throughout the Old Testament (Luke 24:27), and no Christian proclaimer could preach any Old Testament passage just as a Jewish rabbi would preach it. The fact is that Jesus Christ has come; the promise that was first articulated in Genesis 3:15 and that permeates the entire older testament has come to glorious fulfillment in Christ. We do not impose Christ on any passage, but He is the ultimate frame of reference in the Father's plan and purpose (Eph. 1:9-10; Col. 3:11).[1]

Thus we preach not only what Christ taught and what Christ did out of the Gospels, but we preach who Christ is. The identification of Christ as God in the flesh, as the eternally begotten Son of the Father, pre-existent with the Father and the Holy Spirit, miraculously conceived by the Holy Spirit, sinless in His life, dying for us vicariously in a substitutionary death, and raised again bodily on the third day—these are the recurring and spacious themes of Christian proclamation. This proclamation involves us in the constant use of pivotal New Testament narrative passages.

Foggy and hazy identification of Jesus Christ is the prelude to the distortions of the cults. One of the sure marks of a cult is error as to who Jesus Christ is. Strong Christological affirmation such as is found in Murray Harris's *Jesus as God* stands in sharp contrast to the interminable evasions of a massive treatise like Edward Schillebeeckx's *Jesus: An Experiment in Christology*.

Yet, the parish preacher turns seasonally to the great gospel pericopes to preach again from the most familiar texts of Scripture. I always found in my years of pastoring local churches that Advent/Christmas and Passion Week/Easter presented the year's greatest pulpit challenges. We have preached and preached these passages and strain for some fresh insight. We realize how desperately our people need clear teaching as to what is central and vital about the incarnation of our Lord during the weeks leading up to Christmas. We are not advised to rant and rave about the travesty of commercialization, but rather to open great texts that interpret the meaning and significance of the Christ-event in human history.

Our purpose in this chapter is to give special attention to the signal events in the life and ministry of Jesus and to suggest some approaches that may trigger creativity in our task. In preaching Palm Sunday annually and straining to find a variant in the theme, I shall argue that we make a serious blunder if we preach a sermon on the donkey who carried Jesus. In preaching on the trial of Jesus I think it is a mistake to preach on Pilate's wife. The theme of our preaching is to be the person and work of Jesus Christ, and all of these peripheral details have significance only in relation to the Lord Jesus Himself.

While the highly selective Gospels are in no sense biographies of Jesus in the traditional sense, I feel strongly that there is value in classic "lives of Christ," such as those written by F. W. Farrar and S. J. Andrews. Everett F. Harrison's magnificent *A Short Life of Christ* brings back to mind the matchless lectures Harrison gave in my seminary days. John Stott's *Life in Christ* is tastefully done, and old reliables like Edersheim's *Life and Times of Jesus the Messiah* are still worth their weight in gold for background-ing our preaching of the gospel narratives.

Our persistent premise in this study is that there is a great dif-ference between preaching out of a text and preaching the text. We may think we are biblical (and indeed clever) by mining and excavating something choice and true out of a text, but our chal-lenge is to preach what the text represents. What is the author wanting to put across? Resisting all efforts to "humanize" Christ in various movements of our time, we need to hold stoutly to both the uniqueness of Christ and the total relevance of Christ.[2] This preaching will be owned of God to the salvation of souls and the upbuilding of the church.

PREACHING THE NATIVITY OF JESUS

> *This is the Month, and this the happy morn*
> *Wherein the Son of Heav'ns eternal King,*
> *Of wedded Maid, and Virgin Mother born,*
> *Our great redemption from above did bring.*
> JOHN MILTON, ON THE MORNING OF
> CHRIST'S NATIVITY, 1629

The celebration of the birth of Christ hath been esteemed a duty by most who profess Christianity. (George Whitefield, sermon in 1812)

He appeared in a body. (1 Tim. 3:16b)

The Word became flesh and lived for a while among us. We have seen his glory, the glory of the one and only Son, who came from the Father, full of grace and truth. (John 1:14)

Jesus Christ is the inescapable personality of all history. The unending flow of books (including such blasphemous recent titles as A. N. Wilson's *Jesus: A Life* and Gore Vidal's *Live from Golgotha*, which seeks to argue that it was Judas Iscariot who was crucified), as well as feature films and plays (*Jesus Christ Superstar* is in currency again), all bespeak our fixation with Christ. George Cantor spent his life trying to prove that Jesus was the natural son of Joseph of Arimathea. Bishop John Shelby Spong's recent treatment of the Advent and Christmas themes seeks to argue that Mary conceived Jesus as a result of rape or sexual abuse and that Jesus may have married Mary Magdalene at the wedding in Cana.[3] Reginald Fuller's treatment of the nativity narratives discounts historicity almost entirely and sees John 1:14 as applying to Christ's baptism, not His incarnation. Here is a prominent Episcopal "scholar" denying the virginal conception of our Lord.[4]

Each year the Christian proclaimer steps into this atmosphere of skepticism and general cynicism. Even among the more low-church and free-liturgy traditions there is increasing concern that preaching on Christmas Sunday alone is not enough to stem the secularistic tide. Throughout my ministry I have preached an Advent series during the four Sundays prior to Christmas. In today's greater mobility, so many of our own people are gone the Sunday before Christmas and on Christmas Eve or Christmas Day itself (when so many visitors are present from afar), I need a good head start on interpreting the meaning of Christ's incarnation. Commercial interests are starting earlier and earlier in their sales promotions; so the preacher might well consider projecting a series for the four Sundays of Advent.

Certainly this annual series will extend beyond the nativity narratives in Matthew and Luke. I have preached a series from the Prologue of John's Gospel, or from Isaiah 9:6 ("His Name Shall Be Called"), or the four Servant Songs of Isaiah (42:1-9; 49:1-13; 50:4-11; 52:13–53:12), or certain passages in the Psalms and other prophets. Other series on "Advent Texts from Timothy and Titus" or "Advent Texts from Hebrews" or the "Why Christ Came" texts from 1 John are exceedingly rich. One year I preached a more theological series using the theme "Let us go even now to Bethlehem," with the titles:

Bethlehem and Eden (Gen. 3:6-15)
Bethlehem and Babel (Gen. 11:1-9)
(man reaching up or God coming down)
Bethlehem and Calvary (Phil. 2:3-11)
Bethlehem and the Ascension (Heb. 2:9-18)
Bethlehem and Eternity (Heb. 10:5-17)

Michael Green puts in a helpful word in urging us to consider the eschatological dimension—Christ has come/Christ will come again.[5]

Surely the great themes of the eternal pre-existence of our Lord, His miraculous and supernatural birth, a Chalcedonian Christology and all that would affirm His full deity and full humanity require strong emphasis. But again and again we must return to the bedrock historical narratives that are altogether basic and foundational for all that we believe. We may preach on "The Characters of Christmas" or "The Emotions of Christmas," but the bottom line must be the Lord Jesus Christ. If our focus is on "The Wisdom of the Wise Men," our preaching may be off-center. We need to see and feel Christ. Preaching on "Precious Names of our Wonderful Lord" can be a fresh approach.

Every effort in our time seems to be bent on divesting Christian faith of its "mythological" and supernatural trappings, but this, as Donald Bloesch well reminds us, is to revise, not to reaffirm, "the faith once delivered to the saints."[6] Redactional studies, even by some more conservative scholars, view the story of the Magi as midrashic and historically suspect. Thus care must be taken in the use of commentaries. Careful excavation of the nativity narratives is essential, and superb brief treatments such as Leon Morris's *The Story of the Christ Child: A Devotional Study of the Nativity Stories in Luke and Matthew* are indispensable.[7] The "Songs of Christmas in Luke" make an exquisite study, as does a series that begins with Luke 1:5-25, "Great in the Sight of God," and continues on with messages found in Luke 2. Some may be drawn to a first-person sermon, and this is fine if the focus turns to Christ. It is not advisable for the storyteller to play the Lord Jesus Christ.

One year I took up the journey motif and preached on "The Five Journeys of Advent," extending over to the last Sunday of the year. The messages were:

The Journey of Faith (Luke 2:1-7)
The Journey of Inquiry (Luke 2:8-20)
The Journey of Hope (Matt. 2:1-12)
The Journey of Refuge (Matt. 2:13-18)
The Journey Home (Matt. 2:19-23) (Year's End)

For some pump priming on individual passages for special occasions, we can be jogged to some new insights by collections recently assembled by Warren Wiersbe or Curtis Hutson, or by rich classic collections edited by Wilbur M. Smith[8] or the priceless piece by Samuel Zwemer.[9] We have choice studies of the *Magnificat*[10] and of Mary, our Lord's mother.[11] Our struggle here is for freshness and forcefulness.[12]

The focus must be on the person and work of the Lord Jesus Christ. Certainly to preach the narrative of Luke 1:26-38 on the annunciation made by the angel Gabriel to the Virgin Mary, we are facing a sequence in which our Lord's mother is crucially involved. The movement of the text is:

Chosen by God
Empowered by God
Responsiveness to God

But this is God-centered.

If done carefully and clearly and with strong emphasis on Matthew 1:21, 23, one can use Joseph, not as the focus but as a contrast. Three times the angel appeared to Joseph in a dream. As God deals with Joseph in the Matthew 1:18-25 text, we do see a progression:

Struggling in darkness—he learns Mary is pregnant.
Struggling with a dilemma—he was minded to put her away.
Struggling with a decision—"fear not; take her as your wife."

But it would be a mistake to lament that Joseph is the forgotten man of Christmas, because we are not to center on Joseph but on Jesus. The Matthew narrative is crystal-clear on the virginal conception of our Lord. This is the fulfillment of Isaiah 7:14, and this is stated in the passage.

We need to preach the virgin birth of Christ from these passages; here history and theology meet. God has given us all we need to know, and we must preach it. The emphasis on the Virgin Birth proclaims the deity of our Lord, protects the doctrine of the two natures of our Lord, and preserves the sinlessness of our Lord. Rather than getting off on the villainy of the innkeeper (which is textually unjustified) or succumbing to seasonal sentimentalities, let us preach the story of the shepherds' wonder and worship centered around the angel's proclamation (Luke 2:10-12), which essentially states:

> The good news of the Savior is joyful.
> The good news of the Savior is universal.
> The good news of the Savior is powerful.

PREACHING THE MINISTRY OF JESUS

> It is literally true that this century is face to face with that Great Figure as no century has been since the first. (D. S. Cairns)

> Not for a single instant did the faintest shadow come between Him and His Heavenly Father. He was without sin. (D. W. Forest)

> The evidence does not indicate that Jesus was partly God and partly man, that He did some things as God and others as man. Rather He was one Person, albeit a Person with divine and human characteristics. (Leon Morris)

> "All things have been committed to me by my Father. No one knows the Son except the Father, and no one knows the Father except the Son and those to whom the Son chooses to reveal him." (Matt. 11:27)

What sections of Scripture are dearer to the heart of Christians or clearer on central aspects of Christian experience and life than the stories of Jesus, since Christianity is Christ? Here we have opportunity to preach on both the deity and the humanity of our Lord (recalling a deeply moving message by the late P. W. Phillpot on "Our Comfort in Christ's Humanity"). Many through the years have mined this ore with creative preaching.[13] But no one has excelled what G. Campbell Morgan did in *The Crises of the Christ* as he expounded the salient events in the life and ministry of Jesus with his characteristic exegetical and theological acuity.[14]

Let us not fail to preach on the childhood and youth of Jesus as set forth in Luke 2:40-52. The growth of Jesus is summarized in Luke 2:40—"And the child grew and became strong; he was filled with wisdom, and the grace of God was upon him." With regard to Jesus at age twelve in the temple, some may choose to preach "Supposition or Certainty" from the 44th verse, "thinking he was in their company" (as did J. Stuart Holden) or "Lost in the Temple"; but this is to preach out of the text and not the text itself. This pericope is about the unusual and unique person that Jesus is, even with His miraculous affinity with us. These narratives are spare and in marked contrast to the extravagant apocryphal stories in circulation. Here we grapple with what no one has ever dealt with more helpfully than Geerhardus Vos in his masterful *The Self-disclosure of Jesus*—namely, the issue of messianic consciousness.[15] Of the years leading up to the beginning of Christ's public ministry, Dr. Luke says most meaningfully: "And Jesus grew in wisdom and stature, and in favor with God and men" (2:52).

The baptism of Jesus is an important narrative. In an extended series on "The Supernatural Christ" I preached on Luke 3:15-23, using the title "The Belovedness of Jesus." Each of the epochs in the life of Jesus is pregnant with lively truth for our lives today. When the Father bears testimony to the Son, we have heaven's verdict on the first thirty years of the Savior's earthly sojourn: "You are my Son, whom I love; with you I am well pleased" (Luke 3:22).

The threefold temptation of Christ in the wilderness touches a vital nerve in all of our lives because Jesus was tempted as we are tempted (Heb. 2:18; 4:14-15). The trinity of temptation familiar to us from the Garden of Eden and 1 John 2:15-17 is certainly in clear evidence here. One can tell this story in one sermon, bridging both to individual Christians and/or to the Church corporately, emphasizing the subversion of the Church in our time. The three temptations are so powerfully applicable:

The temptation to indulgence.
The temptation to independence.
The temptation to importance (using the Matthean order).

Or the expositor can preach three sermons, one on each tempta-tion, using titles something like those I read years ago:

"The Snare of the Shortcut"
"Playing to the Gallery"
"Forcing the Issue"

This narrative is exceedingly rich. We need more here than an exegetical outline with illustrations. The outline needs to bridge from the text to life today.[16]

The transfiguration of our Lord is a much neglected theme. Indeed, it is not mentioned in the six greatest creeds of the Church. The focus must not be spiritual loneliness, or the shallow sugges-tion of Peter about establishing a conference center. Here we need to preach the Savior. In my opinion one of the best chapters ever written on the metamorphosis of the Master is by Wilbur Smith, who quotes David Smith's view to the effect that "It was designed to reconcile them to the incredible and repulsive idea of Messiah's sufferings by revealing to them the glories which should fol-low."[17] What a theme to preach! So here we have in fact:

The preview of glory
The pattern of godliness (cf. Rom. 12:2; 2 Cor. 3:18)
The preeminence of the Son of God

Similarly, the Palm Sunday procession needs exposition as a prophetic manifestation (cf. Zech. 9), a public presentation, and a personal identification (Matt. 21:10-11). Certainly the preacher will use this great festal day to use texts that trumpet the Lordship and kingliness of Christ, but there is also much to emphasize in the deficient worship of the multitude and the tears of our Lord Jesus on that occasion. What a privilege it is to preach Christ!

PREACHING THE AGONY OF JESUS

"For even the Son of Man did not come to be served, but to serve, and to give his life as a ransom for many." (Mark 10:45)

The story of Christ is what once, somehow and somewhere, we came to Christ through. (Frederick Buechner)

For Christ died for sins once for all, the righteous for the unrighteous, to bring you to God. (1 Peter 3:18)

"But I, when I am lifted up from the earth, will draw all men to myself." He said this to show the kind of death he was going to die. (John 12:32-33)

When we come to preach the passion narratives of our Lord, we are at the heart and core of the Gospel (1 Cor. 15:2-5). The whole Christ-event has as its supreme purpose and goal the exercise of our Savior's mediatorial office as the perfect sacrifice and sin-bearer. The whole Old Testament from Genesis 3:15 on points toward the efficacious redemption procured and provided by God's Messiah. In prophecy, type, and ritual symbol, the way was being prepared for the vicarious, substitutionary atonement of Christ. The suffering servant of Isaiah 53 is Jesus the Messiah (Acts 8:30-35).

The principle that "without the shedding of blood there is no forgiveness [for sin]" is embedded in the sacrificial system of the Old Testament and was fulfilled in the work of Him of whom John the Baptist preached, "Look, the Lamb of God, who takes away the sin of the world" (John 1:29). The modern aversion to the Cross and the ridicule of "the gospel of gore" and "the slaughterhouse religion," as some put it, express exactly the first-century scorn of the Cross as a "stumbling block" and "foolishness" (1 Cor. 1:22-23). Four times the New Testament tells us the story of the death of Jesus on the cross. Though spare in detail, these narratives are heavily freighted with the theology of our salvation.

While many in Christendom today view the theology of the Cross as "a relic of a bygone age," the scandal of the Cross is nothing new. Justin Martyr made reference to the fact that "they say that our madness (mania) consists in the fact that we put a crucified man in second place after the unchangeable and eternal God, the Creator of the world" (*Apology*, I, 13.4). The blood of the Cross has always been at the heart of the primary proclamation of the forgiveness of sins. Understandably, Spurgeon described his preaching method as opening the text and running across country as fast as possible to the cross on Calvary. As seasonably and regularly the preacher inevitably comes to the crown

184

jewels of our most holy faith, what shall we say about their more powerful use?

The road to the Cross really begins with the birth of Jesus, for He was born to die. The Cross was eternally in the heart of a loving and just God (Rev. 13:8). Christ's predictions of His death and the pathway He trod toward the cross so resolutely (Luke 9:51) are fruitful areas for sermonic exploration. The emphasis in the Gospels is on preparation for the passion (cf. Luke 9:31). We have already referred to Robert Gundry's more recent commentary on Mark's Gospel, which he entitled *A Commentary on His Apology for the Cross*. Preaching through the events of Passion Week itself requires meticulously careful researching of the data. Leon Morris's helpful *The Story of the Cross* helps us with sequence and detail.[18] The case is still the strongest for Christ being crucified on Friday and hanging on the cross from 9 A.M. until shortly after 3 P.M. The use of popular research such as Jim Bishop's *The Day Christ Died* can assist us in the pictorial depiction of the events of those momentous days.[19]

In preaching the events of Holy Week we can most profitably ponder all aspects of the Upper Room Discourse, the Garden of Gethsemane, the arrest and trial of Jesus, and the *Via Dolorosa*; but the steady focus should constantly be the redemptive mission of Christ. We need to meditate on the extraordinary pressures of the Garden and the physical wounds of Jesus; but we must beware of that emphasis that makes response to the sufferings of Jesus more emotional sympathy than repentant faith (cf. Jesus' own words, "do not weep for me," Luke 23:28). We need to understand the physiology of the crucifixion, but the burden of our sins imputed to Christ must be seen as the chief suffering of the Savior.[20]

We must beware, it seems to me, of preaching Christ's prayer for the removal of the cup in the Garden of Gethsemane as in any sense His quailing or faltering before the sacrificial offering He had come to make. I see the suffering of Jesus as so great as to threaten His premature death in the Garden, and hence His prayer was to be spared so that He might go on to the cross; and indeed His prayer in the Garden was answered (Luke 22:43; Heb. 5:7). One of the finest examples of a series of narrative sermons on these events is the Lutheran Oscar A. Anderson's *With Him All the Way*.[21] Schilder's massive trilogy (*Christ in His Sufferings*,

Christ on Trial, and *Christ Crucified*) is most worthwhile, although a little heavy and at points idiosyncratic.[22] My favorite examples of preaching these narratives must be F. W. Krummacher's *The Suffering Savior*[23](one can never be the same after pondering his sermon on "Lord, is it I?") and F. A. Tholuck's *Light from the Cross*.[24]

Preaching the seven last words of Jesus is always holy ground. In one recent anthology my own sermon on the second word, entitled "The Transformation of a Terrorist," seeks to set forth the peerless drama in a brush-stroke outline:

    I.   Ruined by sin.
    II. Reviewing the Son.
    III. Repenting for sin.
    IV. Recognizing the Savior.
    V. Receiving salvation.[25]

Some striking treatments of these great themes include: Russell Bradley Jones's *Gold from Golgotha,* Lehman Strauss's *The Day God Died,* Spurgeon's *The Passion and Death of Jesus,* and Bishop William Nicholson's *The Six Miracles of Calvary,* which treats some of the more often overlooked aspects of Christ's sufferings, such as the torn veil, etc.[26]

Other notable preaching on the atoning work of Christ would have to include J. Sidlow Baxter's *The Master Theme of the Bible,* Neil Fraser's *The Grandeur of Golgotha,* and William L. Clow's incredible rich volumes of sermons *The Day of the Cross* and *The Cross in Christian Experience.*[27] What we are dealing with here is the rather stark narratives of the Gospels that require the interpretive analysis of the epistles of the New Testament. We read of the mighty acts of God, and we hear the Savior's calls from Calvary, but Paul's word to the Romans gives us the overarching frame of reference that we need: "But God demonstrates his own love for us in this: While we were still sinners, Christ died for us" (Rom. 5:8).

So the expositor needs positive doctrinal studies like Leon Morris's *The Apostolic Preaching of the Cross* and James Denney's *The Death of Christ.* We need the solid old standbys like Hodge, Smeaton, and Crawford. But we also need preachers like Martyn Lloyd-Jones (*The Cross*) and John Stott's unique *The*

Cross of Christ or Marcus Loane's *Life Through the Cross* or F. J. Huegel's *The Cross of Christ: The Throne of God.*[28]

Not long ago I attempted a series that I called "The Geography of Golgotha," in which I sought to blend story and theology: "Up to the Cross" (Ex. 12), "At the Cross" (Luke 23:32-43), "On the Cross" (Rom. 3:21-31), "In the Cross" (Rom. 6:1-14), "By the Cross" (Heb. 10:19-25), "With the Cross" (Matt. 16:21-28), "Against the Cross" (Phil. 3:17–4:1), and "Through the Cross" (Eph. 2:11-22). There are no greater themes than these, and no higher a privilege than to proclaim the unfathomable riches of His grace.

PREACHING THE VICTORY OF JESUS

"Why do you look for the living among the dead? He is not here; he has risen!" (Luke 24:5-6)

The reason why the resurrection is so pivotal, is that it validates and vitalizes all the other basic doctrines.
(Professor T. A. Kantonen)

Paul was preaching the good news about Jesus and the resurrection. (Acts 17:18)

Christ is risen! In fact, the very existence of the New Testament proclaims it. Unless something very real indeed took place on that strange, confused morning, there would be no New Testament, no Church, no Christianity.
(Frederick Buechner)

Although every Lord's Day reminds us of the foundational fact of Christ's bodily resurrection, the pastor-teacher makes an annual trek to the exquisite narratives of the four Gospels that set forth the miracle so directly. Wilbur M. Smith often remarked on the impressive reserve of the descriptions—no particular effort to describe the appearance of Christ as such, no blaze of glory, the utter absence of extravagance. We marvel at the artless simplicity and the indefinable loveliness of these narratives.

The first denial of the Resurrection is in Scripture itself (Matt. 28:11-15), and we are not surprised that relentless assaults and onslaughts have been directed at the resurrection of our Lord through the centuries. Paul goes logically to the heart of the matter when he argues: "And if Christ has not been raised, our preaching is useless and so is your faith" (1 Cor. 15:14). The preacher must make abundantly clear, therefore, that Christ's resurrection body is as literal and actual as the bread and fish that He ate in it.

The Muslims believe that Christ only swooned on the cross and did not in fact die there; and hence they deny the Resurrection. One sect in Islam actually believes that Jesus was buried in Srinagar, Kashmir. But religious liberals do little better in their assertion, "I do not believe in the physical resurrection of Jesus Christ. . . . The resurrection cannot be understood as the return of a physical body from the grave," or in Paul Tillich's notion that the resurrection is "a symbol of eternal life" (the word picked up by David Buttrick in his woefully inadequate treatment of the resurrection of Christ in his *Homiletic*).[29] In the face of Schonfield's outlandish theory (*The Passover Plot*) that Jesus, Joseph of Arimathea, Lazarus, a Judean priest, and an anonymous "young man" arranged a feigned death on the cross by taking a drug, the Easter preacher of "Now is Christ risen from the dead" is well advised to review the apologetical basis of our confidence that the resurrection of Christ is the best-attested fact in history.[30] "We did not follow cleverly invented stories when we told you about the power and coming of our Lord Jesus Christ, but we were eyewitnesses of his majesty" (2 Peter 1:16).

The Easter preacher seeking rhythmic variation will sometimes preach from an Old Testament text (such as Ps. 16 or Isa. 26:19 or Job 19:25) and will most assuredly preach from one of the great resurrection texts in Acts or in the epistles or in the Apocalypse (cf. Rev. 1:9-20). Still, we come again and again to the familiar gospel narratives for a fresh word of confidence and hope for our hungry hearers. Careful study of the documents indicates that Christ came walking out of the grave alive early on Sunday morning. The stone was rolled away by the angel, not to let Christ out but to allow witnesses to see in.

The respective accounts are complex in their relationship but without essential conflict.[31] Christ appeared ten times on record after the Resurrection, half of which occasions were on Resurrection Day. Titles such as "The Up-and-Coming Christ," "Ground-Breaking," and "Grand Opening" pick up the scriptural slant on this epochal and defining event. A series of sermons on the resurrection appearances and/or on the Christ of the forty days would only strengthen the vital impressions of what R. A. Torrey termed "the cornerstone of Christian doctrine." The Resurrection is mentioned 104 times in the New Testament, and every sermon in the book of Acts save one is really a resurrection sermon.

Since the narratives tend to be lean and quite spare, we probably will have a difficult time keeping the homiletical seams from showing unless we use a dramatic monologue or first-person sermon around one of the characters of the Easter account. Several preachers of my acquaintance have creatively presented the resurrection message through the eyes of Pontius Pilate or Joseph of Arimathea. But this is not everyone's cup of tea.

Building upon "Come and see the place where he lay" (Matt. 28:1-8), I have preached on "That Incredible Invitation":

> Emptiness—how forlorn and bleak they were.
> Evidence—"They entered and found not the body of the Lord Jesus."
> Experience—others went and found it so also
> (cf. Luke 24:24).

Stressing more of the dialectic of response, one might preach on "Wavering or Worshiping?" out of Matthew 28:1-17:

> A dreadful wrongness
> A dynamic rightness
> A diverse responsiveness (Matt. 28:17)

In the Markan account, we have more of Peter's perspective:

> The resurrection brings the reality of forgiveness.
> The resurrection brings the reality of fellowship.
> The resurrection brings the reality of freedom from fear.

Recognizing that the first person to see the living Christ was Mary Magdalene, the account in John's Gospel shows us "The Brightness of a Boundless Light" in her experience:

We can see the blessedness of deliverance—Christ liberated her.
We can sense the bleakness of deprivation—Christ was
taken away.
We can certify the brightness of discovery—Christ is alive!

Preaching on "The First Easter Sunday Evening Sermon" or
on "Christ's Final Beatitude" (for Thomas, John 20:24-29) opens
up magnificent opportunities.

Probably some of the most powerful classical sermons on the
resurrection are those of H. P. Liddon in his monumental *Easter
in St. Paul's*. Superlative examples of superb preaching on these
themes will also be seen in C. Ernest Tatham's *He Lives* (especially
on "When the Risen Lord Prepared Breakfast on the Beach" from
John 21), Neil Fraser's *The Glory of His Rising*, J. Vernon
McGee's *The Empty Tomb*, Marcus Loane's *Our Risen Lord*, and
Donald Grey Barnhouse's *The Cross Through the Empty Tomb*.[32]
The anthologies by Wilbur Smith and Samuel Zwemer also present gems for our perusal.

Attention to these commanding themes should not deflect us
from following on to preach the ascension of Christ, the session
of Christ, and the present ministry of Christ for believers from the
right hand of the Majesty on high. Our theme here is the exalted
Christ—the story goes on! What is possibly more imaginable or
more daring or more exciting than these portrayals of our conquering and victorious Christ! *Christus vere resurrexit!*—"Christ
truly arose!"

CHAPTER ELEVEN

The Exquisite Vignettes of Bible Biography

These things happened to them as examples and were written down as warnings for us, on whom the fulfillment of the ages has came.

1 COR. 10:11

These were all commended for their faith, yet none of them received what had been promised. God had planned something better for us so that only together with us would they be made perfect.

HEB. 11:39-40

. . . and then of course there is the cast of characters. Who can count their number? Who can describe their variety?—patriarchs and judges, kings and courtesans, peasants and priests; in short, men and women of every possible sort, heroes and scoundrels and some, like ourselves, who from time to time manage to be something of both. The central character, of course—the one who dominates everything and around whom all the others revolve—is God Himself. The Bible is God's book.

FREDERICK BUECHNER[1]

The heroes of mankind are the mountains, the highlands of the moral world.

A. P. STANLEY

If our objective is to preach subcutaneously—that is, to get under the skin of our hearers—we shall increasingly value both the brief and the more extensive character sketches of Scripture. Stories about other people and their experiences are high-interest factors for the communicator. The pages of the Bible abound with personalities. The long genealogical lists in Scripture not only serve to trace the Messiah's lineage but also disclose the Lord's great fascination with and concern for people. The Apostle Paul tended to be something of a prickly pear in terms of disposition, but his epistles carry the names of ninety-nine different persons mentioned in one connection or another. The book of Acts gives us 110 different names of persons in its annals of the primitive church.

The instinct of the communicator to put biblical principle into shoe-leather and personal terms is sound. Don Hewitt, the creator of *60 Minutes*, has distilled his philosophy as follows: "It's what little kids say to their parents: 'tell me a story.' Even the people who wrote the Bible knew that when you deal with issues you tell stories. The issue was evil: the story was Noah. I've had producers say, 'We've got to do something on acid rain.' I say, 'Hold it. Acid rain is not a story. Acid rain is a topic. We don't do topics. Find me someone who had to deal with the problem of acid rain. Now you have a story.'"[2] Think of how the Bible grapples with the problem and enigma of human suffering. We are told the story of Job, whose piety and prayerfulness were legendary. Then life tumbled in on him. The question is dealt with in terms of a narrative.

In today's communications climate we cannot presuppose great familiarity with Bible characters as was formerly the case in western thought generally. Widespread biblical illiteracy, even in evangelical and fundamental circles, is shocking and disturbing. Passing allusions to biblical scenarios are risky. It is better to deal more in depth with one or two specific cases. Other cautions will be referenced in the course of this chapter.

Most instructively, even in Paul's most concentrated theological discourse he uses the biographical and the autobiographical. As he argues in Romans for the doctrine of justification by faith alone apart from the works of the law, he turns (in Rom. 4) to two great Old Testament examples of justification by faith— namely, Abraham and David. The vital theological principle is personalized. Then in his section on sanctification Paul utilizes his own experience with the law (Rom. 7). This is the common practice of biblical writers (consider Heb. 11, James 2, 1 Peter, 2 Peter, Jude, etc.).

The view of H. Grady Davis, the influential homiletical theorist, is sound at this point: "We overestimate the power of assertion, and we underestimate the power of a narrative to
communicate meaning and influence the lives of our people."[3] The
profoundly moving biographical resources of the Bible offer us
such opportunities. The widely-read volume of the late Roy L.
Laurin, entitled *Meet Yourself in the Bible*, makes a survey of
these resources. Several volumes by Herbert Lockyer, and the
more recent *Peculiar Treasures: A Biblical Who's Who* by
Frederick Buechner, also delve into these resources.

In the Bible we have major characters and minor characters
(in terms of treatment), persons at the head of the pack and little
people, men and women, persons of all ages, more positive and
more negative persons. We have what are called flat characters in
which only a single facet of personality is developed, as in the
cases of David's wives Abigail and Abishag. Or we have what are
called round or full characters, in whom a more complete nuancing of personality is achieved, as in the cases of David's wives
Michal and Bathsheba.

The Bible does not present us hagiography but true biography, in the sense that it shares with us the flaws and failures of its
heroes (with but few notable exceptions, one of whom is Daniel
the prophet). This is one of the marks of the supernatural origin
and nature of the Bible and sets it apart from so much other literature. We turn now to analyze our impressive assets.

OUR AIM

> The characters of the Old Testament and the New walk our
> streets; their temperaments and problems are ours; and the
> way they meet them, for good or evil, comes close to us when
> brought close by the preacher ... the people of the Bible are
> all about us in modern clothes; they are the most effective
> instruments on which the preacher can lay his hands.
> (Halford Luccock)[4]

> But he [Jesus] said, "I must preach the good news of the
> kingdom of God to the other towns also, because that is why
> I was sent." And he kept on preaching in the synagogues of
> Judea. (Luke 4:43-44)

In analyzing further our preaching of the biographical narratives of Scripture, we need to be reminded of what it is we are called to preach. Preaching in the tradition of the Enlightenment is anthropocentric; preaching in the tradition of the Reformers is theocentric and christocentric. Our evident peril in preaching Bible biography is that we lapse into anthropocentric preaching, becoming overly psychologistic and moralistic.

No one has more forcefully and helpfully kept our feet to the fire on this issue than Sidney Greidanus in his important book *The Modern Preacher and the Ancient Text: Interpreting and Preaching Bible Literature*. Greidanus calls us to the preaching of the biblical text and insists on serious inquiry into the literary genre of the text we are going to preach. Although he skips poetry and apocalyptic, he quite thoroughly and satisfactorily canvasses the other primary genres. While I would have some differences with Greidanus on certain matters of definition and criticism, I feel strongly that he has addressed head-on the critical necessity of anchoring the sermon in solid exegesis.[5]

Most properly Greidanus has a major concern with the preaching of Bible characters, and it is imperative that we come to terms with his analysis and something of a corrective that I submit needs to be made. His discussion on this issue comes in his section on improper ways of bridging the gap between the ancient text and the modern world. We are clearly again, as always, wrestling with "the then and the now" question.

For Greidanus, "imitating Bible characters" is in the same category as allegorizing, spiritualizing, and moralizing. He scores Faris Whitesell strongly for his remark that "The life experiences of Bible people illustrate certain timeless and universal truths which preachers can apply to life today," or Andrew Blackwood's observation that "The biographical sermon is one which grows out of the facts concerning a biblical character, as these facts throw light upon the problems of the man in the pew."[6]

We are well reminded by Greidanus that "biblical characters are not presented as ideal persons" in the Bible, and that there are great challenges in analyzing whether we have something descriptive or prescriptive in the narrative, determining what is indeed the author's intention, and, most critically, seeing the danger of horizontalizing our preaching and losing the Godward dimension that is the essence of preaching. Of course, all of these challenges exist, and these dangers lurk in whatever literary genre we use. He quotes Noth to the effect that we "cannot use the individual human figures of biblical history as its subjects, either as 'ethical models,' which they in fact never are, or as exemplary 'heroes of faith' since in the biblical narratives they are never so presented, or as representatives of true humanity whose experiences are to be imitated."[7]

Greidanus argues with Clowney that we cannot legitimately use David's victory over Goliath as an example of bravery because our circumstances are so different. But how far shall we carry this? Is Greidanus establishing a canon for principalization which will make 1 Corinthians an irrelevancy to us because its situation is so different from ours? The issue of Scripture as model is difficult, but if some err in too quickly and broadly asserting the existence of models, isn't Greidanus going too far to the other extreme?

But whatever lack of congruence exists between young David and our lives, isn't the point of the passage that God gives the victory? And God gives the victory to the weak and unexpected. Did not our Lord use Elijah and Elisha as illustrations of the principle that a prophet is without honor in his own country (cf. Luke 4:24-27)? Does not the writer of Hebrews use Old Testament figures as examples of faith? And are we not to emulate their faith? Paul and James both use Abraham as an example of faith. Job's perseverance is cited by James, and the prayer life of Elijah is viewed by that apostle as exemplary. Balaam is a negative example to both Peter and Jude. I find Scripture itself abounding with what Greidanus proscribes for the preacher.

Of course, we need the reminder and the regimen of most carefully seeking and assessing the underlying principle and trying to be sensitive to genuinely comparable situations; but I think Greidanus has built something of a straw man. We can identify with biblical characters at many points, because in many cases the Scripture instructs us to do so (see 1 Cor. 11:1; Heb. 13:7; etc.). Greidanus himself emerges with some encouragement for "controlled identification."[8] He concedes that Samson is a model for Israel, as was Jonah. I regret that he puts Charles W. Koller, Lloyd Perry, and Faris Whitesell into the category of "anthropocentric preaching."

It is quite clear that one can preach any of the literary genres anthropocentrically. One can psychologize the epistles and moralize the gospel accounts. Greidanus is absolutely correct in his basic parameters of concern, but he is inadequate and inconsistent on the matter of preaching Bible characters. We need to put ourselves (as much as we can, for this is not easy) in the place of the original hearers of the Scripture. We need to be concerned about the author's intention. We need to recognize with Greidanus that the biblical writers can have a primary and a secondary purpose for the inclusion of materials.

The work of Greidanus has well called us to greater rigor and concern that all of our preaching be God-centered (1 Cor. 1:31).

OUR APPROACH

It must be remembered that the Bible was not given to reveal the lives of Abraham, Isaac and Jacob, but to reveal the hand of God in the lives of Abraham, Isaac and Jacob; not as a revelation of Mary and Martha and Lazarus, but as a revelation of the Savior of Mary and Martha and Lazarus. (Charles W. Koller)[9]

If the story has been properly told, the truths one wishes to enforce will already be so clear that they can be driven in and clinched quickly. (Ilion T. Jones)[10]

Sapienta (divine wisdom) without eloquentia (the best human expression) will do good; eloquentia without sapienta will do no good, and will often do harm; but the union of sapienta with eloquentia is ideal. (St. Augustine, in *De Doctrina Christiana*)

We have seen the minimal interaction with narrative in homiletical theory in John Broadus, the venerable and still influential homiletical theorist (1827-95). Even in the fourth edition of his standard textbook, just over two pages are devoted to narrative, and that under the category of ways of explaining the text.[11] This is to seriously underestimate the importance of biographical narrative in Scripture. Biography is not only used to illustrate principle, but reappearing characters tend to interconnect pericopes, as in the book of Acts where such characters as Stephen, Philip, and Barnabas keep bobbing up in both positive and negative ways.

Gifted preachers such as Clarence E. MacCartney and Clovis G. Chappell tended to preach series on different Bible characters under a commanding motif. I have preached a series from John's Gospel on "Immortal Interviews," studying the seven interpersonal episodes in the fourth gospel and matching the seven miracles and the seven messages centering on the "I am" passages. It is even better and more preferable to preach through a series on a single Bible character.

Abraham, "the father of all who believe," is seen in all of Scripture as "the friend of God," a man of faith. I have outlined a series something like this:

> Theme: *The Trail Leading to the Trusting Life*, or *The Formula of Faith*
> Series prayer: "Lord, increase our faith . . ."
> F. B. Meyer: "Abraham was great through his faith in God—
> and that faith was at first but a silver thread, a tiny streak,
> an insignificant sinew, not stronger than that which trembles in the humblest and weakest believer."[12]
> Geerhardus Vos: "Abraham's whole life was a school of faith
> in which the divine training developed this grace from
> step to step."
> 1. "God's Imperial Summons to Separation" (Gen. 11:31–12:9)
> 2. "Regression Revisited" (Gen. 12:10–13:4)
> 3. "Settler or Pilgrim?" (Gen. 13:5-18)
> 4. "The Pathway to the Promises" (Gen. 14:1-24)
> 5. "A Vision on the Tablelands of Trust" (Gen. 15:1-21)
> 6. "A Valley on the Tablelands of Trust" (Gen. 16:1-16)
> 7. "New Unfoldings from the Father" (Gen. 17:1-27)
> 8. "New Fellowship with the Father" (Gen. 18:1-33)
> 9. "Spiritual Undulation in the Faith Cycle" (Gen. 20–21)
> 10. "Faith's Painful Crisis" (Gen. 22) (the sacrifice of Isaac)
> 11. "Sunshine and Shadows in Life's Evening Hour" (Gen. 23, 25)

Similarly one can preach through the life of Jacob using a theme like "The Crucible of Character," showing how God made a saint out of a crook. Or the Joseph cycle can be preached under a theme like "The Sufferings and the Glory," showing how a sovereign God weaves a tapestry of integrity, utilizing some dark and somber threads. The life of Moses is scattered over so much space in Scripture that possible concentration on one rich section like the call of Moses can be a profitable study.[13]

The book of Judges gives us opportunity to preach from largely negative characters like Samson (although still cited as a man of faith in Hebrews 11:32). In developing a largely negative character such as Judas Iscariot (in a sermon like "Why Did Judas Sell Jesus?") the preacher needs positive classic and contemporary examples by way of balance. Paul Johnson's moving *Intellectuals* (1988) is a good example of how to make positive points out of the negative instance. The preacher should not neglect the distinguished women in Scripture (Abraham Kuyper has a notable series of sermons on women of the Bible).

Gideon in the book of Judges opens an opportunity to preach from the life of what some would see as a negative character:

Theme: *The Hesitant Hero*
1. "The Angel Under the Oak Tree" (Judg. 6:1-18)
2. "Jehovah-Shalom" (Judg. 6:19-24)
3. "Daring the Devil" (Judg. 6:25-32)
4. "The Test and the Trust" (Judg. 6:33-40)
5. "Preparing the People" (Judg. 7:1-14)
6. "Mighty in God" (Judg. 7:15-25)
7. "A Snare to God's Servant" (Judg. 8)

In order to achieve a more principial sense, proper names and past tenses should be avoided in titles and mains. Minor characters should be preached with the same general criteria in mind, such as Jabez (1 Chron. 4:9-10), or Benaiah, one of David's mighty men, of whom we read, "He also went down into a pit on a snowy day and killed a lion" (1 Chron. 11:22). Frank Boreham's priceless outline would be apropos for a brief devotional on some occasion:

I. A difficult place—a pit.
II. A difficult time—a snowy day.
III. A difficult task—to kill a lion.

On occasion the preacher must be more synthetic than analytic. For example, in preaching the whole book of Ruth in one sermon rather than in a series, and focusing on the theme of "God's Providential Care for His People," the communicator might consider something like the following:

198

I. Extremity (Ruth 1).
II. Industry (Ruth 2) (what a vivid story!).
III. Discovery (Ruth 3) (one could start here and use flashback).
IV. Expectancy (Ruth 4).

Preaching the life of David with ongoing reference to the Psalms is an approach Alexander Maclaren long ago recommended. This means that in preaching about David's sin with Bathsheba, we would expound Psalms 32 and 51.

The lives and ministries of Elijah and Elisha are especially relevant in our time of moral, social, and spiritual decline. Messages on the great revivals of Scripture are particularly rich and pungent. We have not really seen or experienced what Scripture and history describe as revival. Micaiah, the son of Imlah, who stood against the 400 false prophets in the strength and power of God, is typical of what we need today (cf. 1 Kings 22:1-28).

Charles Dickens had great skill in developing characters, and his novels are worth studying. Think of his genius in depicting a Mr. Micawber, Uriah Heep, the Padsnaps, Sam Weller, Miss Havisham, Smike, old Fagin, Quilp, Mrs. Gamp, Mrs. Jellyby, Sidney Carton, and on and on. Analysts such as John Mortimer have commented on how Dickens "agonized over his plots, suffered with his characters and knew black despair when ideas failed to come on his endless walks." Perhaps a willingness on our part to pay a price would help us get into the bones of Bible characters and present them more grippingly.

OUR APPLICATION

For everything that was written in the past was written to teach us, so that through endurance and the encouragement of the Scriptures we might have hope. (Rom. 15:4)

All Scripture is God-breathed and is useful for teaching, rebuking, correcting and training in righteousness, so that the man of God may be thoroughly equipped for every good work. (2 Tim. 3:16-17)

*Lives of great men all remind us
We can make our lives sublime,*

And departing, leave behind us
Footprints on the sands of time.

HENRY WADSWORTH LONGFELLOW

But how can we make the move from the biographical story-line to life and experience today? Andrew Lloyd Webber's musical *Joseph and the Amazing Technicolor Dream Coat* captures the verve and excitement of the old story, but how can we apply it in preaching?

Helpful in a basic and generic way are Andrew Blackwood's classic *Biographical Preaching for Today* and a contemporary volume patterned very much after it by Roy DeBrand entitled *Guide to Biographical Preaching: How to Preach on Bible Characters.*[14] Suggestive in its research and biblical background are the volumes by William S. LaSor, *Great Personalities of the Old Testament* and *Great Personalities of the New Testament,* not unlike Melvin Grove Kyle's much older piece, *Mooring Masts of Revelation.*[15] Biographical fiction drawing on careful study of the biblical data can be helpful—for example, Marion Wyse's *The Prophet and the Prostitute,* telling the story of the domestic tragedy of the prophet Hosea and his family.[16] Difficult issues abound here, such as did God tell Hosea to marry Gomer when she was a prostitute, or did she become unfaithful subsequent to marriage?

Old preachers of Bible characters can help us—such outstanding practitioners as William Taylor who served the Broadway Tabernacle or George Matheson, the blind Scottish preacher. Few have been so prolific as F. B. Meyer, to whom we have made reference in relation to Abraham. Many have benefited from his printed sermons on Jacob, Joseph, Moses, Joshua, David, Elijah, Jeremiah, John the Baptist, and the Apostle Paul. His application is practical and veers toward the Keswick deeper-life movement, of which he was a valued part. No more famous a course of preaching on Bible characters has ever taken place than that by Alexander Whyte in Edinburgh (1836-1921). He did six extended series, and he dealt not only with the pivotal personalities but with the likes of Nimrod, the Queen of Sheba, and Apollos. The final series focuses on "Our Lord's Characters." Whyte majored on the themes of sin and grace. This is a massive and suggestive resource.[17]

We should not overlook Jewish storytellers such as Abraham

Heschel and Elie Wiesel.[18] Conversancy with Jewish folklore and viewpoints can greatly enrich our own Old Testament story-telling.[19] Even the most familiar Bible biographies need fresh infu-sions of inspiration and insight. Jonah's life and ministry have been a favorite of mine, and I have certainly preached this dozens of times in a series of seven or more (often a series of four). Yet Eugene Peterson's new *Under the Unpredictable Plant: An Exploration in Vocational Holiness* has opened some totally new vistas and horizons in my thinking.[20] Developing the obedi-ence/disobedience dialectic, Peterson offers what he describes as Christian midrash on the Jonah passages. Though disappointing in his reluctance to take any stand on the historicity of Jonah, Peterson has a real "zinger" here.

The first six chapters of the book of Daniel are really bio-graphical in nature and are almost scary in their relevance to our cultural situation today, in which believers really must be coun-tercultural in order to reach and win their culture. The parallels with Daniel and his friends in a viciously idolatrous and pagan culture are explosive. I cite my own poor efforts to seize this trea-sure for a congregation in a series of messages on the theme "Cameos of Character and Courage." I developed six messages:

1. "The Daniel Dilemma" (Dan. 1) (Daniel faces the crunch at age fourteen or fifteen)
2. "Living Near the Knuckle" (Dan. 2) (Daniel in sync with God's plan)
3. "When Nonconformity Is Necessary" (Dan. 3)
4. "A Declaration of Dependence" (Dan. 4)
5. "Antidote to Approval Addiction" (Dan. 5)
6. "The Precedence of Prayer" (Dan. 6) (Daniel's amazing durability)

I just gloat over the richness and relevancy of these great chapters.

The general pattern is to steep and immerse ourselves in the biblical text and in the biblical backgrounding that is so impor-tant for effective narrative preaching. Then we lay out the series, identifying a God-centered motif, using continuous and running application from square one. A New Testament example that draws on several literary genres for the series has to do with the spiritual pilgrimage of Simon Peter, one of the disciples of Jesus.

Lloyd Douglas's stereotypical bumbling bumpkin must really yield to John MacGinnis's *Peter: The Fisherman-Philosopher*. Peter's two epistles show us the theological and intellectual calibre of the man. He certainly is "the American disciple," and one with whom we can all quite readily identify.

> Theme:"You Are . . . You Will Be" (John 1:42)—The Making of a Man of God
> 1. The call (Matt. 4)—"I . . ."
> 2. The confession (Matt. 16) ". . . will make . . ."
> 3. The collapse (Matt. 26) ". . . you . . ."
> 4. The conversion (Mark 16) ". . . to become . . ."
> 5. The conquest (Acts 2) ". . . fishers . . ."
> 6. The conflict (Acts 10) ". . . of men . . ."
> 7. The confidence (1 Peter) "I will make you to become fishers of men"

Again in this series I excavated the texts, used sources to help me with biblical backgrounds,[21] and got help in bridging to our lives today from several writers and preachers of experience and wisdom.[22]

OUR ADDITION

> When a man preaches to me, I want him to make it a personal matter, a personal matter, a personal matter! (Daniel Webster)

> Coming home from church one snowy day, Emerson wrote: "The snow was real, but the preacher spectral (ghostly)."[23]

> The eyes of everyone in the synagogue were fastened on him, and he [Jesus] said to them, "Today this scripture is fulfilled in your hearing." (Luke 4:20b-21)

> The persuasive representation of reality in an artistic medium answers a deep human need and provides profound and abiding delight in itself. (Robert Alter, in *The Pleasures of Reading*)

As one obsessed with the desire to communicate the truth of the Word of God, I highly value the personal accounts and character sketches of Scripture. They are priceless and powerful assets for the preacher. The story of Zacchaeus in Luke 19:1-10 opens the truth of the salvific mission of Jesus Christ and its implications with extraordinary genius and skill. King Hezekiah's prayer goes miles to help us avoid "the pumping iron" approach to the soul's devotion to God. The woman at the well in John 4 is a real person who met Jesus. We must not drown her in discourses on soul-winning or the weariness of Jesus or fixating on the jewels of worship (John 4:24) or discourses on how her absorption with sex was in fact a thirst for the transcendent. The focus of the passage is on how she discovered who Jesus is.

The characters of Scripture can, of course, be used as illustrations and examples within the sermon; but if we are seeker-sensitive or seeker-focused we must beware of assuming knowledge of the characters or their settings. In fact, most of our regular hearers have a far vaster ignorance of the Bible than many pulpiteers seem to realize. The use of ancient examples also underscores the necessity of finding contemporary-focus illustrations of the biblical principle. The nagging question often becomes, "Does this work in today's world? Show us."

If we will systematically and carefully lay bare what Scripture teaches, we shall intersect with all current problems and issues. Perusal of an evangelical version of "life situation preaching" such as Perry and Sell's *Speaking to Life's Problems* only confirms the relevancy of scriptural address.[24] Biography and autobiography generally, whether Christian or secular—General MacArthur or Winston Churchill or the Durants or Bertrand Russell or whoever—are gold mines for preachers. We find much positive and negative illustration out of the lives of familiar personalities.

But in terms of preaching, should we base a sermon on the life of an extrabiblical character? My own strong persuasion is that the sermon needs to be based on the Word of God. Spurgeon did preach a series of "Pictures from Pilgrim's Progress," but these were not given on the Lord's Day but as a stimulus to pray at a Monday evening prayer meeting.[25] Alexander Whyte preached on ninety Bunyan characters (from both *Pilgrim's Progress* and *The Holy War*), but he did this at a meeting largely for men after the evening service at Free St. George's, Edinburgh.[26] These are priceless. On the occasion of the 300th anniversary of the publication of the immortal allegory, I preached Sunday evening sermons on the theme "With Our Bibles and *Pilgrim's Progress.*" I anchored each message firmly in a scriptural text but used the imagery of Bunyan to illustrate and pictorialize the truth. For example, I took Psalm 42, the reflection of David cast down, in connection with Christian's engulfment in the Slough of Despond. The series created some interest in the press and in the community, and I was even asked to lecture on Wesley and Bunyan to a group of Methodist ministers! This was a somewhat infrequent opportunity for me.

No one preached on extrabiblical characters to greater effect or with more notoriety than Frank Boreham, the eminent Baptist preacher of New Zealand and Australia, who preached well up into the first half of this century. Boreham's essays in their time were, as some wag had it then, "on every preacher's shelves, on every preacher's tongue, and in every preacher's sermons." Though dated and long out of print, Boreham's essays are well worth reading.

Boreham's approach was to preach on a distinguished Christian leader's favorite text and then to weave pertinent and relevant biographical material through the sermon on the text itself. I have used this pattern for a series of Sunday night messages and found good response. Since these works are long out of print and unavailable to many readers, let me identify some salient examples:

> Thomas Chalmer's text—Acts 16:31
> Martin Luther's text—Romans 1:17 ("the righteous will live by faith")
> John Bunyan's text—John 6:37
> John Knox's text—John 17:3
> William Cowper's text—Romans 3:24-25
> Charles Spurgeon's text—Isaiah 45:22
> William Carey's text—Isaiah 54:2-3
> William Wilberforce's text—Luke 18:13
> John Wesley's text—Mark 12:34
> John Newton's text—Deuteronomy 15:15
> David Brainerd's text—John 7:37
> George Whitefield's text—John 3:3
> Philip Melanchthon's text—Romans 8:31
> J. G. Paton's text—Matthew 28:20
> Teresa of Avila's text—John 4:15

The Countess of Huntingdon's text—1 Corinthians 3:11
Charles Simeon's text—Ephesians 3:18[27]

This rich biographical material can be used illustratively with great effect, and this approach could be used with more current, if not contemporary Christian figures, including many within our several traditions that Boreham did not treat. These are worthy and varied materials for good use indeed!

CHAPTER TWELVE

The Special Challenges of the Apocalyptic and Prophetic

A Christian cannot have any other vision of the world in which he lives than an apocalyptic one . . . he must act at every moment as if this moment were the last.

JACQUES ELLUL

Pastoral work is eschatological . . . eschatology is the category we use to deal with matters concerning the end . . . without eschatology the line goes slack and there is nothing pulling us to the heights, to holiness, to the prize of the high calling in Christ Jesus.

EUGENE H. PETERSON

Paul's center is the apocalyptic triumph of the gospel.

J. C. BEKER

"I looked, and there before me was one like a son of man, coming with the clouds of heaven. He approached the Ancient of Days and was led into his presence. He was given authority, glory and sovereign power; all peoples, nations and men of every language worshiped him. His dominion is an everlasting dominion that will not pass away, and his kingdom is one that will never be destroyed."

DAN. 7:13-14

He who testifies to these things says, "Yes, I am coming soon." Amen. Come, Lord Jesus.

REV. 22:20

Even though our times seem overwhelmingly apocalyptic, apocalyptic is obviously a step-child among preachers. Social scientists and political scientists and environmentalists use much apocalyptic imagery, but the pulpit is strangely silent overall. Apocalyptic has to do with the eschatological and the prophetic future. The apocalyptist addresses practical concerns in a time of crisis from the standpoint of a view of continuous history, often making predictive prophecies.[1]

Apocalyptic sections are found in Daniel, Joel, Amos, and Zechariah in the Old Testament, and in the Olivet Discourse (Matt. 24–25; Mark 13; Luke 21) and the book of Revelation (The Apocalypse) in the New Testament. Little attention was given to these truths in the more optimistic nineteenth century, until Albert Schweitzer called attention to the inescapable apocalypticism of Jesus. While he thought Jesus was mistaken, Schweitzer nonetheless pointed out a stubborn fact that had been generally overlooked. Today the "eschatological orientation of biblical theology" (George Ladd) is widely recognized, but little of this has seeped into the pulpit. Date-setting harangues and various prophetic hangups have turned many pulpit communicators aside.

What is even harder to understand is why the renewed interest in narrative preaching has almost entirely ignored apocalyptic. Terrence Tilley in his *Story Theology* brazenly states that "apocalyptic is incompatible with our faith."[2] David Buttrick acknowledges the vast amount of apocalyptic material in the Bible in his "For Further Reading" section in *Homiletic*; but he does not treat the genre in his analysis and says only, "We do not live in expectation of the immediate Parousia!"[3] Thomas Long skips apocalyptic altogether, as does Sidney Greidanus, who at least acknowledges its existence. Even Leland Ryken in his astute analysis of literary forms in the Bible makes only a single reference to apocalyptic.

Apocalyptic is narrative in quality and composition because it presents to us a series and sequence of connecting events that form a *gestalt*. As over against the Greek cyclical view of history, our Bible presents us with a linear view of history, with a beginning point in creation, a decisive mid-point in the death, burial, and resurrection of Jesus Christ, and then a climax and consummation in the *Parousia*, the Second Coming of Christ and the events surrounding it. This is a story that desperately needs to be told. Christianity is more than "morality touched with emotion" as Thomas Arnold of Rugby argued. Christianity is the story of the kingdom of God—past, present, and future.[4]

Fascinatingly, Ernst Kasemann proposed that "apocalyptic is the mother of Christian theology." Jurgen Moltmann has built his "Trinitarian view of history" on this thesis, sharply contrasting Joachim of Fiore (who preached the fulfillment of the promises of God in time, beginning with the Messianic Age and climaxing in the chiliastic age) with Thomas Aquinas (who taught that the fulfillment of the promises would not be in history and time and that hope was an entirely transcendent virtue).[5] By abstracting eschatology, Aquinas effectively destroyed it, and the Church then totally replaced Israel. Joachim, on the other hand (1135-1202), moving from "the concordia of the Old Testament and the New Testament," sees the overlap of the two ages, the permanent election of Israel, and the future salvation of Israel. Indeed, with regard to this subject, Moltmann argues that Joachim is more alive today than Augustine.[6]

Moltmann goes so far as to state that there can be no Messianism without eschatology and no eschatology without chiliasm (the belief in the 1,000-year reign of Christ on earth). One of the great challenges of the biblical narratologist is to preach this great truth about the course of history and its omega point with practicality and strong application. Helpfully, on many of these disputed points there seems to be an emerging consensus among many evangelicals. I cite the recent symposium entitled *A Case for Premillennialism: A New Consensus.*[7] But in this action there is a story to be told!

PREACHING THE PURPOSE OF ESCHATOLOGY

The one last event toward which the whole creation moves . . . (Tennyson)

Give me the hope that will deliver me from fear and faintheartedness. (Dietrich Bonhoeffer)

The judgments might be terrible, but, for the children of God, the Old Testament view of history was always one of hope. (Herbert Butterfield)

> Praise be to the God and Father of our Lord Jesus Christ! In his great mercy he has given us new birth into a living hope through the resurrection of Jesus Christ from the dead. (1 Peter 1:3)

> ... while we wait for the blessed hope—the glorious appearing of our great God and Savior, Jesus Christ. (Titus 2: 13)

One of the distinctive and defining marks of the early Christians was their indomitable hopefulness. With all the genius of the Greeks, the Greeks had little to say about the last things. Their cyclical view of history caused them to look backward at death. "The future was unknown."[8] The *Dialogues of Plato* did not make predictive prophecies. The Golden Age was in the past. The best of human wisdom distilled into, "What has been will be again, what has been done will be done again; there is nothing new under the sun" (Eccles. 1:9).

But the Judeo-Christian worldview stood in stark and sharp contrast. God breaks into history. In the New Testament we have proclamation of the age of fulfillment. The present interval of time is seen as "the last days" (Acts 2:17; Heb. 1:1-2). Our age is an overlap between this age and the age to come. The powers of "the coming age" have broken into this age (Heb. 6:5). We are those "on whom the fulfillment (*teloi*) of the ages has come" (1 Cor. 10:11). History is moving toward its consummation, and believers in Christ are supremely hopeful.

Greeting each other with "Maranatha" ("The Lord is coming"), the early believers exuded a positive outlook, even in the face of martyrdom. Our barbarous age is seeing the eclipse of hope. Truly ours has been a doom boom. The physicians of western culture have been clutched in an abysmal pessimism in the face of the seemingly insoluble moral, social, economic, environmental, and political problems of our times. The approaching end of the second millennium since Christ will see a quickening of eschatological interest. The *QE II* is already fully booked for its cruise on December 31, 1999 (although technically this millennium ends on December 31, 2000).

The Old Testament prophets spoke of the Day of the Lord and the coming of the theocratic kingdom. The smiting stone will crush all the structures of Gentile world power, and the kingdom of heaven will be established on earth (Dan. 2:44-45; 7:13-14).

The Day of the Lord is seen as a complex of events that are largely judgment on a rebellious world. A future golden age of peace and glory is anticipated (Isa. 2:4; 11:1-11; 65:17-25; 66:1-24). In the New Testament the focus moves to the return of the Lord Jesus Christ (the *Parousia*). Many different interpretations circulate on the details of this expected event, but the biblical preacher cannot escape the preaching of God's plan for the ages and what the Bible has to say about the wrap-up of human history. God is going to step into time/space in the eschaton and ring down the curtain on experience as we have known it. This overarching and undergirding reality is the burden of our communication.

A Promised Hope

Some mock and scorn at the thought of a literal second coming of Christ (cf. 2 Peter 3:3ff.). One prominent magazine speaks of those who believe in the Second Coming as "the lunatic fringe of religious life." Yet the Lord Jesus spoke often of His second coming (for example, in John 14:1ff.). He was not talking about the destruction of Jerusalem or the believer's death. The angels at the ascension of our Lord made this explicit: "This same Jesus, who has been taken from you in heaven, will come back in the same way you have seen him go into heaven" (Acts 1:11). One verse out of four in the New Testament bears on the return of Christ. "Second Coming type" is the largest typeface used in publishing. We're talking about an event that old Tertullian in *De Spectaculis* says majestically and magnificently exceeds any prodigious spectacle the world offers. *Christ is coming!*

A Practical Hope

Fixation on the number of hairs on the beard of the he-goat of Daniel 3 or the shape of the nose on the Beast out of the sea is futile and foolish. We bring prophetic study into disrepute by endless obsession with vulture population in contemporary Israel or oil-drilling in Dan. Believing in the imminent return of the Lord Jesus Christ for His Church (as excitingly set forth in 1 Thess. 4:13-18) changes the perspective on all of life. This hope encourages purity of life (1 John 3:3) and a changed lifestyle (Luke 12:35-43). Luther said that the Christian is to live as if Jesus died this morning, rose this afternoon, and is coming back tonight. He also wisely testified that if he knew Christ was coming back soon, he would still plant his apple tree today. Part of the malaise among

North American Christians rises out of our failing to see that we are an eschatological people. Our roots shouldn't go too deeply into this present evil age. *Christ is coming!*

A Powerful Hope

While not all Christians agree, I would argue that not only will Christ's return involve new resurrection bodies for the saints and the final defeat of death, but Christ on His return in glory and power with His saints will express His glory in the created order of earth and will rule for 1,000 years. The whole earth will be changed as His will is done on earth even as it is done now in heaven. Then ultimately there will come the final purging and cleansing of every vestige of sin and selfishness (Rom. 8:18ff.; 2 Peter 3:1-12). So Peter exclaims: "But in keeping with his promise we are looking forward to a new heaven and a new earth, the home of righteousness" (2 Peter 3:13). *Christ is coming!* What an unspeakable privilege and responsibility it is to announce what our great God will be doing to set everything right again!

PREACHING THE PERSONALITIES OF ESCHATOLOGY

> If the end of history lies in personalities, which represent the highest things we know in the mundane realm, then we must face the fact that the purpose of history is not something that lies a thousand years ahead of us—it is constantly here, always with us, for ever achieving itself—the end of history is the manufacture and education of human souls. (Herbert Butterfield)

> The passionate belief in the imminent return of Christ was central in primitive Christianity. (Franz Overbeck, 1872)

> Theology is eschatology. [I.e., eschatology shapes theology.] (Jurgen Moltmann)

> The Lord is near. (The Apostle Paul, in Philippians 4:5b)

Liberalism's massive reconstruction was essentially a struggle against eschatology, but this was to build on sand. Garry Wills has effectively argued in *Under God* that we cannot understand American history without understanding biblical prophecy.[9] Milliast enthusiasms abounded at the time of America's settling;

the nineteenth century was "drunk on the millennium," according to Robert Sanden. Raymond Brown, the eminent Roman Catholic exegete, is certainly right that the Lord's Prayer is an eschatological prayer. London oddsmakers are offering stakes (1000:1) that Christ is not coming back today.

An important entry into preaching eschatological narrative is through prominent and pivotal eschatological personalities. The prime mover in the end-time drama is our sovereign God. History is His story. In the ferment and flux of the book of Revelation the Lamb is on the throne ("throne" is used a dozen times in Revelation to supply the critical point of reference). Whether we are looking at the succession of Gentile world powers and the ultimate demise of all structures arrogantly set up against God as set forth in Daniel 2, or the rider on the white horse who goes forth to judge and make war at the final convulsive Battle of Armageddon (Rev. 19), the figure of focus is our Lord.

"This same Jesus" (Acts 1:11) is coming back for His Church (1 Thess. 4:13-18); and all of the events in relation to the resurrection of believers—their rejoicing at the marriage supper of the Lamb, the rigors of the Judgment Seat of Christ, and their eternal residence in the Father's House—are all in relation to the character and kingly reign of the Lord Jesus Christ. The history of prophetic interpretation should make us cautious in identifications. Even a secular writer like Garry Wills observes, "An understanding of Christian prophecy will be more needed, not less, in the next few years, as 'signs of the times' are read by everyone under the impending deadline of a millennium."[10] Our preaching should be of the Christ who was pierced and who is coming again in power and glory to rescue imperiled Jews, see to their salvation (Rom. 11), and set up His kingdom to rule (cf. Zechariah 12:10).

Martin Luther insightfully argued, "*Diabolos est simia dei*" ("The devil is God's ape"). Certainly Satan himself is a prime actor in the *dramatis personae* of end-time events. His age-long rebellion will climax in the seven-year period we call the tribulation (Dan. 9:24-27). His expulsion from any accusing access to God's presence at the midpoint of the seven-year period will mark the drastic escalation of anti-Semitism and will stiffen the final revolt against God (Rev. 12:7ff.). But Satan, as the archfiend and counterfeiter that he is, will seek to put forward a facsimile of the Holy Trinity with his unholy trinity.

Corresponding to God the Father is that old dragon himself, his infernal majesty, the Devil. He creates a masterpiece, the Antichrist, or the Beast out of the sea (Rev. 13:1ff.), who becomes his effort to duplicate Christ. The second beast out of the earth, the False Prophet (Rev. 13:11ff.), becomes his effort to reduplicate the Holy Spirit. Satan is the great deceiver and imitator. A hypocrite is Satan's imitation of a Christian. The great harlot of Revelation 17 is Satan's version of the bride of Christ, the Church. Satan also pulls off a mock millennium (1 Thess. 5:3). The fact is, as the age draws to a close there will be the church of the Antichrist (the false church) and the Church of the Lord Jesus Christ (the true Church).

Clearly, the sin of man is going to climax in the man of sin (2 Thess. 2:3). This malign figure, half demon and half man, will have a pseudo-resurrection (Rev. 13:3), and the whole world will go wondering after and worshiping the Beast (Rev. 13:12). Jewish eschatology had an anti-Messiah who was to become involved in a period of extreme anguish, known as the "Messianic woes."[11] This personality is really the "serpent's seed" in a climactic sense, who will make a covenant with the nations, including the Jews (Dan. 9:24ff.). Arthur Pink has given us a particularly trenchant study of the twenty different names this evil genius bears.[12] He will come peaceably with flatteries. His claims will be braced by the signs and wonders performed by his cohort and chief henchman (Rev. 13:14; 2 Thess. 2:9-10). He will subdue kings and become strong, and the ten-nation confederacy will give their kingdom to the Beast (Rev. 17:17). Just as the four Gospels present the Lord Jesus Christ, the four horsemen of Revelation 6 present the Antichrist.

The historical likelihood of the emergence of a world ruler who will dominate a world government and an apostate world church seems quite plausible. Even the widely read futurologist Alvin Toffler believes that things will get so bad with massive insoluble problems that one ruler will emerge. Paul Henri Spaak, the distinguished Belgian statesman and leader, has said: "We do not want another committee—we have too many already. What we want is a man of sufficient stature to hold the allegiance of all people and to lift us out of the economic morass into which we are sinking. Send us such a man and be he god or devil, we will receive him."

Isn't this just the picture presented in Revelation 13? Isn't this what our Lord Jesus intimated in John 5:43—"I have come in my Father's name, and you do not accept me; but if someone else comes in his own name, you will accept him"? Even the Jews through the offices of the False Prophet (I believe a Jew himself) will join in heralding and honoring the Antichrist.

PREACHING THE MOUNTAIN PEAKS OF ESCHATOLOGY

> *Distingue tempora, et concordat Scriptura* (Distinguish the times, and the Scripture is at harmony with itself). (Augustine, Sermon XXXII)

> *Mere anarchy is loosed upon the world,*
> *The blood-dimmed tide is loosed, and everywhere*
> *The ceremony of innocence is drowned . . .*
> *Surely some revelation is at hand;*
> *Surely the Second Coming is at hand.*
> *The Second Coming!"*
> WILLIAM BUTLER YEATS, *THE SECOND COMING*, 1920

> "When these things begin to take place, stand up and lift up your heads, because your redemption is drawing near." (Luke 21:28)

> But you . . . are not in darkness so that this day should surprise you like a thief. (1 Thess. 5:4)

We can preach the story of God's plan of the ages biographically—that is, in terms of the commanding figures of Bible prophecy—or we can preach sequentially, in terms of the great salient events through which God will bring human history to its consummation. Many through the ages have spoken of the steps and stages in the divine plan. Such seminal thinkers as Spener, Bengel, and Cocceius in the post-Reformation period are examples of those who saw an *ordo tempora* (an order of times or ages in the economy of God). Bengel shrank from "the typological method of interpretation" (Gottlob Shrenk) and moved toward historical revelation, the actual outworking of the divine plan in the conversion of the Jews, the establishment of Christ's rule on earth, and the end-time. Such a later worthy as C. A. Auberlen believed that "Jerusalem would be the center of the millennial

215

kingdom and that Israel will again rise to the summit of all mankind."[13]

In his recent *Homiletical Handbook* Donald L. Hamilton offers some helpful cautions on our interpretive work in a given apocalyptic passage:

1) Let the text interpret itself (Dan. 2:36-43, 7:17, Revelation 1:20, 17:9-16).
2) Check how figures or symbols are used elsewhere by the same author.
3) Allow the clear parts of Scripture to serve as the basis for unclear parts.
4) How would the original hearers understand the symbolism?
5) Don't force symbols or figures into a preconceived mold.
6) Some figures or symbols need not be understood fully to grasp the passage.
7) Be willing to say "I don't know" on a given point or even passage.[14]

The sizable mass of fulfilled prophecy would seem to dictate that we take the *natural* or plain meaning of the text of Scripture. Girdlestone impressively cites how exactly chronological prophecies have been fulfilled.[15] It is also well to be reminded that "the testimony of Jesus is the spirit of prophecy" (Rev. 19:10). Students of the book of Revelation know how doxological and Christ-centered that wondrously rich book is. To preach these great passages is necessarily to preach the Lord Jesus Christ and His mighty salvation.[16]

Some of the mountain peaks in the prophetic plan would certainly include those discussed in the following pages.

The Covenant Story and the Conversion of Israel

Is there a more moving story than God's faithfulness to His covenant promises made to His ancient people, Israel? The story begins with the call of Abram out of Ur (Gen. 12:1-3) and the promise of the land. Clearly, in later reaffirmations the ownership of the land is permanent, but prosperity and happy possession depended on obedience (Deut. 28–30). Many would feel that as the judgments on Israel have been literal, so the blessings promised must also be literal.

Trace the story through the prophets (Hosea especially) and

on through the words of Jesus (Matt. 23:39; Luke 21:29-33) to the great affirmation of God's unchanging purpose for the Jews in Romans 11. The ultimate conversion of Israel as reiterated in Romans 11:26-27 is actually described in Revelation 7 and 11, where we read about the two witnesses and what will happen in Jerusalem after their martyrdom and ascension. The egregious anti-Semitism of the tribulation period is reflected in Revelation 12:13-17. This story of God's unswerving fidelity to His covenant promise is an incalculable encouragement to the people of God in this age and needs to be told.

The Course of This Present Age and the Midnight of Human History

Clearly, the Church will not save the world and transform society. Jesus in the Olivet Discourse (Matt. 24-25; Mark 13; Luke 21) sketches something of the direction that our world will take as this age draws toward a close. Passages such as 2 Timothy 3:1-9 reflect the perilous times toward which a rebellious world lurches. The love of ourselves, the love of money, and the love of pleasure are virtually preempting all other values in our own culture.

The Coming of Jesus Christ for His Own

Our Savior's promised return (1 Thess. 4:13-18) and His coming in glory to set up His kingdom and rule for 1,000 years are events that need to be chronicled. Exact chronologies may be matters of discussion, but the factors involved need to be drawn out and announced. *Christ is coming!*

The Sequence and Story of the Resurrections and the Scenarios of Divine Judgment

Whether for the believer, for the nations at the *Parousia*, or unforgiven sinners at the final Great White Throne judgment, these need to be carefully and clearly delineated.

The Convulsive Period of Seven Years

Known as the Tribulation, this time needs to be faced. Here we draw on the whole legacy of the Old Testament prophets and their description of "the day of the Lord." The alignment of nations, the character and career of the Antichrist, and the final rebellion at Armageddon are matters that should not be left to the cuckoos and the cultists.

The Establishment of the Millennial Kingdom

The anticipated time when Christ rules and the saints rule with Him is a thrilling epoch of future glory. Preach the story of the new configurations in Jerusalem and the temple (Ezek. 47), and expound the new world order to be inaugurated when Christ reigns. This is incomparable narrative!

PREACHING THE FINAL PICTURE

> The primary point of prophecy is to assure readers that God is going to accomplish His plans, in unique and amazing ways. Its function is both to warn and to comfort, not to assuage our curiosity about what the next year will hold. (D. Brent Sandy, in *Christianity Today*)

> Every instant of time becomes more momentous than ever— every instant is "eschatological," or, as one person has put it, like the point in the fairy-story where the clock is just about to strike twelve. (Herbert Butterfield)

> Then the end will come, when he hands over the kingdom to God the Father after he has destroyed all dominion, authority and power. For he must reign until he has put all his enemies under his feet. The last enemy to be destroyed is death. (1 Cor. 15:24-26)

> "The kingdom of the world has become the kingdom of our Lord and of his Christ, and he will reign for ever and ever." (Rev. 11:15b)

The eschatological and prophetic narrative of Scripture—the story of the consummation of human history—brings us to a decisive and dramatic climax. The book of Revelation is, among other things, the book of outcomes. How will human history end? With a bang and a whimper? With thermonuclear holocaust? Will the return of the glaciers or some other ecological disaster terminate life as we have known it? A popular news magazine recently featured a cover story on "Doomsday Science: New Theories About Comets, Asteroids and How the World Might End."[17]

Biblical prophecy is seldom sequential and chronological, but it does supply us with the pictorial and highly imagistic story of how things will be. One might preach on the question, "Will humanity destroy itself?" and take 2 Peter 3 as the text for exposition. One might divide the text as follows:

I. God has a program, vv. 1-7—Our sovereign God rules; He has a plan.
II. God has patience, vv. 8-9—His purpose is salvation, and that is why the Lord tarries and seems to unduly delay the wrap-up.
III. God has given a promise, vv. 10-18—God will intervene and create a new heaven and a new earth in which righteousness dwells; therefore, a distinctive lifestyle is incumbent upon us.

The final outcome for Israel becomes a thrilling chronicle of divine fidelity, as so many saints have held down through the centuries. As John Owen, the great Puritan preacher, said in 1673: "The Jews shall be gathered from all parts of the earth where they are now scattered, and brought home into their homeland." The outcome for the Church can be preached in several ways. Utilizing the comparisons in Revelation (where we see the contrast between the unholy trinity and the Holy Trinity, as previously noted), we can also draw the contrast between the church of the Antichrist as set forth in Revelation 17–18 and the true Church of Jesus Christ as the bride as set forth in Revelation 19. The apostate super-church that is in collusion with Satan and his minions in the final spasms of rebellion against God is foreshadowed by the false religious system of Babylon in the Old Testament.

William Ernest Hocking in his *The Coming World Civilization* (1956) speaks of what he sees coming religiously: "Thus there will eventually emerge one religion for this one world—in which tradition is fused together into an inseparable whole." Similarly, Ralph Barton Perry urged: "We need a world religion. The essence of a world religion is its equal and undiscriminating appeal to all men. It joins the Christian doctrine of regeneration, the Buddhist doctrine of recurrent desire and its conquest through self-denial, and the more homely wisdom of Confucius." We see how syncretism is moving us in this direction in our own time. The commercial complement of this ecclesiastical amalgam is seen in Babylon's busy bazaar (Rev. 18).

The contrast is, of course, more and more sharply drawn as

the midnight of human history approaches. Truly the new dark ages will come upon us in the spiritual convulsions of the end-time (cf. 2 Tim. 3:1-9). The bride of Christ, "the little flock," now in glorified bodies, will share in the wedding supper of the Lamb (Rev. 19:1-9). This is a story that needs to be told, and we need to do it in such a way that we can hear the silverware rattle. I would divide the exposition as follows:

    I. The invitation to the supper
    II. The presentation before the supper
    III. The celebration at the supper

Here we are truly dealing with what "'no eye has seen, no ear has heard, [for] no mind has conceived what God has prepared for those who love him,' but God has revealed it to us by His Spirit" (1 Cor. 2:9).

Notwithstanding the serious erosion of evangelical belief and preaching in the everlasting punishment of the wicked dead, the Scripture is clear about the judgment at the Great White Throne (Rev. 20:11-15). Mark Twain used to say that he didn't believe in hell but was afraid he would go there. W. C. Fields said he was looking for loopholes. Jesus spoke so clearly about hell that although we understandably feel a deep revulsion, we must tell the story of that place of everlasting separation from God "where the worm never dies and the fire is not quenched." But as Andrew Bonar once said to Robert Murray MacCheyne: "Preach it with tenderness."

The destiny and felicity of believers in Christ needs to be preached as well. "The glory that shall be revealed in us" is a powerful antidote to discouragement and weariness. We have something more than "intimations of immortality" and a few shreds of who-knows-what from near-death experiences. We have the promises of Jesus about the Father's house (John 14:1-6), we have the crystal-clear disclosure about our new bodies (1 Cor. 15), and we have a sharply focused revelation of how the whole of the created world will be emancipated (Rom. 8).

Revelation 21–22 are great chapters that tell the story. These magnificent paragraphs should not be used only at funerals. Here are the critical outcomes. Here is the triumph of God over Satan, of good over evil, of love over hate. A thoughtful man wrote not long ago: "I wish I could stop worrying about death. I think about it every day. The whole subject baffles me. I give people a lot of credit for muddling through when they don't know how the story will end." But believers in Christ know from their Bibles how the story will end. Like the old Quaker exclaimed, "I'm going to live until I die or until Christ comes, and then I'm going to live forever."

In preaching on "The Garden City of God" out of Revelation 21:1-5, for instance, I would incline to keep the sermon God-centered, as is indeed the text:

     I. God builds the city.
    II. God dwells in the city.
   III. God rules from His throne in the city.

Here really is the Christian philosophy of history and the heart of our eschatology. Christians will be with Christ forever and will see His glory (John 17:24). In this life we see in black and white; in the glory we will see in living color. As old Chrysostom said: "If one man could suffer all the sorrows of all the saints in the world, yet they are not worth one hour's glory in heaven." And it is our high privilege and great joy to tell this story and preach this hope.

The Demanding Rigors of the Difficult Passages

The very supernaturalness of the Bible gives to it a darkness as well as a glory.

JAMES BANNERMAN

Shall I suppose that after facing the mysteries in God's work I shall find none in studying His words?

JOHN WILLIAM BURGON

It [the Scripture] is and ever must be true even though I should not succeed in bringing all of the representations of the evangelists into harmony or in solving all the difficulties which an ingenious mind may suggest.

WILLIAM LEE

The common doctrine of the Church is and ever has been that inspiration was an influence of the Holy Spirit on the minds of certain select men which rendered them the organs of God for the infallible communication of his mind and will.

CHARLES HODGE

The Holy Spirit was co-worker with the evangelists in the composition of the gospel and therefore, lapse of memory, error or falsehood were impossible to them.

ORIGEN

"Heaven and earth will pass away, but my words will never pass away."

MATT. 24:35

Every serious student and expositor of the Scripture knows there are difficult passages. All of the literary genres present their unique challenges. As Augustine observed, the Scripture is like a river in which a child can wade and an elephant can swim. The Church has held to the essential perspicuity of Scripture down through the ages—i.e., that the Bible is basically understandable. The International Council on Biblical Inerrancy affirmed the clarity of Scripture particularly in its message about salvation, but did properly deny that all passages of Scripture are equally clear or have equal bearing on the message of salvation.[1]

Luther, for instance, admitted that Scripture bristles with difficulties (and this is not surprising); but it is perfectly clear with respect to all doctrines relating to salvation. As a Luther scholar points out, "Therefore less clear matters must be interpreted in the light of the lucid; and above all, Scripture must be at all times its own interpreter."[2] Consecrated scholarship has made an immense contribution to our understanding of the text, but the humble Spirit-filled believer can grasp what Scripture teaches because it was meant to be understood, and the inspiring Holy Spirit continues to illuminate the authoritative page (cf. 1 John 2:27). Yet as Peter said of the Apostle Paul, "His letters contain some things that are hard to understand, which ignorant and unstable people distort, as they do the other Scriptures, to their own destruction" (2 Peter 3:16).

The narrative sections of Scripture likewise do present their own special challenges and difficulties, which we want now to analyze and understand. These will fall under four basic categories. In so doing, we want to be reminded of the tendency of unbelief and skepticism to construe difficulties as errors or contradictions or serious problems. Faith takes a contrasting approach. It has been well said that "faith cannot bring itself to speak about 'mistakes and contradictions' in Scripture, but it does not deny that Scripture has 'a humble form' which readily offends unbelief. The form of Scripture is analogous to the humble form of God's Son also in this respect: People take offense—until the Spirit persuades them and they begin to love both Jesus Christ and the Scripture."[3]

Biblical faith, like any other system of truth, must be evaluated and judged in terms of its critical radicals—i.e., its central tenets and their consistency and factuality. An approach to a formulation of the nature of biblical authority through an inductive examination of the minutiae will make any conclusion impossible.[4] Thus J. Oswald Dykes scored the point well when he said: "If men must have a reconciliation for all conflicting truths before they will believe any; if they are to see how the promises of God are to be fulfilled before they will obey His commands; if duty is to hang upon the satisfying of the understanding instead of the submission of the will—then the greater number of us will find the road of faith and the road of duty blocked at the outset." We may not resolve and must not seek to force matters of biblical understanding. Westcott quotes Bishop Butler: "The truth of our Religion, like the truth of common matters, is to be judged by all the evidence taken together."[5] That is to say, our system of faith must be taken as a whole.

Augustine first articulated the apologetical principle to be observed here: any solution that affords a possible mode of harmonizing those statements of the sacred writers that present a semblance of opposition is to be admitted before we can allow the existence of a contradiction. That is, the apologist's task is met successfully in advancing even one plausible solution to an alleged problem. Far more comprehensive address to various of these issues can be found in John Halley's compendious *Alleged Discrepancies of the Bible* or in Gleason Archer's most useful *Encyclopedia of Bible Difficulties*.[6] Indeed, some of the knottiest and most thorny problems obtrude in biblical narrative, and we now move on to consider them and how they are to be preached in our times.

THE DIFFICULTY OF PRIMAL HISTORY

If all the animals and man have been evolved in this ascendant manner, then there have been no first parents, no Eden, and no Fall. And if there has been no Fall, the entire historical fabric of Christianity, the story of the first sin and the reason for an atonement, upon which current teaching bases Christian emotion and morality, collapses like a house of cards. (H. G. Wells)

> . . . to him who alone does great wonders,
> His love endures forever.

who by his understanding made the heavens,
His love endures forever.
who spread out the earth upon the waters,
His love endures forever.
who made the great lights—
His love endures forever.
the sun to govern the day,
His love endures forever.
the moon and stars to govern the night,
His love endures forever.

Ps. 136:4-9

The account of creation [in Genesis] is unique in ancient literature. It undoubtedly reflects an advanced monotheistic viewpoint, with a sequence of creative phases so rational that modern science cannot improve on it, given the same language and the same range of ideas in which to state its conclusions. In fact, modern scientific cosmogonies show a disconcerting tendency to be short-lived, and it may be seriously doubted whether science has yet caught up with the Biblical story. (William Foxwell Albright)

Preaching out of primal history (Gen. 1–11) is vital and important because the foundations of everything subsequent are laid there. In these chapters we are introduced to God the Creator and the origins of the universe and our world. Here we meet humankind made in God's image. Here we confront the Fall and the announcement of redemption. Here we confront matters that are critical for faith ("By faith we understand that the universe was formed at God's command, so that what is seen was not made out of what was visible," Heb. 11:3) and the great themes of worship and praise for God's people down through the centuries ("You are worthy, our Lord and God, to receive glory and honor and power, for you created all things, and by your will they were created and have their being," Rev. 4:11).

Yet, preaching these passages is especially challenging (not unlike passages portraying the eschatological consummation) because there is little in our experience analogical to what we read (in Gen. 1–2, for instance). What is more, the long and bitter conflict between creation and evolution embroils the preacher in technical and complex discussions that never seem to end. To appreciate the literary structure and parallels in the Genesis account is all to the good, just so long as we vigorously affirm the reliability and trustworthiness of the creation account and the historicity of Adam and Eve and of the Fall. If we hedge and fudge at these junctures, we are in grave peril. If we lose the early chapters of our Bible as serious history (such as the universal flood in the days of Noah), we will soon lose the last pages of our Bible. Indeed, if the Fall does not require a historical Adam, then how (in the terms of Paul's argument in Romans 5:12-21) can we insist that redemption requires a historical Christ? How we approach and handle this material is crucial.

A recent *Time* magazine cover story on "The Truth About Dinosaurs. Surprise: Just About Everything You Believe Is Wrong" reflects the ferment and flux in the whole field.[7] Classical Darwinianism is gone,[8] and our culture's dog-like devotion to hard science is under serious scrutiny.[9] What Anthony Standen spoke of years ago in his classic *Science Is a Sacred Cow* is now all the more apparent. Micro-evolution, of course! Macro-evolution, no! Macro-evolution has never really been observed, and the necessary transitional fossils have never been found. A Gallup poll in 1991 found that 47 percent of Americans (and a quarter of all college graduates) believe that "God created man pretty much in his present form at one time within the last 10,000 years." The rise of a vigorous creationism in our time has been immensely heartening, though we have continued to face withering fire and opposition from many quarters.[10] Charles Hodge saw the implications of the Darwinian assault on special creation as early as in his salvo of 1874 entitled *What Is Darwinism?* A two-hour CBS special recently on the search for Noah's ark on Mount Ararat was both in text and tone most encouraging to those who believe primal history is not some kind of special meta-history or trans-history but in fact serious history.

The preacher who would share these or many other narratives of Scripture needs to give great care to the exegesis of the passages. Many relevant helps are available.[11] In preaching about the mighty creative work of God out of Genesis 1–2, one should not be unaware of the parallels between Genesis and "the new heavens and the new earth" of Revelation; nor should one miss the fact that what God brings out of formlessness, emptiness, and darkness is a picture of the continuing creative work of God *ex nihilo* in human lives, as Paul reminds us in 2 Corinthians 5:17—

"Therefore, if anyone is in Christ, he is a new creation." The use of slides and multimedia to convey the marvelous and magnificent work of the creative genius of our God will only make more vivid the action-story. While not strongly bringing out the narrative character of these chapters, James Montgomery Boice's sermons are most significant examples; as he observes on Genesis 2, "Adam was no evolutionist!"[12] Francis Schaeffer also treated these texts classically;[13] and although written from a different position, Helmut Thielicke's *How the World Began* is well worth consulting.[14]

Genesis 3, the story of the Fall, is the one chapter in Scripture that, if excised, would leave the whole of the Bible unintelligible, as Archbishop Trench pointed out long ago. We're in the seed-plot of the Bible here. The trinity of temptation is here—"the lust of the flesh," "the lust of the eyes," and "the pride of life"—just as we find them in the temptation of our Lord as described in the Gospels. Then how we need to trace the tragic fallout of human sin as it tears apart the fabric of the first family and eventuates in the awful deluge in the days of Noah. Nor should we forget about the tower of Babel in Genesis 11, which reflects so poignantly the tendency to a collectivism that our human depravity renders idolatrous and rebellious against God.

These are tremendous themes and the foundations for subsequent scriptural appeal and theology. We are to tell the story, and it is a true story!

THE DIFFICULTY OF MORAL AMBIGUITY

O Lord, are you not from everlasting? . . . Your eyes are too pure to look on evil; you cannot tolerate wrong.
(Hab. 1:12-13a)

Will their lack of faith nullify God's faithfulness'? Not at all! Let God be true, and every man a liar. (Rom. 3:3-4)

He who is the Glory of Israel does not lie or change his mind; for he is not a man, that he should change his mind.
(1 Sam. 15:29)

Since God's first concern for His universe is its moral health, that is, its holiness, whatever is contrary to this is necessarily under His eternal displeasure. (A. W. Tozer, in *The Knowledge of the Holy*)

The character of God defines the nature of the good. The moral demands of a holy and righteous God issue out of His own character, as both the Old Testament and the New Testament clearly affirm. So the Lord God says: "be holy, because I am holy" (Lev. 11:44-45). So the Lord Jesus insisted: "Be perfect, therefore, as your heavenly Father is perfect" (Matt. 5:48). God's own character, then, is the sanction of moral and ethical behavior.

But does the Bible seemingly give divine approval for unethical and immoral conduct? Critics of Scripture squeal with glee at certain alleged instances of serious moral ambiguity in the Bible, and the teller of biblical stories is particularly vulnerable because most of these instances rise within narrative portions of the Holy Scriptures. At stake is, then, not only the trustworthiness and infallibility of Scripture but the character of our God.

A prime case would be the clear instruction of God to Abraham that he sacrifice his only son, Isaac (Gen. 22:2). Since human sacrifice was explicitly forbidden in the Old Testament (Lev. 18:21; 20.2), how could God ask Abraham to do this? The fact that human sacrifice was widely practiced among the Canaanites does not help us, because God insisted that His people be distinct and different from the Canaanites. Kaiser's emphasis on God's "right to require human sacrifice" is certainly correct, but is it really that helpful?[15] In telling this story to children and expounding it for adults, how do we handle the difficult order that God addressed to His servant?

The original, as Kurtz points out, literally says, "Make him ascend for a burnt offering," and we know from verse 12 that God did not seek "the slaying of Isaac in fact but only the implicit surrender of the lad in mind and heart."[16] It is helpful to point out that God "did not spare his own Son, but gave him up for us all" (Rom. 8:32). Giving up his son became the great test for Abraham's growing faith. As Oswald Chambers well observes in *My Utmost for His Highest*, "there is continual testing in the life of faith, and the last great test is death." In preaching this narrative, the possible narrative blocks might well be:

I. The testing of the obedience of faith.
II. The suffering of the obedience of faith.
III. The blessing of the obedience of faith.

A further example of possible moral ambiguity comes in Rahab's apparent lie in shielding the two spies who visited Jericho (Josh. 2:4-6). Rahab is a heroine of faith (Heb. 11:31) and is cited as an instance of a faith that works (James 2:25). Walter Kaiser is right in arguing that approving her faith does not give blanket approval to her lie.[17] Is a lie ever justified? Do the ends justify the means? The whole discussion of situation ethics and the new morality come to the fore and cannot be sidestepped by the narrative preacher. Mark Twain classically focused the argument in his memorable short story "Was It Heaven or Hell?" The story begins with the accusation, "You told a lie?" "You confess it— you actually confess it—you told a lie!"[18]

Scripture nowhere countenances prevarication or mendacity. Rahab had little teaching or insight into God's methods and will. Amazingly, this prostitute (or more probably, a priestess of the illicit Canaanite religion) did seek after God and trust Him, but at this point she did not tell the truth. Compare this with the midwives in Egypt who certainly did not tell the whole truth (Ex. 1:19). Telling the truth does not require that we disclose all that we know, but to purposely deceive is not right.

The Bible reliably records the deceitful statement of the inhabitants of Jabesh Gilead (1 Sam. 11:10), but this is not to lend a divine stamp of approval to their strategy. The Bible gives us the sentiments of the friends of Job and even the lies of Satan, but this is not to endorse the statements. Careful study of all of the passages raised in this category does not indicate any abrogation of the moral law of God as set forth in the Decalogue and in the New Testament. The fact is, there are no benevolent lies.

A curious and troubling case is the parable of the shrewd manager in Luke 16:1ff., in which our Lord Jesus seems to commend questionable behavior (vv. 8-9). Such a renegade as Julian the Apostate alleged that Jesus' words here cast a dark shadow on His morality in that Jesus seems to commend a crook. The steward was in fact as crooked as a dog's hind leg, and he was called to task for his dishonesty; Jesus plainly called him "the dishonest manager." Jesus sharply contrasts the honest with the dishonest (vv. 10-12).

But while recognizing that the man was a rascal and indeed reprehensible, Jesus saw something commendable in the man and something that can teach us a lesson. We may not approve of the tenets of a vicious cult but admire and indeed be rebuked by the passionate zeal of the cultists. We could bridge from this striking parable to today's world by saying:

I.   Jesus wants us to be realistic (the manager faced his situation as it was).
II. Jesus wants us to be resolute (the manager pushed down the accelerator).
III. Jesus wants us to be resourceful (the manager framed a shrewd strategy).

It is not God who is unholy but we ourselves. And Jesus will forgive.

THE DIFFICULTY OF VIOLENCE AND LACK OF CIVILITY

". . . the earth is filled with violence." (Gen. 6:13)

"Blessed are the peacemakers, for they will be called sons of God." (Jesus, in Matt. 5:9)

"If you don't have a sword, sell your cloak and buy one." (Jesus, in Luke 22:36)

But if you do wrong, be afraid, for he [the ruler or government leader] does not bear the sword for nothing. He is God's servant, an agent of wrath to bring punishment on the wrongdoer. (Rom. 13:4)

If it is possible, as far as it depends on you, live at peace with everyone. (Rom. 12:18)

The idea of cleansing the Bible of objectionable materials comes out of autonomous man's unwillingness to submit to any authority. The Nazi theorist Alfred Rosenberg tried to excise materials inconsistent with "the Nordic ideal." Radical feminists also take the scalpel to Scripture, as do ultra-pacifists. This is, of course, the height of arrogance and presumption.

The Scriptures faithfully and accurately reflect man's inhumanity to man, beginning with Cain's murder of Abel. But violent solutions to interpersonal problems are always proscribed in terms of the sixth commandment and the violation of the *imago dei* in human beings (1 John 3:12). The biblical case for capital punishment is a recognition of the inviolable dignity of every human being (Gen. 9:6). The biblical storyteller and the narrative preacher will frankly blanch at some of the more vivid and lurid descriptions of depraved violence found in Scripture (for example, the story of the Levite and his concubine in Judges 19–20, especially the gang rape and dismemberment). The problem is not with the truthfulness of the representation but with the prudence of telling the story in gory detail to young children. Maturity, after all, involves a sense of the proper time and place. Some passages will be laid aside for more mature audiences and the right occasion; this may be because the passages in question are of great doctrinal complexity or are too explicit or gruesome for the audience. Scripture itself is reserved in describing the physical sufferings of Jesus, and that for several good reasons.

The portrayal of murder and assault in modern media has become a serious problem, in large part because there is no awareness of moral guidelines, and only 5 percent of the criminals are shown going to trial or even possibly going to trial. "Justice seems to flow from the barrel of a gun" on TV.[19] The impact of a steady diet of violence and crime is clear in a jaded sensitivity that won't allow us to kill the geese who are a scourge in some of our communities but allows us to be appallingly indifferent to the mass-murder of millions of the unborn. The advance of the "right-to-die" movement and the fact that there are now three deaths every day from "involuntary euthanasia" in the Netherlands remind us that we have a serious problem.

The days of the judges were particularly grim, and the story of Jephthah's daughter is frequently cited as something too primitive and sub-Christian for serious communication in our time (Judg. 11:29-40). Jephthah, living in a time of drastic decline and anarchy, made a brash vow, which he kept. Yet Jephthah is listed as a hero of faith (Heb. 11:32). Archer argues that he did not sacrifice his daughter but dedicated her to the Lord's service, while

Kaiser takes the language of the passage more seriously and holds that indeed she was sacrificed, contrary as this was to the will and purpose of God. While Jephthah had zeal without knowledge, he is an example of total dedication.

The cursings in the so-called imprecatory Psalms and the slaughter of the Canaanites are not easy for us either, but clearly there is a reflection here of the "dark lines in the face of God," as one writer put it. God commanded that the Canaanites be exterminated (after a 400-year time of warning; cf. Gen. 15:12-21), just as a surgeon must sometimes amputate a cancerous limb in order to save the organism as a whole. The vile Canaanite religion could have destroyed the whole world from the critical crossroads of Palestine, land-bridge of three continents. No one has helped me more with the cursing in some of the Psalms (for example, Ps. 137:8-9) than C. S. Lewis.[20] Lewis argues that "the absence of anger, especially that sort of anger which we call indignation, can, in my opinion, be a most alarming symptom." The ferocity reflected in these passages accurately mirrors the wrath of God and the hatred of God for evil and selfishness. We too must hate what God hates.

Even the Lord Jesus drove out the moneychangers from the temple on two different occasions. John tells us that "he made a whip out of cords, and drove all from the temple area" (John 2:15). Similarly, we must not see Jesus' cursing the fig tree as a petulant outburst, as the Jewish scholar Robert Klausner tried to maintain (cf. Mark 11:12-14). The fact is that while it was not yet the time for ripe figs, Jesus had every right to expect the little green knobs known as *taksh*, which poor people ate. His curse was symbolic in that the fruitless tree with "nothing but leaves" pictured the nation barren at its heart.

A typical passage that seems a bit ghoulish to us is the story of Rizpah in 2 Samuel 21:8-10. Rizpah had been a concubine of King Saul and had two sons. When her two sons were put to death along with other descendants of Saul, Rizpah climbed the bloody hill where they were put to death, kissed their bloody feet, and wept her heart out. Indeed, from April to October she sat on the Rock of Gibeah, driving the voracious vultures and the wild animals away. Both Tennyson and William Cullen Bryant have magnificent poems entitled "Rizpah."[21] Three qualities of her life are noteworthy and not to be lost even though the setting is quite grim.

I. We see a life that is purposeful—a dedicated mother.
II. We see a love that is pained—this is realism.
III. We see a loyalty that is persistent.

There are many realities in life and in history that are not pretty. The Bible is forthright and candid with respect to them. But the Bible always puts them in a context of morality, compassion, and justice (cf. Mic. 6:8).

THE DIFFICULTY OF OBSCENITY AND MORAL IMPURITY

But the thing David had done displeased the Lord. (2 Sam. 11:27b)

Do not lie with a man as one lies with a woman; that is detestable. (Lev. 18:22)

"But I tell you that anyone who looks at a woman lustfully has already committed adultery with her in his heart." (Matt. 5:28)

It is God's will that you should be holy; that you should avoid sexual immorality; that each of you should learn to control his own body in a way that is holy and honorable, not in passionate lust like the heathen, who do not know God. (1 Thess. 4:3-5)

Do not let any unwholesome talk come out of your mouths, but only what is helpful for building others up according to their needs, that it may benefit those who listen. (Eph. 4:29)

Another category of biblical narrative poses a different kind of challenge. As we have sought to oppose pornography and the junk sex so rampant in our time, we have heard it alleged that the Bible itself is scatological, if not obscene, and that its contents should be banned if other similar material comes under an interdict. Shades of Clarence Darrow, Thomas Paine, and Robert Ingersoll! Bold and bumptious critics are heard to say that David and Jonathan had a homosexual relationship, as did Paul and

Timothy, and that Jesus had a harem, the chief representative of which was Mary Magdalene. Shocking and scandalous as these unsupported allegations are, they must be addressed, as must other issues in this general area as we prepare biblical texts for preaching.

The Bible forthrightly and frankly addresses the whole of human behavior, including the issues of God-given human sexuality. No false modesty is to be observed in the narrative or didactic parts of Holy Scripture. Many of the sacred books of the East are blatantly pornographic and could not be sent through the mail in our country for many years. But the Bible always discusses sexual conduct within a frame of reference that draws the line clearly and carefully between natural and unnatural acts, between acceptable and deviant behavior.

The disrespectful and immodest behavior of one of Noah's sons is described in reserved language, but the behavior is condemned and punished (Gen. 9:20ff.). The adultery of Judah and Tamar is set forth in plain language, as is the defiance of Onan (Gen. 38); but the guilt that God attaches to these persons is clearly and consistently presented. Efforts to "bowdlerize" or make the Bible genteel are ill-advised.[22] We need this direct address to the moral ambiguities and the sexual revolution of our times.

The heroes of the Bible are not shielded; we see them "warts and all." Samson's reprehensible exploits and King David's grievous adultery with all of its tragic concomitants are seen as immoral and unacceptable to God. Likewise, homosexual acts are seen in the Torah as *toeva* or abominable, and Orthodox Jews so hold to this day. As one of the distinguished chief rabbis in Israel today has written: "Judaism, unlike the Ancient Near East, Greece, Rome, the Far East, and Arabic cultures, stood alone in urging a sexual revolution, and insisting on exclusively heterosexual behavior. This is largely because Judaism sees the family as the bedrock of sane society, and understands homosexuality to be the family's most lethal enemy."[23] Today it is plainly Athens versus Jerusalem again. So indeed we are told of Amnon's rape of his half-sister, Tamar (2 Sam. 13:1-21); but we are left in no doubt whatever that this depraved behavior is punishable and is a part of the sad moral unraveling that took place in Israel in the wake of King David's heinous sin.

Certainly in telling the story of Ruth and Boaz we cannot miss the erotic overtones in the developing romance; and the curious custom reflected in Ruth 3 is not easy to understand or explain today, though clearly Boaz and Ruth were chaste and upright persons. The infidelity of Hosea's wife is discussed discreetly and delicately (Hos. 1–3.). The degradation of Gomer and her subsequent purchase by Hosea are seen as a vivid depiction of human moral and spiritual declension, and the Lord's "covenant love" is powerfully reflected. The late Donald Grey Barnhouse would preach this narrative with unrivaled skill.[24] The Apostle Paul picks up the action as a principial disclosure of God's restoring grace (Rom. 9) and of what will yet happen to God's ancient covenant people at the end of the age.

Certainly there are a few bawdy passages in Shakespeare as well, but with all of the candor and directness of the bard, his clear commitment to the moral and ethical standards of Scripture is clear. As Samuel Taylor Coleridge himself observed about Shakespeare:

> *no innocent adulteries,*
> *no interesting incests,*
> *no virtuous vice.*

A. H. Strong, the revered systematician, well observed that Shakespeare depicts vice, but he does not make it alluring. The same is true of the Bible.

In our day of bold and brazen attacks on biblical moral strictures, sexual confusion, and feminist crusades to revise biblical and Christian language, we are persuaded of the absolute nature of biblical authority and the biblical ethic and find ourselves increasingly at odds with the prevailing currents in our culture. Some go so far as to insist that preaching a male figure as the Savior is sexist. Government support of obscene and blasphemous art that in no sense has any "redeeming social value" merely tightens the situation in which we find ourselves as Christian communicators in an increasingly "X-rated" society.

To be sure, in preaching the narrative of Joseph's resisting the temptation of Potiphar's wife (Gen. 39) or David's sin with Bathsheba (2 Sam. 11) or expounding the description of the toboggan slide to idolatry in Romans 1:18-32, we do not want to foster and encourage the kind of behavior we are urging people to avoid. We must not be so graphic as to make the scenes of Scripture uncomfortably lurid for those presently caught in great sexual temptation. The same goes for any illustrative material being used.

We are finding ourselves hurtling toward what some call "the homosexual millennium." With the legitimizing of gay marriages, the boom of gay theater and gay fiction, and the pressure to lift the ban on gays in the military, we must be all the more concerned and careful to make clear the Bible's direct address to the evils of homosexual expression. We must not dodge the clear and unequivocal teaching of Genesis 19 and what God hated there. This must always be accompanied by explicit teaching as to what the power of God and the gospel can do to transform and change human lives (1 Cor. 6:9-11).

Totally contrasting approaches to moral issues are to be seen in two quotations. Dan Aykroyd asserted at John Belushi's funeral, "Real greatness gives great license for great indulgence." This is the spirit of our age and is addressed in Scripture in Romans 1 and 2 Timothy 3. On the other hand, Abraham Lincoln argued in his debates with Stephen Douglas, "No man has the right to choose to do evil." Holy Scripture raises up the standard of righteousness, and all of its materials bear upon this objective. The Christian communicator needs to claim the high ground and preach the story. The alternative is clear: "To the pure, all things are pure, but to those who are corrupted and do not believe, nothing is pure. In fact, both their minds and consciences are corrupted. They claim to know God, but by their actions they deny him. They are detestable, disobedient and unfit for doing anything good" (Titus 1:15-16).

IV

OUR SUMMONS

O give me that book! At any price, give me the book of God! I have it: here is knowledge enough for me. Let me be homo unius libri.

JOHN WESLEY

Do your best to present yourself to God as one approved, a workman who does not need to be ashamed and who correctly handles the word of truth.

2 TIM. 2:15

CHAPTER FOURTEEN

Enlarging Imagination and Creativity

If we lose the sense of the wonder of our commission, we shall become like common traders in a common market, babbling about common wares.

JOHN HENRY JOWETT

Imitation is suicide.

RALPH WALDO EMERSON

Imagination is the supreme work of preparation.

G. CAMPBELL MORGAN

Imagining is the queen of the faculties.

BAUDELAIRE

The first element on which your preaching will largely depend for power and success, you will be perhaps surprised to learn, is imagination, which I regard as the most important of all the elements that go to make up the preacher.

HENRY WARD BEECHER

"Your sons and daughters will prophesy, your young men will see visions, your old men will dream dreams. Even on my servants, both men and women, I will pour out my Spirit in those days."

ACTS 2:17-18

The contemporary situation for the communication of the Word of God is one that calls for freshness. In today's competition for attention and the soul-deadening media blitz that relentlessly pummels our conscious awareness, we can only lament the fatal lack of imagination in much preaching. Joseph Sittler some time ago bemoaned that many preachers have become "dull and soggy in the brain . . . they have become dull functionaries . . . ordination was their intellectual stopping-place." Our critics are all too right in alleging that modern conservatives have been brainwashed by the rationalism we reject.

Thus the renewal of interest in preaching the narrative sections of the Bible is most timely for us because the pictorial and imaginative aspects of Scripture are powerful and appealing in our time in special ways. The hour summons preachers to bestir and stretch imagination and creativity in handling all of the genres of Scripture but especially biblical narrative. Creativity essentially means doing it in a way others don't, and creativity in preaching is saying it in a way others don't say it. We need to shake loose from our custom-crusted ways, from the clichés, the stereotypical, the predictable. All of us who preach need new breakthroughs into more imaginative and creative modes of thought and expression, along with an undying loyalty and commitment to what the text says. That is the concern and focus of this chapter.

We must aim beyond presenting what someone termed "a mild, soporific commentary on the biblical text." We need some volcanic action with sizzling hot lava flows—an occasional whirlpool in our preaching. When some preachers expound Noah and the ark, we can hear it rain. When some share Isaiah's vision of the seraphim, we hear their wings whoosh and swish. The question before us is, how can we escape state-of-the-art gridlock? Sometimes in preaching we feel like we're trying to pedal a bicycle that has slipped its chain. The answer is not a rhetoric of copiousness or an increase of energy level, because we may drive in the nail so hard we split the wood.

One preacher was diagnosed as being "completely lacking in narrative sweep" through information overkill; what we are looking for is narrative grace. Granted, some seem to be born torrentially creative, but all of us can make progress from where we are and so get beyond what seems to be something akin to the narration of train schedules. You may think you have the imagination of a grapefruit, but you can grow and develop.

Thanks be to God that the biblical material is so alive. After all, the elaboration of the inconsequential can only be inconsequential. Even a gifted actor can do only so much with a poor play. Samuel Johnson said of the plot of *Cymbeline*: "It is impossible to criticize imbecility." Taking in Scripture is not like eating cotton candy three times a day. Our sermons can be all icing and no cake. We need the substance of the Word processed and packaged with excitement and skill.

Flat, unadorned prose will not do. Indolent repetition of hackneyed phrases will not carry the message. Creative lassitude must surrender its pasteboard characters and reach for nugget characterizations. Some Rubenesque amplitude, some Swiftean rhetoric of the outrageous, some Tolstoyan spaciousness and grandeur, some Carlylean volubility are needed. The Romans were not innovative in architecture, but they were effective adapters. Our styles will differ; my tendency to windiness and more elephantine style is very different from Anthony Powell's "sly, slow-motion style." James Fennimore Cooper's use of language was as wooden as we can carve; no blast-furnace prose there. What we must declare war on is sloppy thinking and sloppy use of language. Our enemy in preaching narrative is musty prose and the loss of lyricism. Spurgeon's fertility in illustration contrasts with many of us whose well of anecdotes has run dry. What's the antidote? Where's the remedy? What does the cure cost? These are the issues before us.[1]

UNDERSTANDING IMAGINATION AND CREATIVITY

A major and too-little-remarked evil in our time is the systematic degradation of the imagination. The imagination is among the chief glories of being human. When it is healthy and energetic, it ushers us into adoration and wonder, into the mysteries of God. When it is neurotic and sluggish, it turns people, millions of them, into parasites, copycats, and couch potatoes. The American imagination today is distressingly sluggish. Most of what is served up to us as the fruits of imagination is, in fact, the debasing of it into soap opera and pornography.

Right now, one of the essential Christian ministries in and to our ruined world is the recovery and exercise of the imagination. Ages of faith have always been ages rich in imagination. It is easy to see why: the materiality of the gospel (the seen, heard and touched Jesus) is no less impressive than its spirituality (faith, hope and love). Imagination is the mental tool we have for connecting material and spiritual, visible and invisible, earth and heaven. (Eugene H. Peterson, in *Under the Unpredictable Plant*)

What is the imagination, and how does it relate to creativity? Martin Ryle has spoken of imagination as "some sort of special seeing in the theater of the mind." Imagination fuels and feeds creativity. Imagination is a vision of possibilities. Imagination is the capacity to see. Mary Warnock describes imagination as productive intuition, "seeing the design, pattern and essence of things." Robert D. Young talks about imagination as impulses, flashes of insight, a kind of excitement. David Tracy tells us that imagination is the productive process of art; i.e., imagination furnishes us with the ideas for the story, and the story that eventuates as the end product is the creation.

Students of imagination agree that imagination is intentional in character. Edward S. Casey points to aspects of spontaneity—effortlessness—surprise in imagination, involving hypothesizing, pretending, and anticipating. All of this is predicated on a certain independence and freedom of the mind. We're looking at what it means to be originative. Some individuals are just extraordinarily so. Johann Sebastian Bach wrote a cantata every week. Alistair Cooke has pointed out that the brilliance of Anthony Trollope was such that when novel after novel continued to come from him, meeting standards stratospherically high, Trollope gradually became accepted as commonplace. This is another problem. Yet, we can all be intentionally more imaginative and creative than we presently are.

Creativity, the result of imagination, is now mainstreamed in American business and industry. "The hot topic right now is creative problem-solving," agrees Betty Edwards, whose *Drawing on the Right Side of the Brain* has sold well over a million copies. Carl Rogers maintained that creative people are the people who are open to experience. Abraham Maslow saw creative imagination as "peak experience." The gestation period is not long. Young cites Robert Frost stepping outdoors, "stopping by the woods on a snowy evening"; A. E. Housman on one of his long walks; Descartes brooding before the fire; Newton watching the apple; Gibbon in the Roman ruins; Hobbes who always carried pen and ink.

We're describing a process that proceeds within the different rhythms of our individuality. It doesn't happen in exactly the same way for any two persons. It is perceiving, understanding, relating, shaping, unifying, analyzing. William James believed that "the mind is at every stage a theater of simultaneous possibilities." Creativity involves the art of connection. It requires staying loose and is concerned about loose ends and dangling threads. Creativity necessitates risk-taking. As Denise Shekerjian points out, noticing has a cousin—curiosity. British historian Herbert Butterfield cites Sherlock Holmes's solving a case by pointing out that a dog had not barked and observes: "Detective stories may not in other ways be true to life, but it is the case in human affairs that the same set of clues, envisaged at higher level of thought . . . may produce a new map of the whole affair, an utterly unexpected story to narrate."

Imagination works in three ways, John Ruskin used to argue. (1) It is penetrative (it probes and digs); (2) it is associative; and (3) it is contemplative. Andrew Blackwood categorized the three kinds of imagination used by the preacher:

1. Descriptive–what is there.
2. Constructive–what is implied.
3. Creative–what could be there.

The Bible is full of images and should truly encourage creativity. God Himself is the great Creator who makes all things new. Christian faith and doctrine should free the artist and the poet because there we face the ultimate mysteries.

Why is it, then, that so many Christian communicators seem so image-poor? Casey is right when he holds that "the habit of suppressing mental imagery characterizes people who deal with abstract ideas." Here is our danger. The failure of creativity is at the symbolic level. What dampens imagination and hence creativity is frequently an unconscious Lockianism, a practical utilitarianism in which beauty, poetry, and art are dismissed. Unfortunately, Christians can be bamboozled right at this point and begin to fade out. The preacher can become like a wrung-out sponge.

Then we descend into a Louvre of clichés and sound bites. We fail to appropriately represent our ingenious God! And constipation of the imagination is ultimately life-threatening. C. E.

Robinson wrote in *Hellas*, concerning the ultimate decline of classical Greece in terms that are applicable to us: "Stagnation of the human spirit sets in when ritualism is made a substitute for worship; when technical skill takes precedence over the search for beauty; or when pedantry obscures the true appreciation of literature." Clichés are prefabricated formulae that save us from the arduous task of thinking.

Creativity, as Warnock reminds us, is not embellishment or special effects. It is the recovery of craftsmanship. It is not cleverness; it is commitment. It lifts us out of the loop of TV reruns. It definitely is what we need more of now!

APPRECIATING IMAGINATION AND CREATIVITY

The soul never thinks without a picture. (Aristotle)

Beauty is a certain kind of order. (Aristotle)

If the hearers need teaching, tell the truth by means of narrative. (Augustine)

> *Let chaos storm!*
> *Let cloud shapes swarm!*
> *I wait for form.*
> ROBERT FROST

Preaching must have a shape. The content of Scripture must be arranged and processed. This packaging we call structure or shape. The relationship between form and content is critical and subtle, as we have observed. At this juncture imagination and its offspring, creativity, need to enter the picture. As Charles Rice puts it:

> Image evokes image, story calls forth story, life speaks to life. . . . But all of this depends upon the exegete/interpreter/preacher's capacity to live in the symbol, in this case in the very language and images of the text, to dwell in the house which the text provides. That capacity, an art of the imagination, is of the essence in forming sermons.[2]

In his inaugural address in January 1993, President Bill Clinton employed the commanding metaphor of the seasons in calling for American renewal. He cited Galatians 6:7 and spoke of sowing and reaping. His reference to "forced spring" was described by William Safire as an "offbeat and thought-provoking figure of speech."[3] At this point we are in the sphere of the imagination and its creativity in communication and discourse. Here is where we see how "story continues to replace system in the minds of believers late in this century," as Martin E. Marty puts it. This is what makes our inquiry into preaching narrative so timely.

The danger here is the evident move away from a text-centered locus to a focus on context and the performance itself. The dethroning of the text in our time is ominous. As the emphasis moves away from the product to the process, from seeing to saying, our peril is that of losing the text, a la Allen Ginsberg who views the written text as a tragic disembodiment. Robert Alter's view that "the persuasive representation of reality in an artistic medium answers a deep human need and provides profound and abiding delight in itself" is seen as "oppositional" by those addicted to interpretive pluralism. "Reality?" We have already noted Thomas Long's placing interpretation itself in the imagination. This is to abandon the text.

No one shows us the folly of this misuse of imagination more than Paul Ricoeur who states: "The imagination is par excellence, the instituting and constituting of what is humanly possible; in imagining possibilities, human beings act as prophets of their own existence." This is the assertion of autonomous man following Kant and Coleridge.[4] We must retain our insistence that there is a difference between reality and fantasy and that ontological reality is defined by special revelation in Scripture. Hans Christian Andersen had it right: "Out of reality are the tales of our imagination fashioned."

The ultimate resting-place of the current trend is seen in Gerald Graff's dismissal of coherence: "Narrow canons of proof, evidence, logical consistency and clarity of expression have to go. To insist on them imposes a drag on progress. Indeed, to apply strict canons of objectivity and evidence in academic publishing today would be comparable to the American economy's returning to the gold standard; the effect would be the immediate collapse of the system." This is properly called by Robert Hughes "the fraying of America."[5]

But on the other hand, "a thing of beauty is a joy forever."

Too often our launch in the sermon is like Edward Bulwer-Lytton's pot-boiler: "It was a dark and stormy night." No wonder no one reads him today. It was said of him that he could not bring himself to discard any of his research. Stuff it in! Cram it down! It is so high-density, it sinks of its own weight.

Yogi Berra's maxim says it all: "You can observe a lot by just watching." How re-ionizing it is for the communicator to watch a master like Thomas Mann trace four generations of a North German family in *Buddenbrooks*, or the first-time novelist Jeffrey Eugenides's brilliant use of a collective narrator, of which a critic wrote: "Mr. Eugenides is blessed with the storyteller's most magical gift, the ability to transform the mundane into the extraordinary."[6]

Business and industry provide us with positive and negative examples of those who are intensely imaginative and those who are not, as Tom Peters shows us in his brilliant *Thriving on Chaos: Handbook for a Management Revolution*. Yankee impatience must yield to a "think and do" approach. In training for service with the Mossad, the Israeli spy organization, Victor Ostrovsky was challenged to strike up a conversation with a guest visiting an apartment on the third floor. He bought two wine bottles, ingeniously got into the building, and dropped the wine bottle outside the apartment in which the guest was visiting. He rang the bell and explained he had dropped the bottle and wondered if he might have something with which to clean up the mess. As the man and his guest assisted, Victor suggested they share the other bottle. He stayed there for two hours and learned the life story of both.[7] This is both *chutzpah* and imaginative creativity.

In preaching on the deceitful and deficient consecration of Ananias and Sapphira in Acts 5, I found myself looking for my launch and entry into the text. An ad featuring the "Wellington Counterfeit" diamond sufficed: virtually indistinguishable from a fine diamond, defies detection, flawless and fiery, even experts have been fooled, "you cannot trust your eyes to see any significant difference," etc. The true versus the sham in spiritual commitment.

STIMULATING IMAGINATION AND CREATIVITY

Come Holy Spirit,
Fill the hearts of those who would be faithful,
Kindle in them the fire of Love.

Send forth your Holy Spirit
And they shall be created
And they shall renew the face of the Earth.

AN ANCIENT PRAYER[8]

You cannot be too blatant or too subtle. You have to find the right salient message. (Kathleen Harty)

Imagination is conjuring up inside one, by use of a very specific intellectual muscle, that which is absent or elusive, by making it concrete. (Frederick Buechner)

The question is how this intellectual muscle can be strengthened and built. Without capitulating to the current drift "from doctrinal proposition to narrative theology," or to the reductionistic notion that preaching deals with poetic fiction challenging the prose world, we readily acknowledge we need to tell the story and use language far more imaginatively. We need to be specialists in imagery, pictures, symbols, and joyful metaphor. Our speaking needs not only to be explanatory but evocatory. We need to practice the hypothesizing, projecting, and anticipating that will allow artistry to communicate passionate urgency.

What we face by way of an obstacle is the fact that at age five 90 percent of the children measure high in creativity; at age seven 10 percent measure high in creativity; among adults 2 percent measure high in creativity. Something in our education and culture seems to deaden imagination and creativity. Perhaps the fast pace of life that has no time for creative brooding or the mindless bondage to television explains this in part. Or perhaps Irving Babbit was correct in his contention that only as imagination is anchored in ultimate reality will it draw us toward a comprehensive and proportionate view of life. With the loss of the sense of a universal moral order, we lose coherence and the base for ethical imagination.[9]

A significant and suggestive piece came out of Public Television's series on *The Creative Spirit*. The thesis of the book behind the series is that creativity is not a luxury for the few but can be cultivated and stimulated by children and adults, by individuals and communities. The series analyzes the creative moment, the art of listening, and what it is that kills creativity. The all-important incubation stage is analyzed and how we make "the creativity stew" is described.[10]

If we want to break ranks with the gray, colorless legions who have become comatose conformists in our culture, we need to jump-start imagination and creativity. Edward de Bono has helpfully urged us to to use lateral thinking. If we hold to a bicameral theory of the brain, then we want to use not only the left hemisphere, which is logical, sequential, and analytic, but to utilize the right hemisphere also, which is pictorial and imagistic. In other words, we should want not only to think more deeply but to think more broadly. This kind of thinking is not the private preserve of people with high intellectual endowment or extraordinary education. Random input, the creative pause, and sensitizing techniques are all part of the picture. We need to break out of the stifling routines that stultify creativity.[11]

My own reading and research have indicated virtual unanimity on the point that if we want to stimulate creativity we need to read, read, read. Literature refines our sensibilities. Learning how to read a book and loving to read books can open new doors of perception for everyone. Mortimer Adler's *How to Read a Book* is the starting-place. Robertson Davies, the eminent Canadian novelist, urges us to read selectively, to listen to the inner music of a writer's words, and then to reread books that really bring pleasure and profit.

Winston Churchill's way with words and his eloquence doubtless sprang from his being immersed in Edward Gibbon and T. B. Macaulay. Lincoln drew on the Bible, Shakespeare, and the beautifully natural poetry of Robert Burns. Charles Darwin, on the other hand, neglected his responsive faculties and stopped all reading of poetry and listening to music. C. S. Lewis always acknowledged that it was George MacDonald who "baptized his imagination" when he was reading *Phantastes*, again, during his Irish vacation in 1923. Think of the creative uprush in his *The Chronicles of Narnia* and his science fiction trilogy. Even the more massive production of J. R. R. Tolkien never ceases to amaze and thrill us.

John Broadus, no less, identified what he felt were factors in cultivating the imagination: (1) Study art and nature. Just dip into Holldobler and Wilson's monumental study of the 8,800 known species of ants. (2) Read imaginative literature and drama.

(3) Stay close to people—be a people watcher and a people lover. (4) Keep up your life of prayer and devotion—your linkage with the great Creator. (5) Use the imagination you have rather than complaining about what you lack. Indulge the habit of saying, Let us suppose, or imagine that, or, Can you conceive . . . ?

In her striking study, Denise Shekerjian shows that overfamiliarization is a trap we must seek to avoid. Try a shift of scenery, a little travel, even if it is to the adjoining county. Creativity requires risk-taking. Build some resilience:

1. Maintain a variety of projects.
2. Choose your friends wisely.
3. Learn from errors and disappointments.
4. Leave problems and come back to them later.
5. Retain plasticity and openness—feed curiosity.[12]

An appropriate prayer for those who want to be truly creative has been shared with us by Louise Pugh Corder:

> *Each morning is a fine new creation—*
> *A fresh canvas on which to paint my day.*
> *Help me look upward for inspiration.*
> *Master Artist, guide my plans, I pray.*
>
> *May I begin my work with grateful praise,*
> *Apply my brush with fervent prayer,*
> *My hand held by your steady hand, Lord,*
> *Warm colors spread with loving care*
>
> *Though I may paint no masterpiece,*
> *The art that's wrought is Yours and mine.*
> *I humbly ask, "Help me erase*
> *My willful flaws in our design."*

SUSTAINING IMAGINATION AND CREATIVITY

He who was seated on the throne said, "I am making everything new!" (Rev. 21:5a)

> *O Holy Spirit,*
> *As the sun is full of light, the ocean full of water,*
> *Heaven full of glory, so may my heart be full of Thee.*

Vain are all divine purposes of love
and the redemption wrought by Jesus
except Thou work within,
regenerating by Thy power,
giving me eyes to see Jesus,
showing me the realities of the unseen world.

A PURITAN PRAYER

Then he said, "Write this down, for these words are trust-worthy and true." (Rev. 21:5b)

Since Scripture itself is so full of powerful imagery and peer-less creativity, should not we who herald and expound its trea-sures be exercised to echo and reflect something of the same? Yet, frequently our sermons are victims to cookie-cutter and copycat conformities that seem dull by comparison and lethally pre-dictable. We want also to recognize that the preacher should not be a mirror but a lens. How can we experience more than occa-sional flashes of imagination and creativity unless we know some-thing of a foundation of inspiration?

As already noted, we are indeed what we eat. Too much pas-sive TV intake only jades imagination. Many will find poetry feed-ing right-brain development. T. S Eliot spoke of poetry as "an ever new raid on the inarticulate." Robert Frost said that good poetry begins with "a lump in the throat." This is the kind of material that stokes imagination. The short story has obvious commonal-ity with the narrative sermon. Read some of the gripping stories of the French writer Guy de Maupassant (who can ever forget his biting "The Necklace"?) or-of William Sidney Porter (O. Henry) with his surprise endings (as in "The Gift of the Magi"). Longer fiction and essays can also be helpful in sustaining imagination and creativity; but I believe that poetry and the short story have particular value in this regard. Bret Harte, Ring Lardner, Eudora Welty, and Paul Gallico should be mentioned as unusual crafts-men of the short story.[13]

Involved in the process must be a commitment to reflection and probing review. Stephen Crane, the Methodist minister's son who wrote the great Civil War novel *Red Badge of Courage* and some significant short stories, in one stretch of his short life was silent for the space of three days. When asked "why?" he replied, "I want to sharpen focus." Such a disconnect would not be plausible for most of us, but the principle is important. The homiletical black hole or the free-fall or the dry-hole can only be avoided if we branch out and broaden our exposure. I was surprised recently, when using Isak Dinesen's fable *Babette's Feast* as an opening point-of-contact in relation to the lavish, reckless, warm grace of God, how many people in an average congregation identified with the imagery.

We live in an age of dilution. How shall we counteract this without becoming too high-density and top-heavy? We don't want our congregations to drown in redundant minutiae. Cartoonish confusion in which transitions and linkages fade out or Gatsby-like evasiveness will do us no good. We are not aiming at a surrealistic mush of mirror images but rather a tactile, almost caressive prose. We communicate at three levels: meaning, feeling, and deciding. We need affinity for the big picture without being overly schematic. Occasionally we need a cymbal-crash conclusion, a Wagnerian exit.

Great music can also assist us. We all have our tastes, but for me the classical music stations or attending an evening concert on the lawns at a nearby outdoor music performance locale does much for me. A visit to an art gallery or an exhibition of paintings feeds and fuels my juices. People such as Francis Schaeffer and Hans Rookmaaker have helped me appreciate what art reveals of what a culture is. All of the arts are commentary on culture. The fact that there is something of a return to form in many of the arts and a crossback from open form to formal poetry again says something to us about our culture's weariness of formlessness and has important implications for our preaching.

Art and beauty can also stir and jog creative logjams. Richmond reported that before William Blake would paint, "he used to fall on his knees and pray that his work might be successful."[14] I have found it useful to study the lives and art of craftsmen such as the English painters Holman Hunt, Leigh Hunt, George Romney, John Singleton Copley, or Thomas Gainsborough. Paul Johnson has led me to John Constable and his "narrative painting." Described as "a highly cerebral and deliberative painter," Johnson particularly cites Constable's brilliant color and his love for painting clouds.[15]

Goethe was right in observing that "we perceive the visible world through light, shade and color." Painting is a form of language. It should tell the truth. Gericault's ability to paint horses and Turner's unusual gifts are worth mentioning. Turner is probably the greatest of all. Turner's modesty and use of new colors (cobalt blue, chrome yellow, and emerald green) must be mentioned. Of him Johnson says, "He read widely all his life, seized on ideas, thought about them, transformed them, and applied them in his art."[16] To understand color, he studied optics. Something analogous to preaching is happening here. Photography has points of similarity, but we as preachers are more painters than photographers. Turner felt affinity both to the poet Shelley as well as to the scientist Faraday. James Whistler is another who has moved me, as well as some of the French impressionists.

At this point the imagery of Rudyard Kipling expresses it for us:

When Earth's last picture is painted,
and the tubes are twisted and dried,
When the oldest colors have faded,
and the youngest critic has died,
We shall rest, and, faith, we shall need it—
lie down for an aeon or two,
Till the Master of All Good Workmen
shall put to work anew.

And those that were good shall be happy:
they shall sit in a golden chair;
They shall splash at a ten-league canvas
with brushes of comet's hair;
They shall find real saints to draw from—
Magdalene, Peter and Paul;
They shall work for an age at a sitting,
and never be tired at all!

And only the Master shall praise us,
and only the Master shall blame;
And no one shall work for money,
and no one shall work for fame;
But each for the joy of the working,
and each, in his separate star,
Shall draw the Thing as he sees It
for the God of Things as They Are!

CHAPTER FIFTEEN

Enhancing Relevancy and Application

In the middle of the square at Wittenberg stood an ancient wooden chapel, thirty feet long and twenty wide, whose walls, propped up on all sides, were falling into ruin. An old pulpit made of planks, and three feet high, received the preacher. It was in this place that the preaching of the Reformation began. It was God's will that that which was to restore His glory should have the humblest surroundings. It was in this wretched enclosure that God will, so to speak, that His well-beloved Son should be born a second time. Among those thousands of cathedrals and parish churches with which the world is filled, there was not one at that time which God chose for the glorious preaching of eternal life.

M. D'AUBIGNE

On the next Sabbath almost the whole city gathered to hear the word of the Lord. . . . At Iconium Paul and Barnabas went as usual into the Jewish synagogue. There they spoke so effectively that a great number of Jews and Gentiles believed.

ACTS 13:44; 14:1

The problem preachers face is how to integrate explication and application so that the whole sermon comes across as relevant communication.

SIDNEY GREIDANUS

The preaching of the Word of God is absolutely central in the divine methodology for the promulgation of revealed truth in this age. Biblical preaching in its various forms is preaching that asserts and affirms what the Bible says. More specifically, expos-

255

itory preaching is preaching that faithfully sets forth what a text of Scripture says, so that the sermon says what the text says. The critical difference for our purposes here is between preaching out of a text and preaching the text. Since God has promised to bless His Word, our primary dedication should be to actually preach what the text says.

Such biblical preaching must give attention to setting forth both the meaning of the scriptural text and the significance of that meaning for daily life here and now. Two extremes should be avoided. On the one hand, we have preachers who are trapped in the text. To them, the sermon is little more than exegesis with illustrations. This is not biblical preaching. Striking "the preaching arc" moves us from the truth as it is advanced in the Word to life as it must be lived in this world. This general pattern of moving from the matters of belief and conviction to the matters of behavior and application is to be observed repeatedly in Scripture. This is the concept in John Stott's *Between Two Worlds*. This is, as Stott argued in an earlier work, the necessary melding of proclamation and appeal.[1] One without the other is impossible.

On the other hand, we sense in the wide appeal of narrative preaching in our time some considerable allergy and aversion to direct application. Just tell the story and don't push its direct relevance too hard, we are told. Trading on Fred Craddock's reliance on Kierkegaard's advocacy of indirection, many favor letting the hearers supply their own conclusions. Open-endedness is so much more appealing in the current revolt against authority. But Holbert is mistaken in citing Nathan preaching to David as an example of indirection.[2] "Thou art the man" would seem to be quite direct in point of fact.

From within our understanding of what the Bible is and what preaching is to be as a consequence, we must insist that "all Scripture is God-breathed" and is "useful for teaching, rebuking, correcting and training in righteousness" (2 Tim. 3:16-17). Our direction here is for direct (not indirect), explicit (not implicit) application of the biblical text. We are inveighing here not only for the inerrancy of Holy Scripture but for the *sufficiency* of Holy Scripture. The pattern of the Holy Spirit's work is persuasion (cf. John 16:8-11), and we see the prominence of persuasion in apostolic preaching (consider the use of *peitho* in the book of Acts).

Application is often most difficult, especially in the narrative passages. Didactic/teaching passages frequently state the applicatory point, but only occasionally do we find the text itself actually stating the principial truth to be drawn from the passage. This is why we probably see more heresy in the framing of the application than in the actual explanation of the meaning. Thus we need to explore in this chapter many of the facets of the often arduous responsibility of application in preaching.

Right now in the whole area of computers and computerization, it is the development of application that is selling. Theoretical capability will get us nowhere. The urgent concern is for the application of the data and theory. Our thesis here is that the Bible is powerfully relevant. We do not need to make the text relevant; rather, our task is to share and show its extraordinary relevance. One of the startling publishing events of our time is the sweeping popularity of Robert Calasso's retelling of the ancient Greek and Roman myths and legends.[3] Translated into more than a dozen languages already, this work is captivating "aesthetically, intellectually and imaginatively." Calasso speaks of that which has never taken place. Can we who speak of that which has taken place in Christ not aspire to preaching God's eternal truth home to hearts?

APPLYING WITH INTEGRITY

> ... a real and a true understanding of the truth always does lead to application. So that if a person does not apply the truth, his real trouble is that he has not understood it. For if a person is gripped by a truth and sees what it means and what it implies, of necessity he must apply it.
> (D. Martyn Lloyd-Jones)

> The sermon which starts in the Bible and stays in the Bible is not Biblical. (Charles L. Rice)

> Where the application starts, there the preaching begins. You haven't started to preach until you say "You."
> (Charles H. Spurgeon)

The case is not overstated when we insist, "Preaching is application." The teaching component in preaching has to do with meaning; the application component has to do with significance.

Preaching is not to be approved or applauded but applied![4] The weakness of the contemporary sermon conclusion is a sure reflection of the contemporary weakness in theology.

Some preachers have a cruising mentality and degenerate into mere word-spinners. The result is opaque sermons that are very thin, consisting of empty moralism presented by purveyors of psychology. We need exegetical conscience. "The word of God is . . . sharper than any double-edged sword" (Heb. 4:12). It both hurts and heals. The Word reflects both the goodness and the severity of God. It is law and gospel, although not always in that chronological order. Frequently it is gospel-law-gospel, with an ever-deepening appreciation for the grace of law.

Market-driven preachers will say, "peace, peace" when no peace exists. The purpose so easily becomes that of accommodating and catering to those who "will not put up with sound doctrine" but will tolerate only those who "say what their itching ears want to hear" (2 Tim. 4:3). Jesus gave "hard sayings" that substantiate the principle that the truth as preached will both reveal and conceal (cf. Isa. 6:9ff.).

Our dedication as preachers must be to avoid any distortion of the Word of God; and "by setting forth the truth plainly we commend ourselves to every man's conscience in the sight of God" (2 Cor. 4:2). In an epochal article William H. Willimon confesses: "When I was in seminary, someone told us that the gospel must be translated into the thought forms of the modern world or we would not be heard. The preacher is the bridge between the world of the Bible and the world of the 20th century. I've decided that the traffic has been moving in only one direction on that bridge. Our task as preachers is not the hermeneutical one of making the gospel capable of being heard by modern people but the pastoral-political job of making a people who care capable of hearing the gospel."[5] This sounds like what the Holy Spirit is about!

In an important follow-up article entitled "A Second Look at Inductive Preaching," William H. Shepherd, Jr. calls us back to the text and shows the congregation how "the message is derived from the text and applied to the church."[6] If we are to avoid the "jumble of images" in today's entertainment presentations from the pulpit, we need to discover the message of the text. This is a word that is not over-heard but that is overwhelming. Is it not curious that while many evangelicals are in a market-driven panic to make the gospel relevant to our culture, Willimon calls on us to help contemporary culture to be relevant to the gospel! We are not called to get the gospel into people but to get people into the gospel![7]

Our chief concern in application is to ascertain with all of the tools at our disposal what the main thought of the text is and to be sure that the main thought of the text is the main thought of the application. In advocating continuous and running application rather than compact application (only at the end of the sermon), we are arguing that while each main point or each narrative block is best served by immediate application, the final application in the sermon should be the application of "the big idea" of the sermon.

In a helpful piece Jack Kuhatschek lays down the vital steps:

1. Understand the original situation.
2. Find the general principles.
3. Apply the general principles today to identical situations, comparable situations, or different situations.[8]

We should look for commands, examples, and promises. Indeed, there may be multiple applications that should be stated and then illustrated—biblically, historically, or in contemporary-focus illustrations, with balanced and appropriate personalization.[9]

In no phase of sermonic construction do we more frequently falter than in the making of application. How many times have I duplicated a recent blunder? After a closely reasoned exposition of an extended narrative, I wanted to use a choice and moving closing illustration to thrust the sermon home; but the illustration was slightly different in its thrust and was dissonant. Lloyd-Jones, even with minimal illustrative material, seldom failed to be right on in his application of the didactic passage. But in narrative sections, he too was occasionally off-target, in my judgment.

For example, in preaching on one of his favorite texts, Peter's miracle in healing Aeneas (Acts 9:33-34), Lloyd-Jones sees the miracle as "a parable of the whole function of the Christian church." Aeneas is thus seen as a picture of the sinner. In another great sermon Dorcas is seen as a picture of the recumbent church and needing resuscitation. But do these applications reflect the author's intention in the passages? How parabolic are the miracles? Are not the primary applications to be seen in the accrediting functions of miracles, setting forth the compassion and capability of Christ?

In Acts we read of Philip assisting the eunuch with both the meaning of the scriptural text and its implications for behavior (Acts 8:30-38). Some types of books help us with the big arcs—the overarching ideas of sections and whole books of the Bible.[10] Thus we need both analysis and synthesis in our task.

APPLYING WITH CLARITY

> It is the duty of people of knowledge to get themselves understood. (Peter Drucker)

> By setting forth the truth plainly we commend ourselves to every man's conscience in the sight of God. (2 Cor. 4:2)

> Pray that I may proclaim it clearly, as I should. (Col. 4:4)

> The first law of preaching is lucidity; the second is lucidity; and the third is similarly lucidity. (James Denney)

The perennial danger for the young preacher and for expository preaching generally is content dump. Content overload has become an occupational hazard for the expositor. Too much material leads to compaction and high-density heaviness. Flow is obstructed; interest lags. The early months of the Clinton administration have been analyzed as suffering from "too many ideas, not enough focus!" The same can be said of many sermons. We hear many great truths but are not commanded by any sense of gestalt—organismic unity.

We are advancing on the premise that every passage and each pericope have a main thought or "big idea." This central point is supported and reinforced by materials designed to move it forward and flesh it out. The following basic axiom needs constant repetition: exposition is the art of selection. The preacher must be selective because the preacher can never be exhaustive. The truth of Scripture is so endlessly profound that we can never say all that could be said or even that should be said. John Stuart Mill reminds us, "On all great subjects, something remains to be said." We need to accept that fact. "Gridlock has gripped America,"

Time magazine has stated. But gridlock has also gripped some ser-mons. As we saw earlier, Ronald Ward put it well: the sermon is a monograph, not an encyclopedia. Our objective is a meal, not a menu. Some preaching styles are as crowded as a metropolitan subway at rush hour.

Fidelity to the one main thrust of the passage requires immense discipline. Without this, some sermons roam around aimlessly. Again, the late Clovis Chappell argued that a sermon should be like a journey: it should start, travel, and arrive. Thus application should begin in the introduction. We must stoutly resist the temptation of appealing excursi or rambling bypaths. Asides blow holes in the story-line. To again cite Tim Stafford, we must be willing to kill our darlings; i.e., we must refuse to indulge attractive side-issues. Halford Luccock thought some preachers' handling of the text was like a hippopotamus chasing a pea. Seeking out and staying with the main idea of the text is some-what like trying to pick up a drop of mercury. It is difficult, but we must do it.

Working through complex material and crystallizing the one thing that the sermon should say is hard work, just like all of the other aspects of preaching. Read the classic sermons of John Henry Jowett for examples of clarity like "a cloudless morning." Preaching is to be clarification. Having too many points militates against the clarity of the single main point. Samuel Johnson wisely counseled us to pursue the simplifica-tion of great truth but to distrust such simplification. While seeking new and fresh ways to state God's eternal truth, recog-nizing that the preacher is essentially a translator, we must also be wary of what Solzhenitsyn has called "the reckless cult of novelty," which he describes as "a raucous, impatient 'avant-gardism' at any cost." He sees what is happening broadly in western culture as "an erosion and obscuring of high moral and ethical ideals" stemming from a clamorous contempt for the text and all givens.[11] Our aim is to escape the cookie-cutter con-formities of our time, but not at the expense of jettisoning the authentic message of the gospel.

In the more didactic sections of Scripture, such as Paul's epis-tle to the Romans, it is relatively easy to identify the command-ing motif or "big idea" of a passage. In the more occasional sections of Scripture and in many of the narrative portions, the task is more demanding and difficult. Certainly in preaching about David's son Adonijah and his abortive effort to seize the throne of the declining and decrepit King David (1 Kings 1), we have more than the transcription of another unsavory chapter in the history of the Judean monarchy. But we need to place the action within the biblical and theological delineation of God's purpose to reveal, to redeem, and to rule. Notice the terms that the text uses for Adonijah's advancing his own interests—"Adonijah . . . put himself forward and said, 'I will be king'" (1:5). We must see this as a challenge to God's rule. It is not difficult to see the extraordinarily relevant application of the action of this passage over against the narcissism of our time and "the pervasive shift toward self-seeking, self-indulgence and self-gratification in contemporary America."[12] After all, as William Temple well observed, sin always mean putting self forward.

Again, looking at the military action in 1 Kings 20, we puzzle a bit as to how this narrative should be applied. Andrew Murray has a great sermon on verse 4, the King of Israel's statement, "I and all I have are yours."[13] And Samuel Zwemer has a moving message on the erroneous theory of the Syrians that the Lord God was the God of the hills only and not of the valleys (20:23).[14] Also, I have heard practical preaching on the danger of busy-ness (20:40). These are examples of devotionally proper and very dear topical-textual sermons, but they do not really grapple with the passage as a whole.

Compounding the challenge is the need to preach here from the negative instance. We would prefer the positive, but we must remember that we can't delimit positively, as the Ten Commandments demonstrate. Clearly the overarching idea is: "God Is the Victor." We can break the text down to three narrative blocks. verses 1-12, feint (the King of Israel's unsuccessful deception); verses 13-30, fight (God shows He is the God of the plains); verses 31-43, fault (Ahab's disregard for God's command). Clearly this is a passage that shows how God "makes the wrath of men to praise him," and I would outline the sermon then as follows:

I. God is the victor, notwithstanding men's wily motivation, verses 1-12.

II. God is the victor, notwithstanding faulty miscalculation, verses 13-30.
III. God is the victor, notwithstanding unworthy misdirection, verses 31-43.

The sermon must clearly be about God, His ways, and His character.

APPLYING WITH PRACTICALITY

The Church comes into being when the Word is spoken. (Martin Luther)

Preach with such life and awakening seriousness . . . and with such easy method and with such variety of wholesome matter that the people may never be weary of you. (Richard Baxter)

God dwells in the details. (Mies van der Rohe)

. . . in truthful speech and in the power of God. (2 Cor. 6:7)

Bonhoeffer was certainly correct when he insisted that preaching should be like holding out a juicy red apple to a child and asking, "Would you like it?" or a cup of cold water to a thirsty man and asking, "Don't you want it?" In these terms, Clyde Fant rightly argues that "the preacher must understand that the historic word and the contemporary situation are not mutually exclusive and that preaching unites the two in the act of communication."[15]

Diminution or denial of either axis or pole will have tragic results. As we carefully study and prepare the text for preaching, we must also carefully consider the listeners, and where they are, if we are to shape the application of the text with effect. G. Campbell Morgan believed that the responsibility of application belonged to the Holy Spirit, not to the preacher. Ultimately, of course, this is true, just as ultimately it is the responsibility of the Spirit to illuminate and interpret the Word; but in both cases the Holy Spirit uses human instruments. Fortunately, Morgan's preaching shows he did not consistently apply his own rule (even as Lloyd-Jones did not consistently apply his distaste for sermonic illustration).

Instructively enough, the *Yale Studies in Communication* show that listeners prefer an explicit to an implicit conclusion, and this is true regardless of the educational level of the hearer.[16] Some fear that specific application lets many off the hook of conviction. But here we rely on the ministry of the Holy Spirit to fit the application when carefully made by the preacher. Care should be taken to avoid too atypical an instance or arguing from the exceptional case. For example, we are not advised to always cite the great saints or the gifted preachers, or only male or female for that matter. We need to seek examples of common folk, both historical and contemporary.

The restoration of Michelangelo's Sistine Chapel ceiling at the Vatican suggests another facet of our challenge. The original work has long since been lost by series of overlay jobs to which spectators have become accustomed. The years have greatly darkened the frescoes. But today, thanks to restoration, we read of "the shock of the Sistine Chapel" as visitors see new brilliance and color. This can happen so easily to the biblical texts that we preach. As we seek to get back to the richness and beauty of the text, we and our auditors will be amazed at what the dirt and dust of the years have concealed. Application will have a new excitement when we live in the matchless and incomparable Word of God!

People want the truth applied to daily life. The new *The Word in Life Study Bible* from Thomas Nelson Publishers has been developed to show "the connection" between the Bible and our own situation today.[17] Such themes as work, economics, ethics, ethnicity, the Church, laity, the family, the city, witness, and women are highlighted.

Achieving practicality in our preaching requires reading and assessing the current situations within culture. It is not enough to condemn divorce; we must face the prevalency of divorce in our culture and the fact that evangelical congregations are demonstrably experiencing the same phenomena as others. We are not immune to sexual abuse of children or wife-beating either. A high percentage of teenagers regard the church as ineffective in responding relevantly to the pressing issues of world problems, morality in government, problems of marriage and divorce, sexual issues, and problems relating to drugs and alcohol, according to the studies of George Gallup, Jr. and Robert Bezilla.

A sobering report from the National Research Council warns

that declining financial stability of families, a decrease in the time parents spend with children, and a failure of education may be leading to "a lost generation of Americans."[18] The study shows that families in every economic class are suffering from growing job worries. There is a climate of increasing anxiety and cynicism about whether government will address any of the basic issues that beset the nation. And this crisis is worldwide. The Church in its worship and preaching needs to face the real world out there.

The Bible speaks to the values, attitudes, and behavior of all time, but this truth must be drawn out and creatively and carefully applied. Using the story of the unnamed prophet from Judah in 1 Kings 13, Paul S. Rees preached a powerfully relevant sermon on "Sidetracked–and Slain." Here is an ancient word that addresses the danger of being enticed and diverted from our God-appointed course. Also, the story of King Ahab and his desire for Naboth's vineyard (1 Kings 21) shows what covetousness and greed can do. These are painfully relevant themes, vividly set forth in the inspired text, speaking right to the issues of pragmatic individualism and consumerism in our own time.

In 1 Kings 22:1-28 we have the stirring story of Micaiah, the son of Imlah, who was willing to stand for God even when he was the only one to do so. I entitled a sermon on this, "On Being Valiant for Truth in a Time of Confusion." My mains were:

I. We need a deepening sense of vocation from God (note verse 14).
II. We need a developing spiritual vision of God (bifocality—verses 17, 19).
III. We need a determined NO VACILLATION before God.

In Micaiah, who could not be bullied or bought, we have a stunningly relevant figure for the spiritual twilight zone in which we live today.

We must not lose touch with what's happening. The Swiss watch industry saw its market share tumble from 65 percent to 10 percent and its profits drop 80 percent because they didn't move from wind-up to quartz soon enough. What does this say to us?

APPLYING WITH URGENCY

Poetry begins with a lump in the throat (Robert Frost)

265

> Human kind
> cannot bear much reality.
>
> T. S. ELIOT

It is written: "I believed; therefore I have spoken." With that same spirit of faith we also believe and therefore speak, because we know that the one who raised the Lord Jesus from the dead will also raise us with Jesus and present us with you in his presence. All this is for your benefit. (2 Cor. 4:13-15a)

Preaching is to the Bible and the inspiring Spirit what the pianist's rendition is to the composer's score and Beethoven. The preacher, like the pianist, is bound to give a faithful and true rendering of the score as written; but no two pianists will be stylistically identical or interpretively uniform. They will have diminuendo and crescendo variations as they progress. Nuancing and pacing will differ as the artists seek to interpret and convey the composer's intention.

In contemporary preaching, application and conclusion are invariably the weakest and least satisfying of the components. This is most regrettable and unfortunate both from the standpoint of effective communication of content and the psychological impact of discourse. Preachers frequently seem to lose steam toward the end, lose control of their data, and become diffuse and preach down as the sermon concludes. This is why we are urging that application begin in the introduction and be built into the message as it develops, thus heightening the sense of appropriate climacteric.

Wise and careful structuring, avoidance of premature climax through time control, and appropriate disinvestment of emotion early on can save the best until last. Even in delivery we are advised, as the old maxim has it, "Start low, start slow, rise higher, catch fire." A thirty-minute sermon with time allocation to the narrative blocks or main points of twelve minutes, eight minutes, and four minutes (with three minutes for introduction and conclusion respectively) is asking for disaster.

Effective flow is also influenced by what can only be denominated as passion. Whether stylistically we are more oratorical or more conversational, we all need some moments of effective intensity consistent with who we are. We can legitimately speak of that "passion without which no major work can be written." There has to be some steam in the boiler, fire in the belly, some enthusiasm and excitement about the truth of God. We must *feel* that truth deep in our own beings. Would it be observed of us that we seem to find each verse of Scripture to be a piece of luscious fruit that we suck dry?

Matthew Arnold lamented, "I am three parts iced over." At some point we want to sense some white-hot heat in the heart. This is because communication is at the level of meaning, but also of feeling and then deciding. Without passion we narrow the prospects of effective persuasion. We are dealing with a fragile reality here. One drop of water will take off the boil. In preaching we are picking the lock, we are breaking the bolt. There is an appropriate sense of discovery. The ability to sensitively personalize preaching is involved here. Do we realize how we come across? The president of Dartmouth had been accused of having a critical, impersonal style. He asked his daughter, "Susan, do you think I'm cold, aloof, and non-communicative?" To which she revealingly replied: "Oh no, Mr. President."

So the elusive sense of urgency that is so vital in telling application rises out of conviction and deeply-held faith, is expressed with passion and great moral earnestness, and is flavored and fueled with fitting personalization. And all of this is related to a pastoral spirit and awareness. We must beware of the pastoral bulldozer. We can come on so strong and be so intimidating that we seem like a neutron bomb in a new, improved, economy size.

The preacher is to speak as a wounded healer. We have both bad news and good news to share. Jesus is our model of urgent and compassionate communication. He spoke directly to the religious upper crust (Matt. 23), and yet His "yoke is easy and [His] burden is light" (Matt. 11:28-30). He respected the capacity of His hearers (John 16:12). Or think how adroitly the Apostle Paul applied truth to the various epistolary situations; reflect on the variations of tone. Or recall the epistle to the Hebrews with its hortatory sections so ingeniously woven through the fabric of the letter. Or restudy how the living Christ in addressing the seven churches of Asia Minor (Rev. 2–3) used local referents, commendation, condemnation, promise, etc. The fact is, Scripture addresses the issues we need to face in our time, and the sermon needs to be given with a sense of the timeless relevance of the Bible in human lives everywhere.

Recently in light of the heavy hit we Christians and Christian leaders are taking in the area of moral lapse and character defect, I found the Elisha cycle in 2 Kings extremely relevant and helpful. Taking as my topic "Cracking the Character Issue," I read as my text 2 Kings 4:1-10, where the Shunammite woman says of Elisha, "I know that this man who often comes our way is a holy man of God." Then, telling the story, I seek to grapple with the inescapability of the character issue in ministry and service. Citing Sykes's *The Decay of American Character* and the incisive volume edited by Digby Anderson, *The Loss of Virtue: Moral Confusion and Social Disorder in Britain and America*, I advanced the proposition, "We can only be godly by knowing God."

The development of the sermon ranged over this part of the Elisha cycle, as it appears to emphasize the character and power of God in divergent scenarios and situations. My narrative blocks in this fairly ambitious undertaking were:

I.   We can see the *revelation* of the power and glory of God.
     The broad canvas: after Elijah's ascent; in the healing of the water; in the mauling of the young men; in the valley full of ditches; in the widow's oil.

II. We can see the *reflection* of the power and glory of God.
     Something of this reality is now visible in Elisha's life as viewed by the woman of Shunem and her husband. Our argument here is that "holiness is nothing less than conformity to the character of God" (Oswald Chambers).

III. We can see further the *reverberation* of the power and glory of God.
     Agreeing with Tozer that "we are called to an everlasting preoccupation with God," I tell the further stories of the Shunammite woman's son; hungry people; a sick foreigner; the floating axhead; and the chariots of God.

In dealing with the character issue, I am pressing for the coherence of the private and the public person. My concern is that charisma without character is calamity. But how do I bring home the truth that it must be the reality and power of God in us and

268

through us? Broadbrushing a series of stories seeks feeling tone in all of our hearts. The structure of the sermon itself seeks to make the statement articulated in the proposition. The sermon must be God-centered, because this is the point of it all. The plea for holiness in life can degenerate to mere moralism unless the dynamic of God Himself grips and moves all of our hearts and lives. Here we are at the crux of the matter of application and relevancy.

CHAPTER SIXTEEN

Encouraging Spirituality and Impaction

The inner world is all important.

WILLIAM BLAKE

The longest journey is the journey inward.

DAG HAMMARSKJOLD

"We will turn this responsibility over to them and will give our attention to prayer and the ministry of the word."

ACTS 6:3B-4

We shall not cease from exploration,
And the end of all our exploring
Will be to arrive where we started
And know the place for the first time.

T. S. ELIOT, IN FOUR QUARTETS

The bottom line in preaching narrative, as in all preaching, must never be seen solely in terms of study, skills, and style. Preaching is spiritual warfare. Preaching is an enterprise that is above all a spiritual ministry totally dependent on an unobstructed right relationship with the Lord. This is not to say that our sovereign Lord cannot use a crooked stick. Who dares to limit what God may choose to accomplish and by whom? Even Balaam's donkey spoke the truth.

The relentless concern of the preacher must therefore be to prepare and preach under the guidance and superintendence of the Holy Spirit of God who alone can bring sinners to Christ and build up the body of Christ. Thus the preacher knows something about persuasion that Aristotle with all of his brilliant analysis did not know. The Holy Spirit is the persuader. Thus the preacher is subject to "the law of the Spirit of life . . . through Christ Jesus" (Rom. 8:2). Failure to observe the laws relating to the culture and nurture of the inner life of faith and godliness will land us in a tragic and pathetic futility.

If we are to feed others, we ourselves must be fed. J. Hudson Taylor was at the core of it when he asserted that "the person who prays, dares and trusts." David Watson put it well: "Nothing is more important than hearing and obeying the Word of God." David Bryant properly insists that "Prayer is love at war." Here we are in our post-Einsteinian universe seeking weekly to swing the pendulum from the then of the biblical past to the now of the American present. By every index culturally and spiritually, we are in the tall grass of confusion and bewilderment.

A whole spray can of clever and brilliant ideas won't do it. Elegant puffery will not avail. Many a sermon seems to have had a thrombosis or hit a homiletical sink-hole. The paradigm of early-church experience is crucial. When those believers were feeling strong pressure that would lead to the confinement and containment of the Word of God, their resort was to prayer and praise and the Word of God. They felt they had to speak; as they testified, "for we cannot help speaking about what we have seen and heard" (Acts 4:20).

Reveling in the magnificence and greatness of their sovereign God, those believers feasted on the riches of revealed Scripture from Psalm 2 (cf. Acts 4:23ff.) and then came to make a request of God: "enable your servants to speak your word with great boldness" (v. 29b). The answer from heaven was prompt and potent: "After they prayed, the place where they were meeting was shaken. And they were all filled with the Holy Spirit and spoke the word of God boldly" (v. 31).

Is is any wonder, then, that the Christians in Jerusalem and environs were stirred to concrete action (Acts 4:32ff.) and that "more and more men and women believed in the Lord and were added to their number" (Acts 5:14) and that as "the word of God spread [t]he number of disciples in Jerusalem increased rapidly, and large number of priests became obedient to the faith" (Acts 6:7)? We can surely understand the sharpened focus of leadership, therefore, on the urgent necessity of giving attention "to prayer and the ministry of the word" (Acts 6:4), allowing nothing to divert and distract them from first things.

In this concluding chapter, I want to factor-analyze some of the critical spiritual ingredients in the preaching task. If indeed our concern in preaching any genre in Scripture coincides with the Apostle Paul's burden, then our concern is: "Pray for us that the message of the Lord may spread rapidly and be honored" (2 Thess. 3:1).

As theology does a disappearing act in contemporary evangelicalism, and as we are being swamped by psychologism from the pulpit and management techniques in the Church, we need to get back to the Word of God and those spiritual disciplines that are requisite for the ever-deepening consciousness of God.

> *God's greatness flows around our incompleteness,*
> *Round our restlessness, His rest.*
>
> ELIZABETH BARRETT BROWNING

SPIRITUAL READINESS

Ripeness is all. . . . (Edgar, in Shakespeare's *King Lear*)

I am so eager to preach the gospel also to you. (Rom. 1:15)

We continually teach that knowledge of Christ and of faith is not a human work but utterly a divine gift—this sort of doctrine which reveals the Son of God . . . is revealed by God, first by the external Word and then inwardly through the Spirit. (Martin Luther)

The miseries of men come from not being able to sit alone in a quiet room. (Blaise Pascal)

The preaching of the Word of God is a daunting task, and were it not for our involvement in partnership with the Holy Spirit, we could only despair. This fact profoundly underscores our total reliance upon the Lord in the whole process of preparation. Are we prepared to preach? We need to prepare with great seriousness. There is no cure for not being prepared. We have a moral and spiritual obligation before God and our hearers to be well prepared. Pearl Harbor lives in infamy in American history as witness to "the blunted edge of preparedness," as one writer put it. As mentioned earlier, recently the renowned Italian opera singer Luciano Pavarotti was hissed and booed by an audience because he was clearly unprepared for his concert. If we preach without sufficient study and planning beforehand, we are taking blocks of invaluable time from our hearers. Multiply thirty minutes by the number of congregants who heard you last. We must be prepared.

But readiness is not only work in the text and the crafting of the sermon to be delivered and the mastery of the material. At this juncture preaching is as much who we are as what we say. This is what James Earl Massey calls "the inwardness" of preaching. He speaks of our sermons as our offspring. The sermon is shaped not only structurally but spiritually. Pianists, Massey observes, must be on the alert against being only "technique aware"—that is, losing the soul, the verve, the flight, the soaring of the music. Cicero, the great Roman orator who influenced Augustine so markedly, greatly emphasized the speaker's character, his or her persona, as key elements in expression.[1] Thus the preparation of the messenger is as fundamental as the preparation of the message.

E. M. Bounds, that extraordinary person of prayer, used to plead: "the character of our praying will determine the character of our preaching." Likewise Martin Luther believed that "He who has prayed well has studied well." Preaching is indeed closet-time. A veteran religious leader was asked to give advice to spiritual leaders, and his first thrust was: "It is absolutely necessary to find time and space to prepare." Can we rise above the mass of impressive trivia that threatens to smother the heart of the Church?

In a remarkable interview after a near-fatal automobile accident Henri Nouwen related how his accident had pushed him "closer to a communion with Jesus." He says: "From the beginning I have tried to stay faithful to the Word of God—not replace it with psychological knowledge." How aptly he states it: "We need affirmation of the self, but also the surrendering of the self. Today we try to claim our full humanity, but we are also called to allow God to transform that humanity." He poignantly observes: "Ministers have to be more radical than anyone in living a contemplative life–which means living a life in which we trust that the love we need will be given to us by God. This is essential to the prayer life."[2]

We all know this and confess the paltriness of our prayer lives. Not at all atypical is the finding that "Generally students' first response to the topic of prayer is to confess how little they pray. They know they ought to. They say they have a guilty conscience from neglecting prayer. They should be more committed, more disciplined and better organized in their prayer life. They ought to try harder (the 'pumping iron' approach to prayer)."[3] While the discipline of a basic regimen is important for all of us, the answer is more than increased self-effort.

Surely James Stewart was right in his driving thesis: "The heart of Paul's religion is union with Christ." Prayer is both the outworking of a personal relationship and the expression appropriate to intimacy with the Lord through the Holy Spirit. Just as the bird lives in the air and the fish lives in the water, the native and normal element for the believer is Christ. Paul exulted, "Life means Christ to me!" (a paraphrase of Philippians 1:21). As von Hugel expressed it: "The passion and hunger for God comes from God, and God answers it with Christ."

In a beautiful little book on prayer, John Guest makes the following suggestion (very much in line with several continuing emphases in this study): "Without the use of the imagination in prayer, there can be little communication that is meaningful—at least to us. The imagination is our ability to create representations of reality—to see things in our mind's eye."[4] It helps to see ourselves at the foot of the cross, or before the throne with our great High Priest's faithful and fervent intercession. We are aided by picturing the persons for whom we pray in their homes or the hospital or nursing home or whatever.

Learning how to engage the text involves us in a spiritual process in which we "watch [our] life and doctrine closely" (1 Tim. 4:16). The hardest sermon to preach is the sermon to ourselves. But if the Lord hasn't been able to ignite and inflame our own spirit with the truth of the Word, how shall we effectively touch others with it. "But what I have I give you" (Acts 3:6a) is the key principle here. Someone has said, "I would rather feel contrition than be skillful in the communication thereof," but we must ask: can anyone who is not contrite really communicate contrition? Shakespeare raised serious question about "those who, moving others, are themselves as stone, unmoved, cold and to temptation slow."

In other words, how can we truly preach the crucified Christ without being possessed by a crucified spirit? The preacher, the man or woman of God, is described by John Bunyan as having "his back to the world, his face toward Heaven, and a Book in his hand." This is spiritual readiness.

SPIRITUAL RIGOR

He wills that I should holy be. (Charles Wesley)

O God, give us some saints. (Lacordaire)

Yes, Father. Yes and always yes. (Francis de Sales)

We Christians will know the truth and the truth will make us odd. (Flannery O'Connor)

I beseech you to seek the Kingdom of God first or not at all. (Henry Drummond)

In reviewing a recent piece of fiction, a commentator locks in on the major obstacle: "The major problem is the unattractive narrator." The narrator is not only unengaging but confounding and confusing. Is this not frequently a serious drawback in preaching? We have stood here with James W. Clarke: "while the preaching of the Word is not the minister's exclusive task, it is his supreme one. It is the central saving activity in history, of God's communication to the world."[5] Jean Balard, a member of the Little Council of Geneva, was asked by William Farel in 1536 why he refused to go hear the sermon as was required by law. He replied that he was willing to listen to the Word of God, but not to those preachers!

If our concern in preaching resembles Paul's desire to "come in the full measure of the blessing of Christ" (Rom. 15:29), then we must pray it down and seek to live it out. Jesus was clear: "Let your light shine before men, that they may see your good deeds and praise your Father in heaven" (Matt. 5:16). Fenelon described Brother Lawrence in terms that give us hope: "gross by nature—delicate by grace."

We cannot separate our speaking from our being. G. K. Chesterton was right on target: "Nothing sublimely artistic has ever risen out of mere art. . . . There must always be a rich moral soil for any great aesthetic growth." There is no substitute for the personal sense of the reality and presence and glory of the Lord in the life of the preacher. MacCheyne confessed: "what my people need more than anything from me is my own personal holiness."

H. G. Wells used to tell the story of an archbishop who one evening felt a strange disquietude. He went to his private chapel to pray, as was his custom. As he knelt before the altar and folded his hands, he began to pray, "Oh, God," and from the altar there came back a voice saying, "Yes, what is it?"' It is related that they found the archbishop the next morning sprawled before the altar obviously having died of shock! Do we expect God to respond and to act?

John Wesley insightfully observed that few Christian organizations enter the third generation with their truths intact. Our tendency is to backslide and slip into dull habit and perfunctory performance. Thus we are capable of deflecting and distorting the message we aim to present. Of one communicator it was reported: "she was too self-absorbed to make her story real or dramatic." A biographer of Michelangelo tells us that one of the problems with which he had to deal was to keep his own shadow off the statue on which he was working. "He found that in the most intricate work he was handicapped by his own shadow. So he devised a candleholder like a miner lamp to use on his forehead. Thus he eliminated the shadow of himself and was able to work in full illumination."⁶ Of course, it is neither possible or desirable to extricate ourselves from the preaching process or product; but we must be concerned about getting in the way of what the living Christ wishes to do.

This explains why preparation for ministry must include concern not only for professional competency but, even more, a concern for a quality of spiritual living. This is why the redoubtable champion of orthodoxy in old Princeton, B. B. Warfield, argued in a memorable article that a theological seminary needs to be a nursery of piety as well as an academy of learning.

Warfield's burdened thesis was that "we need scholar-saints to become our preachers, our missionaries and our teachers."⁷ We need character as well as comprehension. The army recruiter looks for prospective soldiers who have two legs; similarly, the servants of God must balance and hold equally dear truth and its personal and practical application (cf. Mal. 2:1-9). Warfield held that ten minutes on our knees will give more operative knowledge of God than ten hours over our books. One seminarian lamented, "I went to become a saint, I became a technocrat." This is tragic, but it happens.

The glorious but sobering fact is, as Augustine expressed it, "God wants to give us good things, but our hands are always full of other things." Augustine spoke of his own earlier days as a mere rhetorician as days (brilliant as they were) of "so much smoke and wind." Can we rise above what John Kenneth Galbraith calls "the culture of contentment" to seek after God? If the Holy Spirit is indeed the taste and the promise of what is to come, do we want, as one writer has expressed it, "the Spirit to be like airline coffee, weak but reliable and administered in small quantities? Or do we want the Spirit to be a can of soda, bubbly and ubiquitous, and capable of easy ownership?" Or do we rather truly desire the fullness of His power and presence?

Are we determined to bridge "the ethics gap" so prevalent in the North American church? There was no genuine communication between Edgar Bergen and Charlie McCarthy. This cannot be our relationship to the God we represent. Religious activity can be an anesthetic to the empty life. We can seek to escape from God in the service of God. Allusion to God will not suffice. That alone would mean that the cupboard is bare. What is needed is the assertion and affirmation of God out of lives that are possessed by Him and obsessed with Him.

There is no easy or quick way to avoid the problem cited above. In an age that gobbles up opportunities for university doctoral degrees without attending classes, we have to break ranks with the passive throng if we are to truly know God and keep His commandments.

SPIRITUAL RESOLVE

> Love and unity . . . are not possible without fundamental repentance and sincere spiritual rebirth, both personally and corporately. For truly we are to blame for everything. (Father Zosima, in Dostoyevsky's *The Brothers Karamazov*)

"I have not hesitated to preach anything that would be helpful to you. . . . I have declared to both Jews and Greeks that
they must turn to God in repentance and have faith in our
Lord Jesus. . . . I have not hesitated to proclaim to you the
whole will of God." (Acts 20:20-21, 27)

The turmoil and tensions of our times test the resolve of the
Christian communicator. Many Siren voices would lure us away
from fidelity to the Scriptures and their message. Merton Rice, the
able Methodist preacher in Detroit during the last generation, had
a motto engraved in stone that stood as a constant reminder:
"Preach the Word." Every ten days he sent a telegram to his
preacher son that simply read: "Preach the Word." This needs to
be our determined resolve. We must not sidetracked on any
account.

In the drift and decomposition of North American culture, the
biblical preacher feels increasingly countercultural; but this is in
the interest of changing culture. Educational activists using the
language of postmodernism urge students to use their own lives
as texts in order to explore their own politically correct bound-
aries. The Christian communicator must hold our generation's
feet to the fire, As E. Michael Jones argues, "In the intellectual life,
there are only two ultimate alternatives: either the thinker conforms desire to truth or he conforms truth to desire."[8]

But it is increasingly lonely on the ramparts of a society that
is hell-bent on self-gratification with no thought at all for God's
glorification. How disconcerting it is to realize that the United
States has the highest rate of teen pregnancy in the world, with a
third of them ending in abortion. Ours is what Henry Adams
described as "an age festooned with ego," an age in which the
human self brooks no constraint. The biblical view of homosexuality is more and more laughed and mocked out of court.
Minnesota State University advises students not to enter the field
of social work "if they have negative thoughts about homosexuality," especially if they are from "strong religious backgrounds."
Students will not be tolerated "if they view homosexuals as per-
verse or sinners." It is not okay in this case, we are told, to "love
the sinner but hate the sin."[9]

The prevailing mood in many quarters is to adjust and accommodate the message to the latest fad and whim. One well-known

evangelical professor twists himself into a veritable pretzel to fit the latest psychological paradigms. He says: "If our sin is viewed as causing the death of Jesus on the cross, then we ourselves become victims of 'a psychological battering' produced by the cross. When I am led to feel that the pain and torment of Jesus' death on the cross is due to my sin, I inflict upon myself spiritual and psychological torment." What else is conviction for sin? Is true guilt an aberration?

Issues like these and the high media saturation of our times confront the Christian communicator with an unavoidable decision: what shall we preach? Shall we give good advice on better living and spend our pulpit time lamenting U.S. foreign policy? Shall we allow the Church to be transmuted into what Clinebell calls "a smorgasbord of small groups, workshops, classes and retreats designed to meet the needs for nurture and growth support for individuals and families"? We need to focus clearly in this regard on the principle Larry Crabb articulates so well when he says: "Fellowships that attend more to relationships than to the truth upon which relationships can be built run serious risks."

At this point I agree with Stanley Hauerwas that we really need the "telling of a counter-story," centered on Jesus Christ, "a story that exposes the liberal fiction of national communities that transcend cultural differences."[10] Spurgeon in his day saw the grave danger of trying to entertain and please people in order to win them to Christ. "From speaking out as the Puritans did," he observed, "the Church has gradually toned down her testimony, then winked at and excused the frivolities of the day. Then she tolerated them in her borders. Now she has adopted them under the plea of reaching the masses."

We have more and more "911 Christians," who see God as existing to enhance their own desires. One cartoonist has spoken of "the lite church, with fewer commitments, home of the 7.5 percent tithe, 15-minute sermons, 40-minute worship services. We have only 8 commandments—your choice. We use just 3 spiritual laws and have an 800 year millennium. Everything you've wanted in a church . . . and less!"[11]

King Saul capitulated because, as he put it, "I was afraid of the people and so I gave in to them" (1 Sam. 15:24). George Eliot's character Lydgate in *Middlemarch* caves in to the constant pressure of compromise and conformity. Will we as preachers crumble also and become part of the crowd careening toward total spiritual inertia? What makes the topics under discussion in this study socially critical is the hope expressed by Mark Ellingsen, formerly of the Institute for Ecumenical Research in Strasbourg and a writer whom we have met previously in these pages, that narrative a la Hans Frei and canonical hermeneutics a la Brevard Childs would "bridge the Evangelical-Ecumenical gap" and replace the "old model of biblical inerrancy."[12]

The practical issue for the Bible preacher is constantly whether we should trim and shave and hedge and sidestep what Scripture clearly means and intends to teach. Walter Brueggemann calls us to "daring speech" in our proclamation. "There are many pressures to quiet the text, to silence this deposit of dangerous speech."[13] While I would argue that God's truth comes in both prose and poetry in Scripture, there is something powerful in the story. The risks are worth it and shall be amply rewarded. *Tell it like it is!*

SPIRITUAL RESILIENCE

The stuff that comes easily is dull reading. (Joseph Conrad)

What I live by, I impart. (Augustine)

Boredom is an unappreciated force in human history. (Robert Nisbet)

He sends his command to the earth, his word runs swiftly. (Ps. 147:15)

But as for you, continue in what you have learned and have become convinced of, because you know those from whom you learned it, and how from infancy you have known the holy Scriptures, which are able to make you wise for salvation through faith in Christ Jesus. (2 Tim. 3:14-15)

Undeniably the Apostle Paul communicated in order to be understood. As he wrote to one group of Christians, "For we do not write you anything you cannot read or understand" (2 Cor. 1:13). But it is frequently tough going, as he indicates: "Come back to your senses as you ought, and stop sinning; for there are some who are ignorant of God—I say this to your shame" (1 Cor.

15:34) . In the light of this, one of the paramount qualities needed in the preacher is patient persistence, the resiliency to bounce back from rebuff and repudiation, a divinely given vision of the goal.

Using a stroke-and-sting strategy, the pastorally sensitive preacher must face realistically the spiritual battle for attention. St. Anesthesia is our foe—the desensitization caused by the media blitz and the overstimulation of our time. Couch potatoes will become pew potatoes. The entertainment industry is shaping the worship situation in many of our churches. We send children and youth off to closely age-graded alternatives during the preaching and foster an unwillingness to listen to anything that is not exactly targeted. There can never be great preaching if there is not great listening.

Aaron Copeland spoke of "talented listening." I believe that good preaching rises out of good listening. In this the preacher needs to be a model, and unfortunately many of us preachers are notoriously bad listeners. Sometimes it seems the preacher is shooting blanks; there is no real contact. Technical virtuosity will not do it. Blindfolded prophets cannot lead. Our concern is to bring a congregation to the listening point. This calls for respect and stillness that allow us to hear.

In a thoughtful proposal Lloyd Steffen observes: "Listening is a moral act . . . an act of attending to the other that discloses the strangeness of otherness, disrupting our comfortable self-images and threatening to undo our everyday experience of ourselves (and others) as familiar and basically unified personalities."[14] But this is a process, and we make steps forward and then slip backwards. Our concern is that of Jesus: "Ephphatha. . . . Be opened!"

But will we stay with it? Will we persevere? The spiritual quality of stick-to-it-iveness is not easy to sustain. When we are turned down, will we turn tail? When the critics rant and the carpers ridicule, do we look for the exit? When there seems to be no flicker of response, are we tempted to toss in the towel? When misunderstood and maligned, do we write our resignation?

In 1889 an editor informed Rudyard Kipling, "I'm sorry, Mr. Kipling, but you just don't know how to use the English language" and refused his manuscript. George Orwell's magnificent spoof on the collectivisms of our time (*Animal Farm*) was rejected in 1945 with the words: "it is impossible to sell animal stories in the U.S.A." And a publisher turned down *The Diary of Anne*

Frank with the canard, "The girl doesn't, it seems to me, have a special perception or feeling which would lift that book above the 'curiosity' level." William Butler Yeats's early poems were turned down as "absolutely empty and void . . . absolute nullity. . . . I would not read a page of it again for worlds" (and they became world-famous). Irving Stone's *Lust for Life* about Vincent Van Gogh was first characterized as "a long, dull novel about an artist."[15] What if any of these writers had pulled back and ceased and desisted? How much does it take to turn *us* back?

Illustrating the principle Paul enunciates in 2 Corinthians 6:9—"always 'going through it' yet never 'going under'" (*Phillips*)—is Abraham Lincoln's path to the presidency:

> Failed in business in 1831.
> Defeated for the legislature in 1832.
> Second failure in business in 1833.
> Suffered nervous breakdown in 1836.
> Defeated for Speaker in 1838.
> Defeated for Elector in 1840.
> Defeated for Congress in 1843.
> Defeated for Congress in 1848.
> Defeated for Senate in 1855.
> Defeated for Vice President in 1856.
> Defeated for Senate in 1858.
> Elected President of the United States in 1860.[16]

The journeys of Disraeli and Winston Churchill were similar. Worthwhile accomplishment is not necessarily an instant phenomenon. If we are truly heliotropic, like plants turning toward the source of life, we shall continue on and reach the goal (Heb. 12:1ff.).

In William Manchester's classic treatment of Winston Churchill, he quotes from an unpublished essay of the young Churchill entitled "The Scaffold of Rhetoric," written when he was a twenty-three-year old cavalry officer in India. Says Manchester: "The key to a speaker's impact on his audience, he believes, is sincerity. Before he can inspire them with any emotion he must be swayed by it himself. . . . Before he can move their tears, his own must flow. To convince them he must believe." If he has grasped all these, young Winston had written, his is the the most precious of gifts: "He who enjoys it wields a power more durable than that of a great king. He is an independent force in the world. Abandoned by his party, betrayed by his friends, stripped of his offices, whoever can command this power is still formidable."[17]

To us Jesus has said: "I will be with you always, to the very end of the age."

Notes

INTRODUCTION

1. Robert Alter, *The Art of Biblical Narrative* (New York: Basic Books, 1981), p. 63.
2. Eugene L. Lowry, *The Homiletical Plot* (Atlanta: John Knox, 1980), p. 25.

CHAPTER ONE: *Assessing the Remarkable Renaissance of Interest in Narrative*

1. John Harrell, *Origins and Early Traditions of Storytelling* (Kensington, Calif.: York House, 1983), p. 19.
2. Ulrich Simon, *Story and Faith in the Biblical Narrative* (London: SPCK, 1975).
3. Anne Pellowski, *The World of Storytelling* (New York: R.R. Bowker, 1977), p. 19. Another redoubtable classic is Marie L. Shedlock, *The Art of the Story-teller* (New York: Dover, 1915, 1936, 1951).
4. Roger C. Shank, *Tell Me a Story: A New Look at Real and Artificial Intelligence* (New York: Charles Scribner's, 1990), p. 1.
5. Stephen Crites, "The Narrative Quality of Existence," in Stanley Hauerwas and L. Gregory Jones, eds., *Why Narrative? Readings in Narrative Theology* (Grand Rapids, Mich.: Eerdmans, 1989), p. 66ff.
6. Wesley A. Kort, *Story, Text and Scripture. Literary Interests in Biblical Narrative* (University Park, Penn.: Penn State Press, 1988), pp. 9, 12, 120, 145ff.
7. William J. Bausch, *Storytelling: Imagination and Faith* (Mystic, Conn.: Twenty-third Publications, 1984), p. 171.
8. Neil Postman, *Amusing Ourselves to Death: Public Discourse in the Age of Show Business* (New York: Viking Penguin, 1985), p. 19.
9. Marshall McLuhan and Bruce R. Powers, *The Global Village: Transformations in World Life and Media in the 21st Century* (London: Oxford University Press, 1978), as quoted in *Insight*, August 7, 1989, p. 62.
10. Jeremiah Creedon, "The Storytelling Renaissance," *Utney Reader*, March/April 1991, p. 46ff.
11. William Ecenbarger, "Mything in Action: How Fables, Legends and Tales Provide Us with Insights into Life's Mysteries," *Chicago Tribune Magazine*, July 5, 1992, p. 20ff.
12. James Limburg, *Old Stories for a New Time* (Atlanta: John Knox, 1983), p. 7.
13. Thomas E. Boomershine, *Story Journey: An Invitation to the Gospel as Storytelling* (Nashville: Abingdon, 1988), p. 10.
14. Thomas Fleming, "I Love to Tell the Story," *Chronicles of Culture*, August 1992, pp. 12-15.

15. Etienne Gilson, *Reason and Revelation in the Middle Ages* (New York: Charles Scribner's, 1938), pp. 3-33.
16. Crane Brinton, *The Shaping of the Modern Mind* (New York: Mentor, 1953), especially Chapter 7, "The Twentieth Century: The Anti-intellectual Attack," pp. 213-241.
17. Nicholas Ridderbos, "Reversals of Old Testament Criticism," and M. C. Tenney, "Reversals of New Testament Criticism," in ed. Carl F. H. Henry, *Revelation and the Bible* (Grand Rapids, Mich.: Baker, 1958), pp. 335-367.
18. James Barr, *Old and New in Interpretation* (New York: Harper, 1966), p. 18.
19. Garrett Green, *Imagining God: Theology and the Religious Imagination* (New York: Harper, 1989), p. 135.
20. Scot McKnight, *Interpreting the Synoptic Gospels* (Grand Rapids, Mich.: Baker, 1988), p. 123.
21. D. A. Carson, "Recent Developments in the Doctrine of Scripture," in eds. D. A. Carson and John D. Woodbridge, *Hermeneutics, Authority and Canon* (Grand Rapids, Mich.: Zondervan, 1986), p. 32.
22. Robert Roth, *Story and Reality* (Grand Rapids, Mich.: Eerdmans, 1973), p. 20ff.
23. Ronald F. Thiemann, *Revelation and Theology: The Gospel as Narrated Promise* (South Bend, Ind.: University of Notre Dame Press, 1985), p. 1ff.; David H. Kelsey, *The Use of Scripture in Recent Theology* (Philadelphia: Fortress, 1975), pp. 39ff., 172.
24. Peter W. Macky, "The Coming Revolution: The New Literary Approach to New Testament Interpretation," in ed. Donald K. Kim, *A Guide to Contemporary Hermeneutics: Major Trends in Biblical Interpretation* (Grand Rapids, Mich.: Eerdmans, 1986), p. 263.
25. *Ibid.*, p. 267.
26. Jack R. Lundbom, *Jeremiah: A Study in Ancient Hebrew Rhetoric* (Missoula, Mont.: SBL and Scholar's Press, 1975).
27. Francis A. Schaeffer, *Escape from Reason* (Downers Grove, Ill.: InterVarsity Press, 1968).
28. Kevin Vanhoozer, "The Semantics of Biblical Literature," in eds. Carson and Woodbridge, *Hermeneutics, Authority and Canon*, p. 78.
29. Hans W. Frei, *The Eclipse of Biblical Narrative* (New Haven, Conn.: Yale University Press, 1974).
30. Meir Sternberg, *The Poetics of Biblical Narrative* (Bloomington, Ind.: Indiana University Press, 1985), p. 82.
31. Alister E. McGrath, "The Biography of God," *Christianity Today*, July 22, 1991, p. 24.
32. Michael Greenberg, *Theology and Narrative* (Nashville: Abingdon, 1981), p. 185ff.
33. Carl F. H. Henry, "Narrative Theology: An Evangelical Appraisal," *Trinity Journal*, Spring 1987, p. 7 (with a rejoinder by Hans Frei).
34. Hans W. Frei, *The Identity of Jesus Christ: The Hermeneutical Bases of Dogmatic Theology* (Philadelphia: Fortress, 1975), p. 143.
35. *Ibid.*, p. 157.
36. *Ibid.*, p. 165.
37. George A. Lindbeck, *The Nature of Doctrine: Religion and Theology in a Post-Liberal Age* (Philadelphia: Westminster, 1984), p. 121.
38. Northrop Frye, *The Great Code: The Bible and Literature* (New York: Harcourt Brace Jovanovich, 1982), p. xviii.

39. Neil Postman, *Technopoly: The Surrender of Culture to Technology* (New York: Knopf, 1992), pp. 80, 83, 172. A most arresting fictional treatment of this theme is A. N. Wilson's *Daughters of Albion* (New York: Viking Penguin, 1991), p. 191ff.

40. Mark Ellingsen, *The Integrity of Biblical Narrative: Story in Theology and Proclamation* (Minneapolis: Fortress, 1990), p. 7.

41. Richard Lischer, "The Limits of Story," *Interpretation*, 38 (January 1984), p. 33.

42. Kort, *Story, Text and Scripture*, p. xi, 1.

43. Hans Kung, in ed. Don M. Wardlaw, *Preaching Biblically: Creating Sermons in the Shape of Scripture* (Philadelphia: Westminster, 1983), p. 105.

44. Thiemann, *Revelation and Theology*, p. 32. Significant statements from an evangelical viewpoint are to be found in Edward John Carnell, *An Introduction to Christian Apologetics* (Grand Rapids, Mich.: Eerdmans, 1948, p. 161ff.); Herbert Schlossberg and Marvin Olasky, *Turning Point: A Christian World View Declaration* (Wheaton, Ill.: Crossway Books, 1987), especially Chapter 6 on "A Biblical Understanding of Reason"; Gordon H. Clark, *Language and Theology* (Phillipsburg, N.J.: Presbyterian and Reformed, 1980); Gordon H. Clark, *Logic* (Jefferson, Md.: Trinity Foundation, 1985); ed. Paul Helm, *Objective Knowledge: A Christian Perspective* (Downers Grove, Ill.: InterVarsity Press, 1987); Carl F. H. Henry, *God, Revelation and Authority*, in six volumes (Waco, Tex.: Word, 1976), especially Volume I, which deals with myth and faith and logic; James Oliver Buswell, Jr., *A Christian View of Being and Knowing* (Grand Rapids, Mich.: Zondervan, 1960).

45. Gustaf Wingren, *Theology in Conflict* (Philadelphia: Muhlenberg, 1958), p. 163.

46. Quoted in Thiemann, *Revelation and Theology*.

47. Emile Cailliet, "The Book That Understands Me," *Christianity Today*, November 22, 1963, pp. 10-11.

48. Quoted in Frei, *The Identity of Jesus Christ*, p. 171.

49. Terrence W. Tilley, *Story Theology* (Wilmington, Del.: Michael Glazier, 1985), p. 212.

50. Scott Donaldson,, "The Fictions of Stephen Crane," *Chicago Tribune Books*, September 13, 1992, p. 1.

51. Vanhoozer, "The Semantics of Biblical Literature," p. 77.

52. A. N. Wilson, *C. S. Lewis: A Biography* (New York: Fawcett Columbine, 1990), p. 133.

53. Neil Postman, *Amusing Ourselves to Death*, p. 78.

54. Fred B. Craddock, in ed. Richard Lischer, *Theories of Preaching* (Durham, N.C.: Labyrinth Press, 1987), p. 257.

55. Wardlaw, *Preaching Biblically*, p. 13.

56. Daniel Patte, *What Is Structural Exegesis?* (Philadelphia: Fortress, 1976), p. 21.

57. Walter Brueggemann, *Finally Comes the Poet: Daring Speech for Proclamation* (Minneapolis: Fortress, 1989).

58. David N. Moisser, "Narrative Preaching and the Congregation's Story," *The Christian Ministry*, January-February 1991, pp. 8-10.

59. Peter M. Morgan, *Story Weaving: Using Stories to Transform Your Congregation* (St. Louis: CBP Press, 1986).

CHAPTER TWO: *Analyzing the Rich Treasury of Biblical Narrative*
1. For a most insightful set of observations about the inevitability of a kind of circularity in paradigm argumentation, cf. Nigel M. de S. Cameron, *The New Medicine: Life and Death After Hippocrates* (Wheaton, Ill.: Crossway Books, 1991), pp. 160, 169.
2. John W. Wenham, *Christ and the Bible* (Downers Grove, Ill.: InterVarsity Press, 1972); Kenneth Kantzer, "Christ and the Scriptures," *His* reprints, 1966.
3. Edward J. Young, *Thy Word Is Truth* (Grand Rapids, Mich.: Eerdmans, 1957), pp. 31, 49.
4. B. B. Warfield, *The Inspiration and Authority of the Bible* (Philadelphia: Presbyterian and Reformed, 1948), p. 112. For the most thorough exposition of this view, cf. Carl F. H. Henry's six volumes on *God, Revelation and Authority*. A splendid recent articulation of this view of Scripture is to be found in Gordon Lewis and Bruce Demarest, *Integrative Theology* (Grand Rapids, Mich.: Zondervan, 1987), Volume I, pp. 61-171.
5. Adele Berlin, *Poetics and the Interpretation of Biblical Narrative* (Sheffield, England: Almond, 1983), p. 116ff.
6. Gerhard Maier, *The End of the Historical-Critical Method* (St. Louis: Concordia, 1977).
7. Walter Harrelson, *Interpreting the Old Testament* (New York: Holt, Rinehart and Winston, 1964), pp. 63, 80, 205, 318, 408.
8. Garrett Green, ed., *Scriptural Authority and Narrative Interpretation* (Philadelphia: Fortress, 1987), p. 50.
9. *Ibid.*, p. 55.
10. Leland Ryken, *Words of Delight: A Literary Introduction to the Bible* (Grand Rapids, Mich.: Baker, 1987), p. 43.
11. John H. Sailhamer, *The Pentateuch as Narrative* (Grand Rapids, Mich.: Zondervan, 1992), p. 12ff.; cf. John H. Sailhamer, "The Canonical Approach to the OT: Its Effect on Understanding Prophecy," *JETS*, 30/3, September 1987, p. 308.
12. Meir Sternberg, *The Poetics of Biblical Narrative* (Bloomington, Ind.: Indiana University Press, 1985), pp. 41-42.
13. G. B. Caird, *The Language and Imagery of the Bible* (Philadelphia: Westminster, 1980). Note also G. Campbell Morgan, *The Parables and Metaphors of Our Lord* (New York: Revell, 1948).
14. Robert Alter, *The Art of Biblical Narrative* (New York: Basic Books, 1981), p. 63.
15. Eugene L. Lowry, *The Homiletical Plot: The Sermon as Narrative Art Form* (Atlanta: John Knox, 1980), p. 25.
16. Richard G. Moulton, *The Literary Study of the Bible* (London: Isbister and Co., 1896).
17. *Ibid.*, p. 199.
18. Robert Alter and Frank Kermode, eds., *The Literary Guide to the Bible* (Cambridge, Mass.: Belknap/Harvard, 1987).
19. Ryken, *Words of Delight*.
20. Walter C. Kaiser, Jr. *Toward an Exegetical Theology: Biblical Exegesis for Preaching and Teaching* (Grand Rapids, Mich.: Baker, 1981).
21. Elizabeth Achtemeier, *Preaching from the Old Testament* (Louisville: Westminster/John Knox, 1989).
22. *Ibid.*, p. 71.

23. Thomas C. Long, *Preaching and the Literary Forms of the Bible* (Philadelphia: Fortress, 1989).
24. Thomas G. Long, "The Use of Scripture in Contemporary Preaching," *Interpretation*, October 1990, p. 341ff.
25. David Buttrick, *Homiletic: Moves and Structures* (Philadelphia: Fortress, 1987), p. 376.
26. Sidney Greidanus, *The Modern Preacher and the Ancient Text: Interpreting and Preaching Biblical Literature* (Grand Rapids, Mich.: Eerdmans, 1988), p. 17.
27. *Ibid.*, p. 16.
28. David L. Larsen, book review of Sidney Greidanus, *The Modern Preacher and the Biblical Text*, *Trinity Journal*, Autumn 1990, pp. 237-239.
29. Christopher R. Seitz, "The Changing Face of Old Testament Studies," *Christian Century*, October 21, 1992, p. 933.
30. J. Vernon McGee, *Ruth: The Romance of Redemption* (Wheaton, Ill.: Van Kampen, 1943), p. 7.
31. Henry M. Morris, *The Genesis Record: A Scientific and Devotional Commentary on the Book of Beginnings* (Grand Rapids, Mich.: Baker, 1976).
32. R. Laird Harris, *Modern Science and Christian Faith*, by members of the American Scientific Affiliation (Wheaton, Ill.: Van Kampen, 1948), p. 251; Erich Sauer, *From Eternity to Eternity* (Grand Rapids, Mich.: Eerdmans, 1954), p. 106.
33. John H. Sailhamer, "The Pentateuch as Narrative," in *Modern Science and Christian Faith*, p. 16. His commentary on 1 and 2 Chronicles is published by Moody Press (1983).
34. Alfred Edersheim, *Bible History*, Volume II (Grand Rapids, Mich.: Eerdmans, 1962), p. 58ff.
35. George A. F. Knight, *Theology as Narrative: A Commentary on the Book of Exodus* (Grand Rapids, Mich.: Eerdmans, 1976).
36. C. J. Goslinga, *Joshua, Judges, Ruth: Bible Student's Commentary* (Grand Rapids, Mich.: Regency/Zondervan, 1986).
37. Leland Ryken, "'And It Came to Pass': The Bible as God's Storybook," *Bibliotheca Sacra*, April-June 1990, p. 131.
38. Jacob Licht, *Storytelling in the Bible* (Jerusalem: Magnes Press/Hebrew University, 1978), p. 9.
39. Elouise Renich Fraser, "Symbolic Acts of the Prophets," *Studia Biblica et Theologica*, October 1974, pp. 45-53.
40. John Guest, *Jeremiah, Lamentations*, in *The Communicator's Commentary* (Waco, Tex.: Word, 1988).
41. John Bright, *The Authority of the Old Testament* (Nashville: Abingdon, 1967), p. 112.
42. David L. Larsen, *The Anatomy of Preaching* (Grand Rapids, Mich.: Baker, 1989), p. 157ff.
43. Walter Brueggemann, "The Terrible Ungluing," *Christian Century*, October 21, 1992, p. 931.
44. J. Arthur Baird, *Audience Criticism and the Historical Jesus* (Philadelphia: Westminster, 1969).
45. Kenneth Kantzer, "Redaction Criticism: Handle With Care," *Christianity Today's Institute*, and "Redaction Criticism: Is It Worth the Risk?" *Christianity Today*, October 18, 1985, p. 11-I.
46. Randel Helms, *Gospel Fictions* (Buffalo, N.Y.: Prometheus Books, 1990).

Greidanus insightfully analyzes the "shift from the historical to the literary dimension of the biblical texts," *ibid.*, p. 49ff.

47. D. A. Carson, book review, *Trinity Journal*, Autumn 1983, pp. 124-125.
48. William P. Sampson, *Meeting Jesus* (San Francisco: Harper, 1991), p. 163.
49. D. A. Carson, "Matthew," *Expositor's Bible Commentary* (Grand Rapids, Mich.: Regency/Zondervan, 1984), p. 38.
50. Lewis and Bruce, *Integrative Theology*, p. 111.
51. Mjchael Green, *Matthew for Today* (London: Word, 1988).
52. Walter L. Liefeld, *New Testament Exposition* (Grand Rapids, Mich.: Zondervan, 1984), p. 57ff.
53. Michael Hilton and Gordian Marshall, *The Gospels and Rabbinic Judaism* (Hoboken, N.J.: Ktav, 1988).
54. Burton L. Mack and Vernon K. Robbins, *Patterns of Persuasion in the Gospels* (Sonoma, Calif.: Polebridge Press, 1989).
55. John Paul Heil, *The Death and Resurrection of Jesus: A Narrative-Critical Reading of Matthew 26–28* (Minneapolis: Fortress, 1991).
56. Werner H. Kelber, *Mark's Story of Jesus* (Philadelphia: Fortress, 1979).
57. Robert H. Gundry, *Mark: A Commentary on His Apology for the Cross* (Grand Rapids, Mich.: Eerdmans, 1992).
58. For a very choice classic, cf. Doremus A. Hayes, *The Most Beautiful Book Ever Written: The Gospel According to Luke* (New York: Methodist Book Concern, 1913).
59. O. C. Edwards, Jr., *Luke's Story of Jesus* (Philadelphia: Fortress, 1981).
60. Robert C. Tannehill, *The Narrative Unity of Luke-Acts: A Literary Interpretation*, Volume I, *Luke* (Philadelphia: Fortress, 1986).
61. David P. Moessner, *Lord of the Banquet: The Literary and Theological Significance of the Lukan Travel Narrative* (Minneapolis: Fortress, 1989). Note also Hobert K. Farrell, "The Structure and Theology of Luke's Central Section," *Trinity Journal*, Fall 1986, pp. 33-54.
62. R. Alan Culpepper, *Anatomy of the Fourth Gospel: A Study in Literary Design* (Philadelphia: Fortress, 1983).
63. D. A. Carson, *The Gospel According to John* (Grand Rapids, Mich.: Eerdmans, 1991).

CHAPTER THREE: *Advancing Excellence in Expounding Biblical Narrative*

1. Clyde E. Fant, *Preaching for Today* (New York: Harper, 1975), p. 7.
2. David L. Larsen, *The Anatomy of Preaching* (Grand Rapids, Mich.: Baker, 1989), p. 30ff.
3. Charles L. Bartow, *Effective Speech Communication in Leading Worship* (Nashville: Abingdon, 1988), p. 86.
4. Charlotte I. Lee and Timothy Gura, *Oral Interpretation* (Boston: Houghton Mifflin, 1991), p. 3.
5. Thomas Edward McComiskey, *Reading Scripture in Public: A Guide for Preachers and Lay Readers* (Grand Rapids, Mich.: Baker, 1991).
6. Olive Beaupre Miller, ed., *My Book House*, in 12 volumes (Lake Bluff, Ill.: The Book House for Children Publishers, 1958, 1963).
7. Bruno Bettelheim, *The Uses of Enchantment: The Meaning and Importance of Fairy Tales* (New York: Alfred A. Knopf, 1976).
8. Charles H. Spurgeon, *John Ploughman's Talk or Plain Advice for Plain People* (Philadelphia: Henry Altemus, n.d.).
9. Jeanette Perkins Brown, *The Story-teller in Religious Education* (Boston: Pilgrim, 1951).

10. John Harrell, *Origins and Early Traditions of Storytelling* (Kensington, Calif.: York House, 1983).
11. Robin Moore, *Awakening the Hidden Storyteller: How to Build a Storytelling Tradition in Your Family* (Boston: Shambala, 1991).
12. Mary Terese Donze, *Touching a Child's Heart: An Innovative, Encouraging Guide to Becoming a Good Story-teller* (Notre Dame, Ind.: Ave Maria Press, 1985).
13. Ethel Barrett, *Story-telling—It's Easy* (Los Angeles: Cowman, 1960).
14. Anne Pellowski, *The World of Storytelling* (New York: R.R. Bowker, 1977), p. 47.
15. Reg Grant and John W. Reed, *Telling Stories That Touch the Heart* (Wheaton, Ill.: Victor, 1990), p. 23.
16. Harrell, *Origins and Early Traditions of Storytelling*, p. 63.
17. Marie L. Shedlock, *The Art of the Story-teller* (New York: Dover, 1951).
18. Tom Brokaw, in Doris O'Neil, ed., *Life in the Sixties* (New York: Time-Warner, 1989), p. xv.
19. Lyle Wesley Dorsett, *E. M. Bounds: Man of Prayer* (Grand Rapids, Mich.: Zondervan, 1991).
20 *Ibid.*, p. 113.
21. T. H. L. Parker, *Calvin's Preaching* (Louisville: Westminster/John Knox, 1992), pp. 37-38.
22. Douglas Stuart, *Old Testament Exegesis: A Primer for Students and Pastors* (Philadelphia: Westminster, 1980, 1984).
23. Walter L. Liefeld, *From Text to Sermon: New Testament Exposition* (Grand Rapids, Mich.: Zondervan, 1984).
24. Ronald A. Ward, *Hidden Meaning in the New Testament: New Light from the Old Greek* (Old Tappan, N.J.: Revell, 1969).
25. D. A. Carson, *Exegetical Fallacies* (Grand Rapids, Mich.: Baker, 1984).
26. E. K. Simpson, *Words Worth Weighing in the Greek New Testament* (London: Tyndale Press, 1945).
27. G. Ebeling, *Introduction to a Theological Theory of Language* (London: Collins, 1973).
28. Walter C. Kaiser, Jr., "Hermeneutics and the Theological Task," *Trinity Journal*, Spring 1991, pp. 3-14.
29. Larsen, *The Anatomy of Preaching*, pp. 67-71.
30. H. Grady Davis, *Design for Preaching* (Philadelphia: Fortress, 1958), p. 158.
31. Alton H. McEachern, *Dramatic Monologue Preaching* (Nashville: Broadman, 1984). Note also the spacious treatment by Harold Freeman, *Variety in Preaching* (Waco, Tex.: Word, 1987), p. 47ff.
32. James Rose, in Haddon W. Robinson, ed., *Biblical Sermons: How Twelve Preachers Apply the Principles of Biblical Preaching* (Grand Rapids, Mich.: Baker, 1989), p. 51ff.

CHAPTER FOUR: *Keying in on the Meaning for Narrative Preaching*

1. I am obliged to my colleague Dr. Thomas Nettles for these quotes, prominently displayed on his office door.
2. Robert Coles, *The Call of Stories* (Boston: Houghton Mifflin, 1989).
3. Thomas G. Long, "The Use of Scripture in Contemporary Preaching," *Interpretation*, October 1990, p. 341.
4. David Buttrick, *Homiletic* (Philadelphia: Fortress, 1987), p. 376.
5. Bruce Demarest and Gordon Lewis, *Integrative Theology* (Grand Rapids, Mich.: Zondervan, 1987), p. 161.

6. Clark H. Pinnock, *Set Forth Your Case* (Nutley, N.J.: Craig Press, 1968).
7. Clark H. Pinnock, *Biblical Revelation* (Chicago: Moody Press, 1971).
8. Clark H. Pinnock, *A Wideness in God's Mercy: The Finality of Jesus Christ in a World of Religions* (Grand Rapids, Mich.: Zondervan, 1992).
9. Clark H. Pinnock, *Tracking the Maze: Finding Our Way Through Modern Theology from an Evangelical Perspective* (San Francisco: Harper and Row, 1990), p. 47.
10. *Ibid.*, p. 70.
11. *Ibid.*, p. 68.
12. *Ibid.*, pp. 160-161.
13. *Ibid.*, p. 172.
14. *Ibid.*, p. 180.
15. *Ibid.*, p. 182.
16. *Ibid.*, p. 185.
17. Pinnock, *Biblical Revelation*, p. 226.
18. *Ibid.*, p. 208.
19. Don M. Wardlaw, ed., *Preaching Biblically: Creating Sermons in the Shape of Scripture* (Philadelphia: Westminster, 1983), p. 13.
20. Hans Frei, in Frank McConnell, ed., *The Bible and Narrative Tradition* (New York: Oxford, 1986), p. 43.
21. Garrett Green, *Imagining God: Theology and the Religious Imagination* (New York: Harper, 1989), p. 137.
22. Daniel Patte, *What Is Structural Exegesis?* (Philadelphia: Fortress, 1976), p. 21.
23. Anthony C. Thiselton, *The Two Horizons* (Grand Rapids, Mich.: Eerdmans, 1980), p. 355. A very solid and helpful new piece that treats the development of the new hermeneutic is Grant R. Osborne, *The Hermeneutical Spiral: A Comprehensive Introduction to Biblical Interpretation* (Downers Grove, Ill.: InterVarsity, 1991).
24. Dennis Nineham, *The Use and Abuse of the Bible* (London: SPCK, 1978), p. 211.
25. Joe Houston, "Objectivity and the Gospels," in Paul Helm, ed., *Objective Knowledge* (London: Intervarsity, 1987), p. 8ff.
26. William R. White, *Speaking in Stories* (Minneapolis: Augsburg, 1982), p. 20.
27. Fred B. Craddock, *Overhearing the Gospel* (Nashville: Abingdon, 1978); also note Paul Scott Wilson, *Imagination of the Heart: New Understandings in Preaching* (Nashville: Abingdon, 1988).
28. Charles L. Rice, *Interpretation and Imagination: The Preacher and Contemporary Literature* (Philadelphia: Fortress, 1970), p. 95.
29. Thiselton, *The Two Horizons*, p. 436.
30. Patrick Fairbairn, *An Exposition of Ezekiel* (Grand Rapids, Mich.: Zondervan, 1960), p. 132.
31. Walter C. Kaiser, Jr., *Toward an Exegetical Theology* (Grand Rapids, Mich.: Baker, 1981).
32. Frank Kermode, *The Genesis of Secrecy: On the Interpretation of Narrative* (Cambridge, Mass.: Harvard, 1979), p. 136.
33. Fairbairn, *An Exposition of Ezekiel*, p. 49.
34. G. R. Beasley-Murray, "Ezekiel," in *New Bible Commentary* (Grand Rapids, Mich.: Eerdmans, 1953), p. 649.
35. Ralph H. Alexander, "Ezekiel," in *ibid.*, p. 769.
36. Milton S. Terry, *Biblical Hermeneutics* (Grand Rapids, Mich.: Zondervan, n.d.).

37. Bernard Ramm, *Protestant Biblical Interpretation* (Grand Rapids, Mich.: Baker, 1970).
38. Osborne, *The Hermeneutical Spiral.*
39. Duncan S. Ferguson, *Biblical Hermeneutics: An Introduction* (Atlanta: John Knox, 1986).
40. Elliott E. Johnson, *Expository Hermeneutics: An Introduction* (Grand Rapids, Mich.: Zondervan, 1990). An important newer study of immense help her is: Richard L. Pratt, Jr., *He Gave Us Stories: The Bible Student's Guide to Interpreting Old Testament Narratives* (Phillipsburg, N.J.: P & R Publishing, 1990, 1993).
41. Alan M. Stibbs, *Understanding God's Word* (Chicago: InterVarsity, 1950), p. 17ff.
42. Osborne, *The Hermeneutical Spiral,* p. 154.
43. David L. Larsen, *The Anatomy of Preaching* (Grand Rapids, Mich.: Baker, 1989), p. 153.
44. John Sailhamer, in an unpublished paper for *Trinity 2000,* p. 10.
45. Donald Grey Barnhouse, *Genesis* (Grand Rapids, Mich.: Zondervan, 1970), p. 144ff.
46. Robert Alter, *The Art of Biblical Narrative* (New York: Basic Books, 1981), p. 6.
47. *Ibid.,* p. 109.
48. James Montgomery Boice, *The Minor Prophets,* Volume I (Grand Rapids, Mich.: Zondervan, 1983), p. 23ff, drawing upon Donald Grey Barnhouse, *Romans: God's Freedom* (Grand Rapids, Mich.: Eerdmans, 1961), p. 188ff.
49. Patrick Fairbairn, *The Typology of Scripture* (Grand Rapids, Mich.: Zondervan, n.d.).
50. James Strong, *The Tabernacle of Israel in the Desert* (Grand Rapids, Mich.: Baker, 1952). This work has marvelous plans, drawings, and descriptions.
51. Worthwhile volumes on the Tabernacle include J. H. Kurtz, *Sacrificial Worship in the Old Testament* (Edinburgh: T.& T. Clark, 1863), which is particularly rich on sacrifice; W. G. Moorehead, *The Tabernacle* (Grand Rapids, Mich.: Kregel, 1957); Charles W. Slemming, *Made According to Pattern* (Chicago: Moody, 1938); A. B. Simpson, *Christ in the Tabernacle* (New York: Christian Alliance Publishing House, 1896); I. M. Haldeman, *The Tabernacle, Priesthood and Offerings* (New York: Fleming H. Revell, 1925); Louis T. Talbot, *Christ in the Tabernacle* (Los Angeles: Church of the Open Door, 1942).

CHAPTER FIVE: *Constructing the Narrative Sermon*

1. Garry Wills, *Lincoln at Gettysburg* (New York: Simon and Schuster, 1992).
2. James M. Wall, "The Pictures Inside our Heads," *Christian Century,* March 18-25, 1992, p. 291.
3. "Century Marks," *Christian Century,* November 4, 1992, p. 989.
4. Lionel Crocker, *Harry Emerson Fosdick's Art of Preaching: An Anthology* (Springfield, Mass.: Charles C. Thomas, 1971).
5. George Tremblett, *Dylan Thomas: In the Mercy of His Means* (New York: St. Martin's, 1991), p. 15.
6. *Ibid.,* p. 19.
7. Henry H. Mitchell, *Celebration and Experience in Preaching* (Nashville: Abingdon, 1990); Gerald L. Davies, *I Got the Word in Me and I Can*

Sing It, You Know: A Study of the Performed African-American Sermon (Philadelphia: University of Pennsylvania, 1985).

8. Gardner C. Taylor, *How Shall They Preach* (Elgin, Ill.: Progressive Baptist Publishing House, 1977), The Yale Lectures for 1976.

9. Brad Hill, "Preaching the Word in the CEUM: Towards a Theology of Obedience," *Covenant Quarterly*, February 1987, pp. 37-44.

10. John S. McClure, *The Four Codes of Preaching: Rhetorical Strategies* (Minneapolis: Fortress, 1991). The incredible complexity of this presentation bears witness to the problems of constructing a homiletic on the semiotic theory of Roland Barthes or on Abraham Maslow's levels of human need or any other human theoretical base.

11. David L. Larsen, *The Anatomy of Preaching* (Grand Rapids, Mich.: Baker, 1989), pp. 60-71.

12. Stephen Kendrick, "On Spiritual Autobiography: An Interview with Frederick Buechner," *Christian Century*, October 14, 1992, p. 901. For a fascinating argument for mixing genres, cf. Robert C. Shanna, "A Contrarian View of Homiletics," *Preaching* Magazine, March-April 1994, pp. 35-36.

13. Quoted in James Wall, "The Religious Music Without the Words," *Christian Century*, April 15, 1992, p. 387.

14. Eugene L. Lowry, *The Homiletical Plot: The Sermon as Narrative Art Form* (Atlanta: John Knox, 1980), p. 87.

15. Fernand Braudel, *The Structures of Everyday Life*, Volume I (New York: Harper and Row, 1979).

16. Meir Sternberg, *The Poetics of Biblical Narrative* (Bloomington, Ind.: Indiana University Press, 1985), p. 190.

17. Gabriel Fackre, *The Christian Story*, Revised Edition (Grand Rapids, Mich.: Eerdmans, 1978, 1984). This is a multi-volume series in which Fackre seeks to develop a theological narratology in the canonical mode. Generally more conservative, the approach is synthetic, drawing on an unbelievable range of sources. It tends to be Barthian-tinged.

18. James Wall, "Getting Involved with the Details," *Christian Century*, April 24, 1991, p. 451.

19. David Rhodes and Donald Michie, *Mark's Story: An Introduction to the Narrative of a Gospel* (Philadelphia: Fortress, 1982), p. 36.

20. John A. Broadus, *On the Preparation and Delivery of Sermons*, Fourth Edition (San Francisco: Harper, 1898, 1979), p. 132ff.

21. Richard L. Eslinger, *A New Hearing: Living Options in Homiletical Method* (Nashville: Abingdon, 1987).

22. Jacob Licht, *Storytelling in the Bible* (Jerusalem: Magnes Press of the Hebrew University, 1978), p. 9.

23. *Ibid.*, p. 24ff.

24. J. Paul Tanner, "The Gideon Narrative as the Focal Point of Judges," *Bibliotheca Sacra*, April-June 1992, p. 160.

25. Esther McIlveen, "Gideon—A Hesitant Hero," *His*, October 1976, pp. 6-7.

26. Eugene H. Merrill, "The Book of Ruth: Narration and Shared Theme," *Bibliotheca Sacra*, April-June 1985, p. 130ff.; Reg Grant, "Literary Structure in the Book of Ruth," *Bibliotheca Sacra*, October-December 1991, p. 424ff.

27. John A. Martin, "The Structure of I and II Samuel," *Bibliotheca Sacra*, January-March 1984, p. 28ff.; "The Literary Quality of I and II Samuel," *ibid.*, April-June 1984, p. 131ff.; "The Text of Samuel," *ibid.*, July-

September 1984, p. 209ff.; "The Theology of Samuel," *ibid.*, October–December 1984, p. 303ff.
28. A. N. Wilson, *Gentlemen in England* (New York: Viking, 1986), pp. 61, 63.

CHAPTER SIX: *Crafting the Components of the Narrative Sermon*

1. Charles F. Kemp, *The Preaching Pastor* (St. Louis: Bethany Press, 1966). In this and many other volumes, the homiletician of "life-situation preaching" makes his case for what has frequently degenerated into third-rate psychology.
2. Mario Vargas Llosa, *The Storyteller* (New York: Farrar Strauss Giroux, 1989), p. 6.
3. James M. Wells, "What If Peter Had Preached Deductively?" *Preaching*, March-April 1991, p. 40. There is much confusion in the claim that Jesus and the apostles used "the inductive method" in their preaching.
4. Michael J. Hostetler, *Introducing the Sermon: The Art of Compelling Beginnings* (Grand Rapids, Mich.: Zondervan, 1986). A splendid piece.
5. H. Grady Davis, *Design for Preaching* (Philadelphia: Fortress, 1958), p. 202ff.
6. Alice and Kenneth Hamilton, *The Elements of John Updike* (Grand Rapids, Mich.: Eerdmans, 1970), p. 19.
7. William E. Sangster, *The Craft of Sermon Illustration* (Grand Rapids, Mich.: Baker, 1950, 1973). The best single treatment we possess.
8. Jay E. Adams, *Sense Appeal in the Sermons of Charles Haddon Spurgeon* (Grand Rapids, Mich.: Baker, 1975).
9. Richard L. Thulin, *The "I" of the Sermon* (Minneapolis: Fortress, 1989).
10. James M. Wall, "Beyond Blandness in Preaching," *Christian Century*, May 11, 1988, p. 467.
11. David Larsen, *The Anatomy of Preaching* (Grand Rapids, Mich.: Baker, 1989), pp. 119-130, "How Then Shall We Conclude?"
12. Aristotle, *Rhetoric*, I.2; II.1; III.1, 19.
13. Anthony Thiselton, *The Two Horizons* (Grand Rapids, Mich.: Eerdmans, 1980), p. 436.

CHAPTER SEVEN: *Communicating the Narrative Sermon*

1. David J. Hesselgrave, *Communicating Christ Cross-culturally* (Grand Rapids, Mich.: Zondervan, 1991, second edition), p. 88.
2. Stephen Goode, "In Praise of Things Past," *Insight*, March 23, 1992, p. 37.
3. Mortimer J. Adler, *Truth in Religion: The Plurality of Religions and the Unity of Religious Truth* (New York: Macmillan, 1990).
4. William H. Willimon, "Preaching: Entertainment or Exposition?" *Christian Century*, February 28, 1990.
5. Burton L. Mack and Vernon K. Robbins, *Patterns of Persuasion in the Gospels* (Sonoma, Calif.: Polebridge Press, 1989).
6. Marshall McLuhan and Bruce R. Powers, *The Global Village: Transformations in World Life and Media in the 21st Century* (Oxford: Oxford University Press, 1989).
7. Calvin Miller, *Spirit, Word and Story: A Philosophy of Preaching* (Waco, Tex.: Word, 1989), p. 171.
8. Donald Grey Barnhouse, *Teaching the Word of Truth* (Grand Rapids, Mich.: Eerdmans, 1940).

9. William Fitch, "Preaching Amid Smog," *Christianity Today*, December 18, 1970, p. 262ff.
10. William H. Kooienga, *Elements of Style for Preaching* (Grand Rapids, Mich.: Zondervan, 1989), p. 26.
11. *Ibid.*, p. 38.
12. Sarah Lloyd, *An Indian Attachment* (New York: William Morrow, 1984), p. 147.
13. Norman Cousins, "The Communication Collapse," *Time*, December 17, 1990, p. 114.
14. Martin P. Marty, "We Don't Communicate Well," *Christian Century*, December 4, 1985, p. 1135.
15. David Morgan, "Sallman's *Head of Christ*: The History of an Image," *Christian Century*, October 7, 1992, p. 870.
16. John R. Bodo, "Sallman's Christ," *Christian Century*, November 4, 1992, p. 1014.
17. Philip Godwin, "From Coolers to Candidates, a Feel for a Feel-Good Appeal," *Insight*, September 14, 1987, p. 38ff.
18. A. N. Wilson, *C. S. Lewis: A Biography* (New York: Fawcett Columbine, 1990), p. 133.
19. D. Martyn Lloyd-Jones, *Preaching and Preachers* (Grand Rapids, Mich.: Zondervan, 1971), p. 94.
20. John Herman Bavinck, in Hesselgrave, *Communicating Christ Cross-culturally*, p. 583.
21. Gwyn Walters, "The Body in the Pulpit," in Samuel T. Logan, Jr., ed., *The Preacher and Preaching: Reviving the Art in the Twentieth Century* (Phillipsburg, N.J.: Presbyterian and Reformed, 1986), p. 460.
22. Reid Buckley, *Speaking in Public* (New York: Harper and Row, 1988).
23. Richard M. Weaver, *Language Is Sermonic: Richard N. Weaver on the Nature of Rhetoric* (Baton Rouge, La.: Louisiana State University Press, 1970).
24. Kenneth Hamilton, *Words and the Word* (Grand Rapids, Mich.: Eerdmans, 1971); Richard M. Weaver, *The Ethics of Rhetoric* (Chicago: Henry Regnery, 1953); Gordon H. Clark, *Language and Theology* (Phillipsburg, N.J.: Presbyterian and Reformed, 1979); Gordon H. Clark, *Logic* (Jefferson, Md.: Trinity Foundation, 1985).
25. R. B. Lanning, "Preaching in America Today," *Banner of Truth*, May 1986, p. 28.
26. Raymond E. Brown, *The Epistles of John* (Garden City, N.J.: Doubleday, 1982), pp. 329-361.
27. E. M. Bounds, quoted in Roy L. Laurin, *Epistle of John* (Wheaton, Ill.: VanKampen, 1954), p. 91.
28. Robert MacKenzie, *John Brown of Haddington* (London: Banner of Truth, 1918), p. 105.
29. Dennis F. Kinlaw, *Preaching in the Spirit* (Grand Rapids, Mich.: Francis Asbury Press, Zondervan, 1985).
30. James Forbes, *The Holy Spirit in Preaching* (Nashville: Abingdon, 1989), p. 25; Tony Sargent, *The Sacred Anointing* (Wheaton, Ill.: Crossway Books, 1994).
31. *Ibid.*, p. 54.
32. Donald R. Sunukjian, "The Preacher as Persuader," in *Walvoord: A Tribute* (Chicago: Moody Press, 1982), p. 290.

CHAPTER EIGHT: *The Unique Charms of the Parable*

1. Thomas J. Peters and Robert H. Waterman, Jr., *In Search of Excellence: Lessons from America's Best-run Companies* (New York: Harper, 1982), p. 61.
2. John R. Brokhoff, *Preaching the Parables* (Lima, Oh.: C.S.S. Publishing, 1987), p. 13.
3. J. Stuart Holden, *Some Old Testament Parables* (London: Pickering and Inglis, 1934).
4. Herman Harrell Horne, *Jesus—The Master Teacher* (Grand Rapids, Mich.: Kregel, 1964).
5. Richard Robert Osmer, *A Teachable Spirit: Recovering the Teaching Office in the Church* (Louisville: Westminster/John Knox, 1990).
6. Clark M. Williamson and Ronald J. Allen, *The Teaching Minister* (Louisville: Westminster/John Knox, 1991).
7. James Montgomery Boice, sermons in *Bible Study Magazine*, June 1981; July 1981; August 1981; January 1982; February 1982, as preached over "The Bible Study Hour" and later published in book form.
8. Eta Linnemann, *Is There a Synoptic Problem? Rethinking the Literary Dependence of the First Three Gospels* (Grand Rapids, Mich.: Baker, 1992).
9. Jon D. Levenson, "The Bible: Unexamined Commitments of Criticism," *First Things*, February 1993.
10. Grant R. Osborne, *The Hermeneutical Spiral: A Comprehensive Introduction to Biblical Interpretation* (Downers Grove, Ill.: InterVarsity Press, 1991), p. 235.
11. C. H. Dodd, *The Parables of the Kingdom* (London: Nisbet, 1935), pp. 11-12.
12. Milton S. Terry, *Biblical Hermeneutics* (Grand Rapids, Mich.: Zondervan, n.d.), pp. 276-301.
13. G. Campbell Morgan, *The Teaching of Christ* (New York: Fleming H. Revell, 1913).
14. Henri J. M. Nouwen, *The Return of the Prodigal Son* (New York: Doubleday, 1992).
15. Helmut Thielicke, *The Waiting Father: Sermons on the Parables of Jesus* (New York: Harper, 1959).
16. A. M. Hunter, *Interpreting the Parables* (London: SCM, 1964).
17. Henry H. Mitchell, "The Genres: Vehicles for Encounter," *Preaching Magazine*, January-February 1993, p. 42.
18. Nigel Watson, *Striking Home: Interpreting and Proclaiming the New Testament* (London: Epworth, 1987), p. 75.
19. George A. Buttrick, *The Parables of Jesus* (New York: Harper, 1928).
20. William Barclay, *And Jesus Said: A Handbook on the Parables of Jesus* (Philadelphia: Westminster, 1970).
21. Bernard Brandon Scott, *Hear Then the Parable: A Commentary on the Parables of Jesus* (Minneapolis: Fortress, 1989).
22. Brownlow North, *The Rich Man and Lazarus* (London: Banner of Truth, 1960).
23. Frederick Houk Borsch, *Many Things in Parables: Extravagant Stories of New Community* (Philadelphia: Fortress, 1988).
24. Robert Farrar Capon, *The Parables of Grace* (Grand Rapids, Mich.: Eerdmans, 1988); *The Parables of Judgment* (Grand Rapids, Mich.: Eerdmans, 1989); *The Parables of the Kingdom* (Grand Rapids, Mich.: Zondervan, 1985).
25. Lloyd John Ogilvie, *Autobiography of God* (Ventura, Calif.: Gospel

Light, 1979); David Allan Hubbard, *Parables Jesus Told* (Downers Grove, Ill.: InterVarsity Press, 1981); Dan Seagren, *The Parables* (Wheaton, Ill.: Tyndale, 1978); David A. Redding, *The Parables He Told* (New York: Harper, 1976).

26. Kenneth W. Rogahn and Walter M. Schoedel, *Parables from the Cross* (St. Louis: Concordia, 1982).

CHAPTER NINE: *The Sensitive Nuances of the Miracle-Stories*

1. J Gresham Machen, *Christianity and Liberalism* (New York: Macmillan, 1923).

2. J. Gresham Machen, *The Virgin Birth of Christ* (New York: Harper, 1930).

3. Walter Lippmann, *A Preface to Morals* (New York: Macmillan, 1929), pp. 30-32.

4. Richard C. Trench, *Notes on the Miracles of Our Lord* (Westwood, N.J.: Revell, 1953, reprint), pp. 11-12.

5. Wilbur M. Smith, *The Supernaturalness of Christ: Can We Still Believe in It?* (Boston: W.A. Wilde, 1940).

6. Randel Helms, *Gospel Fictions* (Buffalo, N.Y.: Prometheus, 1986).

7. Anton Fridrichsen, *The Problem of Miracle in Primitive Christianity* (Minneapolis: Augsburg, 1972), p. 119.

8. Gerd Theissen, *The Miracle Stories of the Early Christian Tradition* (Philadelphia: Fortress, 1983).

9. Reginald H. Fuller, *Interpreting the Miracles* (Philadelphia: Westminster, 1963), p. 121.

10. Alan Richardson, *The Miracle-Stories of the Gospels* (London: SCM Press, 1941).

11. Colin Brown, *Miracles and the Modern Mind* (Grand Rapids, Mich.: Eerdmans, 1984); *That You May Believe: Miracles and Faith Then and Now* (Grand Rapids, Mich.: Eerdmans, 1985).

12. See Smith, *The Supernaturalness of Christ*, supplemented by my class notes from Fuller Theological Seminary, 1954.

13. Eric C. Rust, "Preaching from the Miracle Stories of the Gospels," in James W. Cox, *Biblical Preaching: An Expositor's Treasury* (Philadelphia: Westminster, 1983).

14. John Wimber, *Power Evangelism* (San Francisco: Harper, 1986).

15. Brown, *That You May Believe*, p. 192.

16. B. B. Warfield, *Miracles: Yesterday and Today, Real and Counterfeit* (Grand Rapids, Mich.: Eerdmans, 1918).

17. David L. Larsen, *Caring for the Flock: Pastoral Ministry in the Local Congregation* (Wheaton, Ill.: Crossway Books, 1991), pp. 175-182.

18. Some truly exemplary preaching on the miracles is in evidence in Ronald S. Wallace, *The Gospel Miracles* (Grand Rapids, Mich.: Eerdmans, 1963); also in works by Charles Allen, William Taylor, and John Laidlaw.

CHAPTER TEN: *The Powerful Scenes of Christ's Birth, Life, Passion, and Resurrection*

1. David Larsen, *The Anatomy of Preaching* (Grand Rapids, Mich.: Baker, 1989), p. 157.

2. Douglas D. Webster, *A Passion for Christ: An Evangelical Christology* (Grand Rapids, Mich.: Zondervan, 1987).

3. John Shelby Spong, *Born of a Woman: A Bishop Rethinks the Birth of Jesus* (San Francisco: Harper, 1993).

4. Reginald Fuller, *He That Cometh: The Birth of Jesus in the New Testament* (Harrisburg, Penn.: Morehouse, 1990).
5. Michael Green, "Preaching the Advent: A Contemporary Approach," *Christianity Today*, January 1, 1965, p. 3ff.
6. Donald G. Bloesch, a review of Theodore Jennings, *Loyalty to God: The Apostles' Creed in Life and Liturgy*, in *Christian Century*, March 10, 1993, p. 275ff.
7. Leon Morris, *The Story of the Christ Child* (Grand Rapids, Mich.: Eerdmans, 1960).
8. Wilbur M. Smith, *Great Sermons on the Birth of Christ* (Boston: W.A. Wilde, 1963).
9. Samuel M. Zwemer, *The Glory of the Manger: Studies in the Incarnation* (New York: American Tract Society, 1940).
10. H. P. Liddon, *The Magnificat* (London: Longmans, Green, 1895); Martin Luther, *The Magnificat* (Minneapolis: Augsburg, 1967).
11. A. T. Robertson, *The Mother of Jesus: Her Problems and Her Glory* (Grand Rapids, Mich.: Baker, 1963).
12. James Montgomery Boice, *The Christ of Christmas* (Chicago: Moody, 1983); Alton M. Motter, *The Preaching of the Nativity* (Philadelphia: Muhlenberg, 1961).
13. D. W. Cleverley Ford, *Preaching Through the Life of Christ* (St. Louis: CBP Press, 1986).
14. G. Campbell Morgan, *The Crises of the Christ* (London: Pickering and Inglis, 1936).
15. Geerhardus Vos, *The Self-disclosure of Jesus* (Grand Rapids, Mich.: Eerdmans, 1954); Oswald Chambers, *The Psychology of Redemption* (London: Simpkin Marshall, n.d.); Oswald Chambers, *Bringing Sons unto Glory* (London: Simpkin Marshall, n.d.)
16. Some good preaching on the temptation of our Lord is to be seen in Helmut Thielicke, *Between God and Satan* (Grand Rapids, Mich.: Eerdmans, 1958); W. Graham Scroggie, *Tested by Temptation* (London: Pickering and Inglis, 1923); James H. Hanson, *Through Temptation* (Minneapolis: Augsburg, 1959); Leonard Ravenhill, *Tried and Transfigured* (Minneapolis: Bethany, 1963); Dietrich Bonhoeffer, *Temptation* (London: SCM Press, 1953). Henri Nouwen speaks of the three temptations as the temptation to be relevant, spectacular, and powerful.
17. Wilbur M. Smith, *The Supernaturalness of Christ: Can We Still Believe in It?* (Boston: W.A. Wilde, 1940), p. 183ff. For some gripping sermons on the Transfiguration, cf. W. M. Clow, *The Secret of the Lord* (London: Hodder and Stoughton, n.d.).
18. Leon Morris, *The Story of the Cross* (Grand Rapids, Mich.: Eerdmans, 1957).
19. Jim Bishop, *The Day Christ Died* (New York: Pocket Books, 1957).
20. Pierre Barbet, *A Doctor at Calvary* (Garden City, N.J.: Doubleday Image, 1963); C. Truman Davis, "The Crucifixion of Jesus: The Passion of Christ from a Medical Point of View," *Arizona Medicine*, March 1965, p. 183ff.
21. Oscar A. Anderson, *With Him All the Way* (Minneapolis: Augsburg, 1948); Hugh Martin, *The Shadow of Calvary* (Edinburgh: Banner of Truth, 1875, reprint).
22. K. Schilder, *Christ in His Sufferings* (Grand Rapids, Mich.: Eerdmans, 1938); *Christ on Trial* (Grand Rapids, Mich.: Eerdmans, 1939); *Christ Crucified* (Grand Rapids, Mich.: Eerdmans, 1940).

23. F. W. Krummacher, *The Suffering Saviour* (Chicago: Moody, 1952, reprint).
24. Friedrich August Tholuck, *Light from the Cross* (Chicago: Moody, 1952, reprint).
25. David L. Larsen, "The Transformation of a Terrorist," in Richard Allen Bodey, ed., *The Voice from the Cross* (Grand Rapids, Mich.: Baker, 1990), pp. 30-39.
26. Russell Bradley Jones, *Gold from Golgotha* (Chicago: Moody, 1945); Lehman Strauss, *The Day God Died* (Grand Rapids, Mich.: Zondervan, 1965); C. H. Spurgeon, *The Passion and Death of Christ* (Grand Rapids, Mich.: Eerdmans, n.d.); William R. Nicholson, *The Six Miracles of Calvary* (Chicago: Moody, 1927, reprint); Arthur W. Pink, *The Seven Sayings of the Saviour on the Cross* (Grand Rapids, Mich.: Zondervan, 1951); A. C. Dixon, *The Glories of the Cross* (Grand Rapids, Mich.: Eerdmans, 1962); Max Lucado, *Six Hours One Friday* (Portland: Multnomah, 1989).
27. J. Sidlow Baxter, *The Master Theme of the Bible* (Wheaton, Ill.: Tyndale, 1973); Neil Fraser, *The Grandeur of Golgotha* (London: Pickering and Inglis, 1959); W. M Clow, *The Cross in Christian Experience* (London: Hodder and Stoughton, 1908).
28. Leon Morris, *The Apostolic Preaching of the Cross* (Grand Rapids, Mich.: Eerdmans, 1955); Martyn Lloyd-Jones, *The Cross* (Wheaton, Ill.: Crossway Books, 1986); John R. W. Stott, *The Cross of Christ* (Downers Grove, Ill.: InterVarsity, 1986); Marcus Loane, *Life Through the Cross* (Grand Rapids, Mich.: Zondervan, 1966); F. J. Huegel, *The Cross of Christ: The Throne of God* (Minneapolis, Bethany, 1935, reprint).
29. David Buttrick, *Homiletic* (Philadelphia: Fortress, 1987), p. 399.
30. Wilbur M. Smith, *Therefore Stand* (Boston: W.A. Wilde, 1945); Josh McDowell, *The Resurrection Factor* (San Bernardino: Here's Life, 1981); William L. Craig, *The Son Rises: The Historical Evidence for the Resurrection of Jesus* (Chicago: Moody, 1981).
31. Merrill C. Tenney, *The Reality of the Resurrection* (New York: Harper, 1963); John Wenham, *Easter Enigma: Are the Resurrection Accounts in Conflict?* (Grand Rapids, Mich.: Zondervan, 1984).
32. H. P. Liddon, *Easter in St. Paul's* (London: Longmans, Green, 1895); C. Ernest Tatham, *He Lives* (Chicago: Moody, n.d.); Neil M. Fraser, *The Glory of His Rising* (Neptune, N.J.: Loizeaux, 1963); J. Vernon McGee, *The Empty Tomb* (Ventura, Calif.: Gospel Light, 1968); Marcus Loane, *Our Risen Lord* (Grand Rapids, Mich.: Zondervan, 1965); Donald Grey Barnhouse, *The Cross Through the Empty Tomb* (Grand Rapids, Mich.: Eerdmans, 1961); cf. also Geoffrey R. King, *The Forty Days: From Calvary to the Ascension* (Grand Rapids, Mich.: Eerdmans, 1962); David L. Larsen, "God's Great Amen," in Richard Allen Bodey, ed., *Good News for All Seasons* (Grand Rapids, Mich.: Baker, 1987), pp. 72-79.

CHAPTER ELEVEN: The Exquisite Vignettes of Bible Biography
1. Frederick Buechner, *The Clown in the Belfry: Writings on Faith and Fiction* (San Francisco: Harper, 1992), p. 34.
2. "Personal Glimpses," *Reader's Digest*, April 1993, p. 136.
3. H. Grady Davis, *Design for Preaching* (Philadelphia: Fortress, 1958), p. 158.
4. Halford Luccock, in Ray E. DeBrand, *Guide to Biographical Preaching: How to Preach on Bible Characters* (Nashville: Broadman, 1988), p. 12.

5. Book Review by David L. Larsen, *Trinity Journal,* Fall 1990, pp. 237-239.
6. Sidney Greidanus, *The Modern Preacher and the Ancient Text* (Grand Rapids, Mich.: Eerdmans, 1988), p. 162.
7. *Ibid.,* p. 163.
8. *Ibid.,* p. 179.
9. Charles H. Koller, in John MacArthur, *Rediscovering Expository Preaching* (Dallas: Word, 1992), p. 271.
10. Ilion T. Jones, in *ibid.,* p. 270.
11. John A. Broadus, *On the Preparation and Delivery of Sermons,* Fourth Edition (New York: Harper, 1979), p. 132.
12. Very fine studies on the life of Abraham have been given by F. B. Meyer, George Morrison, Oswald Chambers, and Ray Stedman.
13. James Hardee Kennedy, *The Commission of Moses and the Christian Calling* (Grand Rapids, Mich.: Eerdmans, 1964).
14. Andrew W. Blackwood, *Biographical Preaching for Today* (Nashville: Abingdon, 1954); DeBrand, *Guide to Biographical Preaching.*
15. William S. LaSor, *Great Personalities of the Old Testament* (Westwood, N.J.: Revell, 1959); *Great Personalities of the New Testament* (Westwood, N.J.: Revell, 1960); Melvin Grove Kyle, *Mooring Masts of Revelation* (New York: Revell, 1933).
16. Marion Wyse, *The Prophet and the Prostitute* (Wheaton, Ill.: Tyndale, 1979).
17. Alexander Whyte, *Bible Characters from the Old Testament and the New Testament* (Grand Rapids, Mich.: Zondervan, 1967, reprint).
18. Elie Wiesel, *Five Biblical Portraits: Saul, Jonah, Jeremiah, Elijah, Joshua* (South Bend, Ind.: Notre Dame Press, 1981).
19. Nathan Ausubel, ed., *A Treasury of Jewish Folklore* (New York: Bantam, 1980); Yaffa Eliach, *Hasidic Tales of the Holocaust* (New York: Avon, 1982).
20. Eugene H. Peterson, *Under the Unpredictable Plant: An Exploration in Vocational Holiness* (Grand Rapids, Mich.: Eerdmans, 1992).
21. Oscar Cullmann, *Peter: Disciple, Apostle, Martyr* (New York: Meridian, 1958); Carsten P. Thiede, *Simon Peter: From Galilee to Rome* (Exeter: Paternoster, 1986).
22. F. B. Meyer, *Peter: Fisherman, Disciple, Apostle* (Grand Rapids, Mich.: Zondervan, 1950, reprint); M. R. DeHaan, *Simon Peter: Sinner and Saint* (Grand Rapids, Mich.: Zondervan, 1954); W. H. Griffith Thomas, *The Apostle Peter: A Devotional Commentary* (Grand Rapids, Mich.: Eerdmans, 1946); Clarence E. Macartney, *Peter and His Lord* (Nashville: Abingdon, 1933).
23. Ralph Waldo Emerson, quoted in Frederick Buechner, *Listening to Your Life* (San Francisco: HarperCollins, 1992), p. 186.
24. Lloyd M. Perry and Charles M. Sell, *Speaking to Life's Problems* (Chicago: Moody, 1983).
25. Charles H. Spurgeon, *Pictures from Pilgrim's Progress* (Grand Rapids, Mich.: Baker, 1982).
26. Alexander Whyte, *Bunyan's Characters,* three volumes (Edinburgh: Oliphant, Anderson and Ferrier, n.d.).
27. F. W. Boreham, *A Bunch of Everlastings* (New York: Abingdon, 1920); *A Casket of Cameos* (Philadelphia: Judson, 1924).

CHAPTER TWELVE: *The Special Challenges of the Apocalyptic and Prophetic*
1. H. H. Rowley, *The Relevance of Apocalyptic* (New York: Harper, 1946); cf. also D. S Russell, *Divine Disclosure: An Introduction to Jewish Apocalyptic* (Minneapolis: Fortress, 1992).
2. Terrence W. Tilley, *Story Theology* (Wilmington, Del.: Michael Glazier, 1985), p. 60.
3. David Buttrick, *Homiletic* (Philadelphia: Fortress, 1987), p. 373.
4. Martyn Lloyd-Jones, *The Kingdom of God* (Wheaton, Ill.: Crossway Books, 1992).
5. Jurgen Moltmann, *History and the Triune God: Contributions to Trinitarian Theology* (New York: Crossroad, 1992), p. 92ff.
6. *Ibid.*, p. 92.
7. Donald K. Campbell and Jeffrey L. Townsend, eds., *A Case for Premillennialism: A New Consensus* (Chicago: Moody, 1992).
8. Ralph Stob, *Christianity and Classical Civilization* (Grand Rapids, Mich.: Eerdmans, 1950), p. 126.
9. Garry Wills, *Under God: Religion and American Politics* (New York: Simon and Schuster, 1990).
10. *Ibid.*, p 24.
11. Samuel J. Andrews, *Christianity and Anti-Christianity in Their Final Conflict* (Chicago: Moody, 1898).
12. Arthur W. Pink, *The Antichrist* (Minneapolis: Klock and Klock, 1979, reprint).
13. Jurgen Moltmann, *The Church in the Power of the Spirit* (San Francisco: HarperCollins, 1977), p. 379.
14. Donald L. Hamilton, *Homiletical Handbook* (Nashville: Broadman, 1992); cf. also R. H. Girdlestone, *The Grammar of Prophecy: A Systematic Guide to Biblical Prophecy* (Grand Rapids, Mich.: Kregel, 1955, reprint); Walter C. Kaiser, Jr., *Back Toward the Future: Hints for Interpreting Biblical Prophecy* (Grand Rapids, Mich.: Baker, 1989); Robert P. Lightner, *The Last Days Handbook* (Nashville: Thomas Nelson, 1990).
15. Girdlestone, *The Grammar of Prophecy*, p. 89.
16. Gilles Quispel, *The Secret Book of Revelation* (New York: McGraw-Hill, 1979). This is a not an interpretation of the Apocalypse but a stunning presentation of plates and historical pictures of great fascination and interest.
17. "Doomsday Science: New Theories About Comets, Asteroids and How the World Might End," *Newsweek*, November 23, 1992, pp. 56-63.

CHAPTER THIRTEEN: *The Demanding Rigors of the Difficult Passages*
1. Norman L. Geisler and J. I. Packer, *Summit II Hermeneutics* (International Council on Inerrancy, 1983), p. 17.
2. John F. Walvoord, ed., *Inspiration and Interpretation* (Grand Rapids, Mich.: Eerdmans, 1957), p. 110.
3. Olav Valen-Sendstad, *The Word That Can Never Die* (St. Louis: Concordia, 1949), p. 51.
4. Everett F. Harrison, "Criteria of Biblical Inerrancy," *Christianity Today*, January 20, 1958, pp. 16-18.
5. B. F. Westcott, *A General Survey of the History of the Canon of the New Testament* (London: Macmillan, 1875), p. 1.
6. John W. Haley, *An Examination of the Alleged Discrepancies of the Bible*

(Nashville: Gospel Advocate, 1967); Gleason L. Archer, *Encyclopedia of Bible Difficulties* (Grand Rapids, Mich.: Zondervan, 1982).
7. "The Truth About Dinosaurs. Surprise: Just About Everything You Believe Is Wrong," *Time*, April 26, 1993.
8. Phillip E. Johnson, *Darwin on Trial* (Downers Grove, Ill.: InterVarsity, 1991).
9. Bryan Appleyard, *Understanding the Present: Science and the Soul of Modern Man* (Garden City, N.J.: Doubleday, 1993).
10. Ronald L. Numbers, *The Creationists* (New York: Alfred Knopf, 1993).
11. Henry M. Morris, *The Genesis Record: A Scientific and Devotional Commentary on the Book of Beginnings* (Grand Rapids, Mich.: Baker, 1976).
12. James Montgomery Boice, *Genesis: An Expositional Commentary*, Volume I (Grand Rapids, Mich.: Zondervan, 1982), p. 108.
13. Francis A. Schaeffer, *Genesis in Space and Time* (Downers Grove, Ill.: InterVarsity, 1972).
14. Helmut Thielicke, *How the World Began: Man in the First Chapters of the Bible* (Philadelphia: Muhlenberg, 1961).
15. Walter C. Kaiser, Jr., *Hard Sayings of the Bible* (Downers Grove, Ill.: InterVarsity, 1988), p. 55.
16. Haley, *An Examination of the Alleged Discrepancies of the Bible*, p. 238.
17. Kaiser, Jr., *Hard Sayings of the Bible*, p. 95.
18. Mark Twain, *The Complete Short Stories of Mark Twain* (New York: Bantam, 1957), p. 474.
19. Michael Parenti, *Make Believe Media: The Politics of Entertainment* (New York: St. Martin's, 1992), p. 115.
20. C. S. Lewis, *Reflections on the Psalms* (New York: Harcourt, Brace, 1958), p. 30; J. Carl Laney, "A Fresh Look at the Imprecatory Psalms," *Bibliotheca Sacra*, January-February 1981, pp. 35-45.
21. Alfred Tennyson, *Selected Poetry* (New York: Modern Library, 1951), pp. 392-396; William Cullen Bryant, *Poetical Works* (New York: Thomas Crowell, 1893), pp. 89-92.
22. Lawrence E. Nelson, *Our Roving Bible* (Nashville: Abingdon, 1945), pp. 123-124.
23. Shlomo Riskin, "Homosexuality as a Tragic Mistake," *Jerusalem Post*, May 1, 1993, p. 23.
24. Donald Grey Barnhouse, *God's Freedom* (Grand Rapids, Mich.: Eerdmans, 1961), p. 188ff.; retold in James Montgomery Boice, *The Minor Prophets*, Volume I (Grand Rapids, Mich.: Zondervan, 1983), p. 21ff.

CHAPTER FOURTEEN: *Enlarging Imagination and Creativity*

1. Daniel J. Boorstin, *The Discoverers: A History of Man's Search to Know His World and Himself* (New York: Random House, 1983); *The Creators: A History of Heroes of the Imagination* (New York: Random House, 1992).
2. Charles Rice, in Paul Scott Wilson, *Imagination of the Heart: New Understandings in Preaching* (Nashville: Abingdon, 1988), p. 21.
3. James M. Wall, "Sowing and Reaping," *Christian Century*, February 3-10, 1993, p. 99.
4. Maria Harris, *Teaching and Religious Imagination: An Essay in the Theology of Teaching* (New York: Harper and Row, 1987), p. 3ff.
5. Gerald Graff, in Robert Hughes, *Culture of Complaint: The Fraying of*

America (New York: Oxford University Press, 1993), p. 77. For a tragic understanding of creativity without a Creator, cf. the work by the systematic theologian from Harvard, Gordon Kaufman, *In Face of a Mystery* (Cambridge, Mass.: Harvard University Press, 1993).

6. Review by Suzanne Berne of Jeffrey Eugenides, *The Virgin Suicides* (New York: Farrar, Straus and Giroux, 1993), *New York Times Book Review*, April 25, 1993, p. 13.

7. Victor Ostrovsky and Claire Hoy, *By Way of Deception: The Making and Unmaking of a Mossad Officer* (New York: St. Martin's Press, 1990), pp. 161-162.

8. Harris, *Teaching and Religious Imagination*, p. 131.

9. Claes G. Ryn, *Will, Imagination and Reason: Irving Babbit and the Problem of Reality* (Chicago: Regnery, 1987).

10. Daniel Goleman, Paul Kaufman, and Michael Ray, *The Creative Spirit* (New York: Dutton, 1992). Note also Warren Wiersbe's *Preaching and Teaching with Imagination* (Wheaton, Ill.: Victor, 1994). A wealth of insight.

11. Edward de Bono, *Serious Creativity: Using the Power of Lateral Thinking to Create New Ideas* (New York: Harper Business, 1992). Also highly recommended to me by my former student, Brent Nelson: Roger Van Oech, *A Whack on the Side of the Head* (New York: Warner, 1983); Roger Van Oech, *A Kick in the Seat of the Pants* (New York: Harper, 1986).

12. Denise Shekerjian, *Uncommon Genius: How Great Ideas Are Born* (New York: Viking, 1990).

13. Laurence Perrine, *Story and Structure* (New York: Harcourt Brace Jovanovich, 1974).

14. Paul Johnson, *The Birth of the Modern: World Society 1815-1830* (New York: HarperCollins, 1991), p. 591.

15. *Ibid.*, p. 611ff.

16. *Ibid.*, p. 623.

CHAPTER FIFTEEN: *Enhancing Relevancy and Application*

1. John R. W. Stott, *The Preacher's Portrait* (Grand Rapids, Mich.: Eerdmans, 1961), p. 33ff.

2. John C. Holbert, "Narrative Preaching: Possibilities and Perils," in *Preaching Magazine*, May-June 1992, p. 26.

3. Roberto Calasso, *The Marriage of Cadmus and Harmony* (New York: Knopf, 1993).

4. D. Martyn Lloyd-Jones, *Darkness and Light: An Exposition of Ephesians 4:17–5:17* (Grand Rapids, Mich.: Baker, 1982), p. 200ff.

5. William H. Willimon, "Preaching: Entertainment or Exposition?" *Christian Century*, February 28, 1990, p. 204ff.

6. William H. Shepherd, Jr., "A Second Look at Inductive Preaching," *Christian Century*, September 19-26, 1990, p. 822ff.

7. William H. Willimon and Stanley Hauerwas, *Preaching to Strangers: Evangelism in Today's World* (Philadelphia: Westminster/John Knox, 1992); William H. Willimon, *Peculiar Speech: Preaching to the Baptized* (Grand Rapids, Mich.: Eerdmans, 1992). Willimon shares with us in the latter book the most serious and incisive criticism of Fred Craddock's approach to preaching that we have yet had (pp. 48-53).

8. Jack Kuhatschek, *Taking the Guess-work out of Applying the Bible* (Downers Grove, Ill.: InterVarsity, 1990); we have already referred to the very helpful and important treatment of application in Elliott E. Johnson,

Expository Hermeneutics (Grand Rapids, Mich.: Zondervan, 1990), pp. 215-306.

9. Richard J. Thulin, *The "I" of the Sermon* (Minneapolis: Fortress, 1989).
10. G. Campbell Morgan, *Living Messages of the Books of the Bible* (Westwood, N.J.: Revell, 1912); J. Sidlow Baxter, *Explore the Book* (Grand Rapids, Mich.: Zondervan, 1960): John Phillips, *Exploring the Scriptures* (Chicago: Moody, 1965); W. Graham Scroggie, *Know Your Bible* (London: Pickering and Inglis, 1940); Charles W. Slemming, *Bible Digest*, four volumes (Grand Rapids, Mich.: Kregel, 1960).
11. Aleksandr Solzhenitsyn, "The Reckless Cult of Novelty and How It Wrecked the Century," *New York Times Book Review*, February 7, 1993, p. 3ff.
12. James Lincoln Collier, *The Rise of Selfishness in the United States* (New York: Cambridge University Press, 1992).
13. Andrew Murray, *Absolute Surrender* (Chicago: Moody, 1897), p. 5ff. Murray shows us biblical depth in his magnificent series on the book of Hebrews; but can the kind of wrenching out of context seen in this sermon really be the right way to use Scripture?
14. All who know Zwemer's class sermons on the birth, death, and resurrection of our Lord know that he can be an eminently biblical preacher.
15. Clyde E. Fant, *Preaching for Today* (San Francisco: Harper, 1967), p. 82.
16. *Ibid.*, p. 249.
17. *The Word in Life Study Bible* (Nashville: Thomas Nelson, 1993).
18. "Adolescents at Risk of Becoming 'Lost Generation,' Report Says," *Chicago Tribune*, June 24, 1993, Section I, p. 15.

CHAPTER SIXTEEN: *Encouraging Spirituality and Impaction*

1. James M. May, *Trials of Character: The Eloquence of Ciceronian Ethos* (Chapel Hill, N.C.: University of North Carolina Press, 1989).
2. Stephen Kendrick, "In Touch with Blessing: An Interview with Henri Nouwen," *Christian Century*, March 24-31, 1993, p. 319.
3. Lawrence A. Wagley, "Prayer for the Hurried, the Undisciplined and the Disorganized," *Christian Century*, March 24-31, 1993, p 323.
4. John Guest, *Finding Deeper Intimacy with God* (Grand Rapids, Mich.: Baker, 1993).
5. James W. Clark, *Dynamic Preaching* (New York: Revell, 1960), p. 16.
6. Quoted in Gene E. Bartlett, "When Preaching Becomes Real," *Pastoral Psychology*, October 1963, p. 20.
7. B. B. Warfield, "The Purpose of the Seminary," in *Selected Shorter Writings*, Volume I (Phillipsburg, N.J.: Presbyterian and Reformed, 1970), p. 374ff.
8. E. Michael Jones, *Degenerate Moderns: Modernity as Rationalized Sexual Behavior* (South Bend, Ind.: Fidelity Press, 1993).
9. *National Review*, July 5, 1933, p. 12.
10. Stanley Hauerwas, in Douglas F. Ottati, "The Spirit of Reforming Protestantism," *Christian Century*, December 16, 1992, p. 1164.
11. *Context*, July 1, 1993, p. 1.
12. Mark Ellingsen, *The Evangelical Movement: Growth, Impact, Controversy, Dialog* (Minneapolis: Fortress. 1988).
13. Walter Brueggemann, *Finally Comes the Poet: Daring Speech for Proclamation* (Minneapolis: Fortress, 1989), The Beecher Lectures for 1989.

14. Lloyd Steffen, "The Listening Point," *Christian Century*, November 21-28, 1990, p. 1087ff.
15. Andre Bernard, ed., *Rotten Rejections: A Literary Companion* (New York: Pushcart Press, 1990).
16. F. Dean Lueking, *Preaching: The Art of Connecting God and People* (Waco, Tex.: Word, 1985), p. 97ff.
17. William Manchester, *Churchill: The Last Lion: Alone, 1932-1940* (Boston: Little, Brown, 1988), p. 210. I am indebted to my brother, Dr. Paul Larsen, for this moving quotation.

Scripture Index

General Index